LOOSENING THE GRIP
A handbook of alcohol information

LOOSENING THE GRIP

A handbook of alcohol information

JEAN KINNEY, M.S.W.

Assistant Professor, Department of Psychiatry, and
Associate Director, Alcohol Counselor Training Program,
Dartmouth Medical School,
Hanover, New Hampshire

GWEN LEATON

Research Assistant, Department of Psychiatry,
Alcohol Counselor Training Program,
Dartmouth Medical School,
Hanover, New Hampshire

Illustrated by
STUART COPANS, M.D.

The C. V. Mosby Company

Saint Louis   1978

The C. V. Mosby Company
11830 Westline Industrial Drive, St. Louis, Missouri 63141

Library of Congress Cataloging in Publication Data

Kinney, Jean, 1943-
    Loosening the grip: a handbook of alcohol information.

    Bibliography: p.
    Includes index.
    1.   Alcoholism—Handbooks, manuals, etc.
2.   Alcoholism—Treatment—Handbooks, manuals,
etc. 3.   Alcohol—Handbooks, manuals, etc.
I.   Leaton, Gwen, 1934-   joint author.
II.   Title.   [DNLM: 1. Alcohol drinking—
Handbooks. 2. Alcoholism—Therapy—Handbooks.
WM274.3 K55L]
HV5035.K56   362.2′92   78-2219
ISBN 0-8016-2673-0

GW/CB/CB   9   8   7   6   5   4   3   2   1

Contributors

FREDERICK BURKLE, Jr., M.D., M.P.H.

Adolescents, CHAPTER 10   Dr. Burkle came to the psychiatry residency program of Dartmouth Medical School after a practice in pediatrics. He has since left chilly New England and is now a psychiatrist on the staff of Maui Mental Health Services in Hawaii.

ROBERT CHAPMAN, M.D.

Medications, CHAPTER 9   Dr. Chapman is an Assistant Professor of Clinical Psychiatry, Dartmouth Medical School. He has been the Director of the Dartmouth-Hitchcock Mental Health Center Comprehensive Alcohol Services Program and has been involved with the training of Medex, Physician's Assistants. His lectures have been incorporated in this handbook.

STUART COPANS, M.D.

CHAPTER 7   Dr. Copans was formerly a Fellow in Child Psychiatry at Dartmouth Medical School. The material on the effects of alcohol abuse on the family has been drawn largely from his lectures to the counselor trainees. Dr. Copans can be found walking around with a pen and sketch pad; he has provided all the illustrations for this handbook. He presently directs the Child and Adolescent Psychiatry Unit at the Brattleboro Retreat and is a consultant to the Alcohol Unit.

BARBARA FEINSTEIN, M.S.W.

The employed, CHAPTER 10   As a social worker in the Boston area, Ms. Feinstein has been involved in the alcohol field in a variety of capacities. She directed a student unit of the Boston College School of Social Work that delivered alcohol services to people in their work settings. She is now authoring a book on social work services in the workplace.

RICHARD GOODSTEIN, M.D.

Suicide prevention, CHAPTER 9;   Dr. Goodstein is an Associate Professor of Clinical Psychiatry and
The elderly, CHAPTER 10   Director of the Ambulatory Care Service of the Dartmouth-Hitchcock Mental Health Center. His lectures on suicide and on the elderly have been edited for inclusion here.

PETER HAURI, Ph.D.

Sleep disturbances, CHAPTER 5

Dr. Hauri is an Associate Professor of Psychiatry and Director of the Sleep and Dreaming Laboratory at the Dartmouth Medical School. His lectures on sleep have been edited for this book.

SUSAN McGRATH

CHAPTER 1;
Sociological aspects, CHAPTER 4

Susan McGrath was a Research Assistant with the Alcohol Counselor Training Program of the Dartmouth Medical School. Intimately involved with the training program since its beginning, her contributions here evolved from a series of lectures she gave to the counselor trainees.

THOMAS MacKENZIE, M.D.

Psychiatric diagnosis, CHAPTER 9

Dr. MacKenzie is currently an Assistant Professor of Psychiatry at the University of Minnesota Medical School. During his tenure as Chief Resident, Department of Psychiatry, Dartmouth Medical School, he kindly accepted the task of distilling psychiatric nosology for the alcohol counselor trainees and contributed it to this book.

HUGH MacNAMEE, M.D.

Adolescents, CHAPTER 10

Dr. MacNamee is an Associate Professor of Clinical Psychiatry in the Division of Child Psychiatry, Dartmouth Medical School, and is Medical Director of West Central New Hampshire Community Mental Health Services. His lectures on adolescents were edited for inclusion here.

TREVOR PRICE, M.D.

Medical complications of alcoholism, CHAPTER 5

Dr. Price is an Assistant Professor of Psychiatry, Dartmouth Medical School, and Assistant Director of the In-patient Service of the Dartmouth-Hitchcock Mental Health Center. He entered psychiatry after a practice in internal medicine. He has been responsible for the bulk of the material available here on the medical complications associated with alcohol use and abuse.

God of Compassion, if anyone has come to thine altar troubled in spirit, depressed and apprehensive, expecting to go away as he came, with the same haunting heaviness of heart; if anyone is deeply wounded of soul, hardly daring to hope that anything can afford him the relief he seeks, so surprised by the ill that life can do that he is half afraid to pray: O God, surprise him, we beseech thee, by the graciousness of thy help; and enable him to take from thy bounty as ungrudgingly as thou givest, that he may leave here his sorrow and take a song away.

AUTHOR UNKNOWN

Preface

Material on alcohol and alcoholism is mushrooming. Books, articles, scientific reports, pamphlets. On present use, past use, abuse. In teenagers, women, the labor force, the elderly. When, where, why. . . .

And yet, if you are in the helping business and reasonably bright, but not an M.D. or Ph.D., and can find an occasional half hour to read but don't have all day to search library stacks, then it's probably hard for you to lay your hands on the information you need when it would be most helpful.

This handbook is an attempt to partially remedy the situation. It contains what we believe is the basic information an alcohol counselor or other professional confronted with alcohol problems needs to know and would like to have handy. The work here isn't original. It is an attempt to synthesize, organize, and sometimes "translate" the information from medicine, psychology, psychiatry, anthropology, sociology, and counseling that applies to alcohol use and alcoholism treatment. This handbook isn't the last word. But we hope it is a starting point.

The Department of Psychiatry, Dartmouth Medical School, has been conducting an Alcohol Counselor Training Program since 1972. The training program has been funded by grant award 2T 31AA00048 from the National Institute on Alcohol Abuse and Alcoholism. The idea for training alcohol counselors must be credited to Dr. Henry Payson. Characteristically ahead of the rest of us, he saw early the important role to be played by the alcohol counselor in the provision of alcohol services.

From the beginning, the Alcohol Counselor Training Program has been a departmental effort. Many of the faculty of the Department of Psychiatry and staff of the Dartmouth-Hitchcock Mental Health Center have con-

tributed to the teaching and training. They have also been very generous in consulting with the training program staff. Their lectures, presentations, and advice have helped shape this handbook. We especially wish to thank

Hill Anderson, M.S.W.	Alex Nies, M.D.
John Corson, Ph.D.	Jim Norton, Ph.D.
Matthew Friedman, M.D.	Frances Nye, M.D.
Ronald Green, M.D.	Peter Silberfarb, M.D.
Patrick Keane, M.S.W.	Thomas Singer, M.D.
Kristi Kistler, R.T.	Katherine Swift, M.D.
Robert Landeen, M.D.	Peter Whybrow, M.D.

The counselor trainees with whom we have all worked have been a vital force in this endeavor too. They have assisted us in separating the important from the trivial, the useful from the useless, and truth from nonsense.

Several other persons have been very important. Their impact, though less easily pinpointed, has been nonetheless incalculable. Jacques Perrault, Chief Alcohol Rehabilitation Counselor at the White River Junction Veterans' Hospital, in his life and work, has shown us what alcohol counseling is all about. Similarly, Father Charles Miller, who has been running a one-man rehabilitation service with the aid of his Boss, has immeasurably widened and sharpened our vision. And a big thank you to all those who know, better than we do, what they put up with as this handbook was being prepared, especially Nick.

Jean Kinney
Gwen Leaton

Contents

Introduction

Remember. . .

Remember back to the time you wanted to learn how to ride a bicycle. . . . A *real* bicycle. A two-wheeler. (Close your eyes.)

Remember the street you lived on. . . . How about the big kids who had their own. . . . Can you feel how eager you were to join them? You could just picture yourself hopping on one of your own and winging off. . . . (Close your eyes and picture that scene.)

Continue in your imagination.

Suppose you had decided to seriously pursue your desire to ride a two-wheeler. Off to the town library, signing out a book on *Riding a Two-Wheeler in 20 Easy Steps*. Glossy pictures, diagrams, and sure enough, absolutely everything you'd need to know, to the smallest detail.

Step 1. Stand beside bicycle.

Step 2. Place hands on handlebars.

Step 3. With foot, push up kickstand.

Step 4. Walk briskly, pushing bicycle.

Step 5. Place left foot on left pedal (if standing on left side) and simultaneously swing right leg over bicycle and place on right pedal. (*Caution:* It is imperative to maintain forward motion during this step. Also critical to see that center of gravity of the body is properly positioned above bicycle.)

Step 6. Depress pedal in clockwise motion with ball of foot. And so forth. . . .

That isn't quite how it happened, is it? Had anyone ever suggested that was how you should go about it, there's no way you would not have spotted the ploy as the super con-job of the year.

So, how did you learn? By trying it! Getting your hands on a bike and simply climbing on! Unless you happened to be the Joe Namath of the cycling set, you didn't smugly cruise down to the playground, either, on that first try. Wobbling along, training wheels, your mother or dad running beside holding the seat . . . spills, scuffs, tears, despair, forgetting how to brake in the crunch, more spills . . . and eventually it all clicked!

Working with alcoholics is pretty much like learning to

ride that two-wheeler. It's a process. A series of trying things that occur over a period of time. Hopefully *Riding a Two-Wheeler in 20 Easy Steps* has convinced you. That means learning by doing—feeling awkward, going shakily in the beginning, having someone close by for support and to provide advice. It will include some blows to your pride, moments of feeling silly or unknowledgeable.

How does this book fit in? It's not a step-by-step guide that you can read—even memorize—and then be a counselor. If it were, it probably would be of little use. At best it can be a guide. As you recall from the days you tackled that bicycle, experience is a big key to learning. While things we read may be of some assistance, it is important that they be put to the test of our own experience. To exhaust the bicycle comparison, riding a bicycle requires doing many different things that people already know how to do. Moving their legs up and down, gripping something in their hands, looking around, balancing, and others. But these activities, when uniquely combined and coordinated, are lumped together and called "riding a bicycle." Counseling, too, involves many familiar activities: talking to people, gathering information, sifting out possibilities, solving problems, etc.

Counseling people about alcohol problems requires some specific knowledge. Alcohol, its uses and abuses, is a far more complex subject than simply alcoholism itself. To narrow your outlook to a focus on the problems of the alcoholic, however tremendous, could leave you forever using only three of the gears on your ten-speed bike.

ONCE UPON A TIME . . .

Imagine yourself in what is now Clairvoux, high in the Swiss hills. Stone pots dating from the Old Stone Age have been found that once contained a mild beer or wine. It probably was discovered very much like fire—nature plus curiosity. If any watery mixture of vegetable sugars or starches is allowed to stand long enough in a warm place, alcohol will make itself. Say you're a caveman named Urg, coming back from a lengthier than usual flight from a dinosaur or some such thing. "Aha!" Some berries or barley left in a bowl in the sun. "Smells a bit funny, but so what! I'm thirsty and hungry and tired." Down it goes. Can you imagine what he thought as his first booze went down?

No one knows what kind of liquor was first, wine or beer or mead; but by the Neolithic Age, it was *everywhere*. Tales of the origin of liquor abound in the folklore. One relates that at the beginning of time the forces of good and evil contested with each other for domination of the earth. Eventually the forces for good won out. But a great many of them had been killed in the process, and wherever they fell, a vine sprouted from the ground. So it seems some felt wine to be a good force. Other myths depict the powers of alcohol as gifts from their gods. Some civilizations worshipped specific gods of wine: the Egyptians' god was Osiris; the Greeks', Dionysus; the Romans', Bacchus. Wine was used in early rituals as libations (poured out on the ground or al-

Ramses III distributed beer to his subjects and then told them the tingling they felt radiated from him!

tar or whatever). Priests often drank it as part of the rituals. The Bible, too, is full of references to sacrifices including wine.

From ritual uses it spread to convivial uses, and customs developed. Alcohol was a regular part of the meals, viewed as a staple in the diet, even before ovens were invented for baking bread. The Assyrians received a daily portion from their masters of a "gallon" of bread and a gallon of fermented brew (probably a barley beer). Bread and wine were offered by the Hebrews on their successful return from battle. In Greece and Rome wine was essential at every kind of gathering. Alcohol was found to contribute to fun and games at a party; for example, the Roman orgies. Certainly its safety over water was a factor, but the effects had something to do with it. It's hard to imagine an orgy where everyone drank water, or welcoming a victorious army with lemonade. By the Middle Ages alcohol permeated everything, accompanying birth, marriage, death, the crowning of kings, diplomatic exchanges, signing treaties, and councils. The monasteries became the taverns and inns of the times, and travelers received the benefit of the grape.

The ancients had figured that what was good in these instances might be good in others, and alcohol came into use as a medicine. It was an antiseptic and an anesthetic and was used in combinations to form salves and tonics. As a cure it ran the gamut from black jaundice to pain in the knee and hiccups. St. Paul advised Timothy, "No longer drink only water, but use a little wine for the sake of your stomach and your frequent ailments." Liquor was a recognized mood changer, nature's tranquilizer. The Biblical King Lemuel's mother advises "give wine to them that be of heavy hearts." The Bible also refers to wine as stimulating and cheering. "Praise to God, that he hath brought forth fruit out of the earth, and wine that maketh glad the heart of man."

FERMENTATION AND DISCOVERY OF DISTILLATION

Nature alone cannot produce stronger stuff than 14% alcohol. Fermentation is a combustive action of yeasts on plants: potatoes, fruit, grain, etc. The sugar is exposed to wild yeasts in the air or commercial yeasts, which produce

God made yeast, as well as dough, and loves fermentation just as dearly as he loves vegetation.

EMERSON

Food without drink is like a wound without a plaster.

BRULL

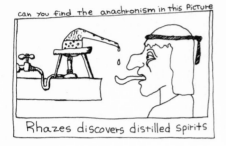

can you find the anachronism in this Picture

Rhazes discovers distilled spirits

an enzyme, which in turn converts sugar into alcohol. Fermentive yeast cannot survive in solutions stronger than 14% alcohol. When that level is reached, the yeast, which is a living thing, ceases to produce and dies.

Now imagine the widespread joy when something stronger came along. In the tenth century an Arabian physician, Rhazes, discovered distilled spirits. Actually, he was looking for a way to release "the spirit of the wine." It was welcomed at the time as the "true water of life." European scientists rejoiced in their long-sought "philosopher's stone," or perfect element. A mystique developed, and alcohol was called "the fountain of youth," "eau-de-vie," "aqua vitae." *Usequebaugh* from the Gaelic *usige beath*, meaning breath of life, is the source of the word "whiskey." The word alcohol itself is derived from the Arabic *al kohl*. It originally referred to a fine powder of antimony used for staining the eyelids and gives rise to speculation on the expression, "Here's mud in your eye!" The word evolved to describe any finely ground substance, then the essence of a thing, and eventually came to mean, "finely divided spirit," or the essential spirit of the wine. Nineteenth century temperance advocates tried to prove that alcohol is derived from the Arabic *alghul*, meaning ghost or evil spirit.

Distilled liquor wasn't a popular drink until about the sixteenth century. Before that it was used as *the* basic medicine and cure for all human ailments. Distillation is a simple process that can produce an alcohol content of close to 93% if it is refined enough times. Remember, nature stops at 14%. Start with a fermented brew. When it is boiled, the alcohol separates from the juice or whatever as steam. Alcohol boils at a lower temperature than the other liquid. The escaping steam is caught in a cooling tube and turns into a liquid again, leaving the juice, water, etc. behind. Voila! Stronger stuff, about 50% alcohol!

Proof as a way of measuring the strength of a given liquor came from a practice used by the early settlers of this country to test their brews. They saturated gunpowder with alcohol and ignited it: too strong, it flared up; too weak, it sputtered. A strong blue flame was considered the sign of proper strength. Almost straight alcohol was diluted with water to gain the desired flame. Half and half was considered 100 proof. Thus, 86-proof bourbon is 43% alcohol. Since alcohol dilutes itself with water from the air, 200-

proof, or 100%, alcohol is not possible. U.S. standards for spirits are between 195 and 198 proof.

ALCOHOL USE IN THE NEW WORLD

Alcohol had come to America in company with the explorers and colonists. In 1620, the *Mayflower* decided to land at Plymouth because, it says in the ship's log, "We could not now take time for further search or consideration, our victuals having been much spent, especially our bere. . . ." The Spanish missionaries brought grapevines to the New World, and before the United States was yet a nation, there was winemaking in California. The Dutch opened the first distillery on Staten Island in 1640. In the Massachusetts Bay Colony brewing ranked next in importance after milling and baking. The Puritans did not disdain the use of alcohol as is sometimes supposed. A federal law passed in 1790 gave provisions for each soldier to receive a ration of one-fourth pint of brandy, rum, or whiskey. The colonists imported wine and malt beverages and planted vineyards, but it was Jamaican rum that became the answer to the thirst of the new nation. For its sake, New Englanders became the bankers of the slave trade that supplied the molasses needed to produce it. Eventually whiskey, the backwoods substitute for rum introduced to America by Irish and Scots settlers in Kentucky, West Virginia, and Maryland, superseded rum in popularity. Sour-mash bourbon became the great American drink.

This is a very brief view of alcohol's history. The extent of its uses, the ways in which it has been viewed, and even the amount of writing about it that survives give witness to the value placed on this strange substance. It has been everywhere, connected to everything that is a part of everyday life. Growing the grapes or grains to produce it is even suspected as the reason for the development of agriculture. Whether making it, using it as a medicine, drinking it, or writing about it, people from early times have devoted a lot of time and energy to alcohol.

WHY BOTHER?

So alcohol happened, why didn't it go the way of the dinosaurs?

Think about the first time *you* ever tasted alcohol. . . . Some people were exposed really early and don't remem-

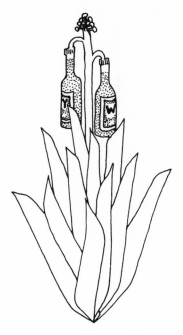

NO, I didn't notice a drink ON THE KitcHen CounTer!

ber the experience of a little sherry in their bottle, or rubbed on their gums when they were teething. Some were allowed a taste of Dad's beer or the Christmas Day champagne at a tender age. Some sneaked sips at the first big wedding or party they were around. Some never even saw it until junior or senior high school. Still others were taught from infancy that it was evil and may not have touched it until college or the army took them away from home. And there are some, who for one reason or another, have never touched the stuff. If you are in the majority, however, you probably encountered it in a variation on one of the above themes.

Maybe you didn't like that first sip of Dad's beer or Aunt Tillie's sherry. Rather than admit it, you decided they must know what was good. So you took a sip every time it was offered. *"As you're fighting your way to the top, it helps to have a taste of what's up there."*

Or perhaps you were around for the preparations for a big do at your house. Ice, soda, and funny-colored stuff in big bottles were lined up with neat things like cherries, oranges, lemons, and sugar. The atmosphere was busy and exciting. When the guests began to arrive, the first thing they got was something from those bottles. Everyone seemed to talk and laugh quite a bit, and after awhile no one seemed to see you. Mom left her drink in the kitchen while she served some of those tasty cheese things she let you try earlier. One quick sip. *"To keep the party going, keep the best on hand."*

Perhaps people in your home drank on weekends, but not you. Mom and Dad said things like, "When you're of age" or "Wouldn't want to stunt your growth" or "This is a big people's drink." Anyway, you weren't getting any tastes. Somewhere along the school trail, you wound up at a party you'd expected to be like all the others you'd been to. Not this time. Someone brought some beer, and everyone else was having some. There might have been a brief flash of guilt when you thought of the folks, but who wants to stick out in a crowd? So you kept up with the gang. Soon you felt as grown-up as you'd ever be. *"On your night of nights, add that sophisticated touch."*

Or perhaps your folks never touched the stuff. They were really opposed to alcohol. They gave you lots of reasons: "It's evil," "People who drink get into terrible trouble," "Vile stuff, it just eats you up," or even, "God's against it." Well, you admired your folks, or were scared of them, or you really believed the part about God's stand. And, anyway, no one pushed you too much. Then came the army or college. It seemed as though everyone drank something, sometime, somewhere. They weren't dropping dead at the first sip or getting into too much trouble that you could see. Even if there was a little trouble, someone said, "Oh, well, he/she was just drunk, sowing some wild oats." Lightning didn't strike. You didn't see the devil popping out of glasses. Just the opposite, most of your friends seemed to be having a lot of fun. *"When the gang gets together. . . ."* Bowling, fishing, sailing, hiking, beaching, everywhere.

It could be that you grew up with wine being served at meals. At some time you were initiated into the process as a matter of course. You never gave it a second thought.

You might have had a religious background that introduced you to wine as a part of your ritual acceptance into manhood or as a part of your particular church's worship.

With time, age, and social mobility, the reasons for continuing to drink become more complex. It's not unusual to drink a bit more than one can handle at some point. After one experience of being drunk, and/or sick, and/or hungover, some people decide never to touch the stuff again. But for most, something they are getting or think they are getting out of alcohol makes them try it again. Despite liquor's real effects on us, most of us search for an experience we have had with it, or want to have with it, or have been led to believe that we can have with its use. *"As an essential part of the Good Life, _____ cannot be excelled."*

Theories to explain alcohol use

The theories advanced to explain the basic why behind drinking alcohol probably all contain some truth. *To escape anxiety*—"It calms me down, helps my nerves." "It helps me unwind after a hard day." *The need for a feeling of power* over oneself or one's environment. Most people don't talk about the latter, but take a look at the heavy reliance of the liquor industry on he-man models, executive types, and beautiful women surrounded by adoring males. People in ads celebrate winning anything with a drink of some sort.

We take a drink only for the sake of the benediction.

PERETZ

The anxiety thesis developed from Freud's work. He concluded that in times of anxiety and stress, people fall back on things that have worked for them in the past. In theory, the things you will choose to relieve anxiety are those you did when you last felt most secure. That neat, secure time might last have been at Mom's breast. It's been downhill ever since. In this case, use of the mouth (eating, smoking, drinking) would be chosen to ease stressful situations. This phenomenon is called *oral fixation*. Another version of the anxiety thesis comes from Horton's studies. He observed that alcohol was used by primitive societies either ritually or socially to relieve the anxiety caused by an unstable environment. Drunken acts are acceptable and not punished. The greater the environmental stress, the heavier the drinking. Therefore, in Horton's view, alcohol's anxiety-reducing property is the one universal key to why people drink alcohol. This theory has by and large been rejected as the sole reason for drinking.

Nonetheless, in our society today, feelings of uneasiness or pressure are often relieved by the businessman's lunch, the cocktail party, etc. Seldon Bacon, head of the Rutgers School of Alcohol Studies, has explored this idea. He describes the original needs that alcohol might have served: satisfaction of hunger and thirst, medication or anesthetic, fostering of religious ecstasy. He maintains that modern, complex society has virtually eliminated these functions. All that is left is alcohol, the depressant, the reliever of tension, inhibition, and guilt. Contemporary society, by creating more and better tensions, has invented new needs that alcohol can meet.

The power theory is one developed by McClelland and friends in the early 1970s. They explored folk tales from both heavy- and light-drinking societies. They discovered that there was no greater concern with relief from tension or anxiety in heavy-drinking societies than in those who consumed less. To carry this further, they conducted a study with college men over a period of ten years. Without revealing the reasons for the study, they asked the students to write down their fantasies before, during, and after their consumption of liquor. The stories revealed that the students felt bigger, stronger, more influential, more aggressive, and more capable of great sexual conquest the more they drank. Their conclusion was that people drink to ex-

perience a feeling of power. This power feeling has two different patterns, depending on the personality of the drinker. What they called *p-power* is a personal powerfulness, uninhibited and carried out at the expense of others. *s-power*, or social power, is a more altruistic powerfulness, power to help others. s-power was found to predominate after two or three drinks; heavier drinking produced a predominance of p-power.

Recently another theory that has popped up from time to time is gaining in popularity. In the article, "Man's Innate Need: Getting High," Weil claims every human being has in him some need to reach out of himself toward some larger experience. And he'll try anything that suggests itself as a way to do that: alcohol, drugs, yoga, meditation, or whatever. Some drugs are commonly known to "blow your mind" or are even designated as "mind-expanding drugs." Weil's evidence for the seeking of altered states of consciousness begins with very young children who whirl, hyperventilate, etc., to produce a change in their experience. When older, people learn that chemicals can produce different states. In pursuit of these states, alcohol is often used because it is the one intoxicant we make legally available. The drug scene is another answer to the same search, plus a dissatisfaction with society. The drug scene also claims "better" highs. Weil states this search arises from the "innate psychological drive arising out of the neurological structure of the human brain." He uses examples of the amazing degree of autonomic control in hypnotized subjects, yogis, etc. In his view, we have put the cart before the horse in focusing attention on drugs, rather than on the

Absinthe makes the heart grow fonder.
ADDISON MIZNER

Wine cheers God and man.
JUDGES 9:13

Wine prepares the heart for love, unless you take too much.
OVID

states people seek from them. He suggests society recognize the need itself and cope with it in a positive rather than a negative way.

The literature abounds with proponents of one or the other theory citing examples and experiments to prove their points. Indeed, there are instances when any theory fits like a glove. From the very earliest recorded times, alcohol has been important to people. That fact is inescapable, and it becomes very tricky business to sort wheat from chaff in the theory area. The trend now seems to be toward a sort of "combination of factors" approach.

Myths

Myths are equally important to people. There are many who think alcohol makes them warm when they are cold (not so), sexier (in the courting, maybe; in the execution, not so), manlier, womanlier, cured of their ills (not usually), less scared of people (possibly), and better able to function (only if very little is taken). An exercise in asking a lot of people what a drink does for them will expose a heavy reliance on myths for their "reasons."

Whatever the truth in the mixture of theory and myth, enough people in this country rely on the use of alcohol to accomplish *something* for them to support a $24 billion a year industry.

THE FLY IN THE OINTMENT—ALCOHOL PROBLEMS

Alcohol is many faceted. With its ritual, medicinal, dietary, and pleasurable uses, alcohol can leave in its wake confusion, pain, disorder, and tragedy. The use and abuse of alcohol has gone hand in hand in all cultures. With the notable exceptions of the Moslems and Buddhists, whose religions forbid drinking, temperance and abstinence have been the exception rather than the rule in most of the world.

As sin or moral failing

Societies have come to grips with alcohol problems in a variety of ways. One of these regards drunkenness as a sin, a moral failing, and the drunk as a moral weakling of some kind. The Greek word for drunk, for example, means literally to "misbehave at the wine." An Egyptian writer admonished his friend with the slightly contemptuous "thou art like a little child." Noah, who undoubtedly had reason to seek relief in drunkenness after getting all those creatures safely through the flood, was not looked on kindly by his children as he lay in his drunken stupor. The complaints have continued through time. A Dutch physician of the sixteenth century criticized the heavy use of alcohol in Germany and Flanders by saying "that freelier than is profitable to health, they take it and drink it." Some of the most forceful sanctions have come from the temperance movements. Axel Gustafson, a temperance leader, wrote that "alcohol is preeminently a destroyer in every department of life." As late as March of 1974, the New Hampshire Christian Civic League devoted an entire issue of its monthly newspaper to a polemic against the idea that alcoholism is a disease. In their view the disease concept gives reprieve to the "odious alcohol sinner."

As a legal issue

Others see the use of liquor as a legislative issue and believe misuse can be solved by laws. Total prohibition is one of the methods used by those who believe that legislation can sober people up. Most legal approaches through history have been piecemeal affairs invoked to deal with specific situations. Excessive drinking was so bad in ancient Greece that "drinking captains" were appointed to supervise drinking. Elaborate rules were devised for drinking at parties. A perennial favorite has been control of supply. In 81 A.D., a Roman emperor ordered the destruction of half the British vineyards.

The sin and legal views of drunkenness often go hand in hand. They have as a common denominator the idea that the drunk chooses to be drunk. He is therefore either a sinner or a ne'er-do-well who can be handled by making it illegal for him to drink. In 1606 intoxication was made a statutory offense in England by an "Act for Repressing the Odious and Loathsome Sin of Drunkenness." In the reign of Charles I, laws were passed to suppress liquor altogether. Settling a new world did not dispense with the problems of alcohol misuse. The traditional methods of dealing with these problems continued. From around 1600 to the 1800s attitudes toward alcohol were low-keyed. There were laws passed in various colonies and states to

deal with liquor use such as an early Connecticut law forbidding drinking for more than half an hour at a time. Another in Virginia in 1760 prohibited ministers from "drinking to excess and inciting riot." But there were no temperance societies, no large-scale prohibitions, no religious bodies fighting.

America's response to alcohol problems

Drinking in the colonies was largely a family affair and remained so until the beginning of the nineteenth century. With increasing immigration, industrialization, and greater social freedoms, drinking became less a family affair. The abuse of alcohol became more open and more destructive.

THE FAMily ThaT Imbibes together
HAS GooD vibes Together.

The opening of the West brought the saloon into prominence. The old and stable social and family patterns began to change. The frontier hero took to gulping his drinks with his foot on the bar rail. Attitudes began to intensify regarding the use of alcohol.

These developments hold the key to many modern attitudes toward alcohol, the stigma of alcoholism, the wet-dry controversy. Ways of looking at alcohol began to polarize America. The legal and moral approaches reached their apex in the United States with the growth of the temperance movement and the Prohibition amendment in 1919.

The temperance movement and Prohibition. The traditional American temperance movement did not begin as a prohibition movement. The temperance movement coincided with the rise of social consciousness, a belief in the efficacy of law to resolve man's problems. It was part and parcel of the humanitarian movement, which included child labor and prison reform, women's rights, abolition, and social welfare and poverty legislation. It originally condemned only excessive drinking and the drinking of distilled liquor, *not all liquor or all drinking.* It was believed that the evils connected with the abuse of alcohol could be remedied through proper legislation. The aims of the original temperance movement were largely moral, uplifting, rehabilitative. Passions grow, however, and before long those who had condemned only the excess use of distilled liquor soon condemned all liquor. Those genial, well-meaning doctors, businessmen, and farmers began to organize their social life around their crusade. Fraternal orders, such as the Independent Order of Good Templars of 1850, grew and proliferated. In a short span of time it had branches all over the United States, with churches, missions, and hospitals, all dedicated to the idea that society's evils were caused by liquor. This particular group influenced the growth of the Women's Christian Temperance Union and the Anti-Saloon League. By 1869 it had become The National Prohibition Party, which was the spearhead of political action. It advocated complete suppression of liquor by law.

People who had no experience at all of drinking got involved in the crusade. In 1874 Frances Willard founded the WCTU in Cleveland. Women became interested in the movement, which simultaneously advocated social reform, prayer, prevention, education, and legislation in the field of alcohol. Mass meetings were organized to which thousands came. Journals were published; children's programs taught fear and hatred of alcohol; libraries developed. The WCTU was responsible for the first laws requiring alcohol education in the schools, which remain on the books. All alcohol use—moderate, light, heavy, excessive—was condemned. All users were one and the same. Bacon, in describing the classic temperance movement, says there was "one word for the action—DRINK. One word for the category of people—DRINKER."

All excess is ill, but drunkenness is of the worst sort.

WILLIAM PENN

By 1895, many smaller local groups had joined the Anti-Saloon League, which had become the most influential of the temperance groups. It was nonpartisan politically and supported any candidate who was Prohibitionist. It pressured Congress and state legislatures and was backed by church groups in "action against the saloon." Political pressure mounted. The major thrust of all these activities was that the only real problem was alcohol, the only real solution, Prohibition. In 1919 Congress passed the Eighteenth Amendment, making it illegal to manufacture or sell alcoholic beverages. The Volstead Act had sixty provisions to implement Prohibition. The act was a messy and complicated affair. There was no precedent to force the public cooperation required to make the act work. From 1920 to 1933 Prohibition remained in effect. Prohibition shaped much of our economic, social, and underground life. The repeal under the Twenty-first Amendment in 1933 did not remedy the situation. Prohibition had failed. The real problems created by alcohol were obscured or ignored by the false wet-dry controversy. The quarrel raged between the manufacturers, retailers, and consumers on one side and the temperance people, many churches, and women on the other. Alcoholics and those with alcohol problems were ignored in the furor. When Prohibition was repealed the problem of abuse was still there, and the alcoholics were still there along with the stigma of alcoholism.

The front door of the Boston Licensing Board was ripped down by the crush to get beer licenses the day Prohibition ended.

Another approach to alcohol problems is that of the ostrich. The ostrich became popular after the failure of Prohibition and is still fashionable today. Problems are often handled with euphemisms, humor, ridicule, and delegation of responsibility, arising from conflicting values and beliefs.

Our inconsistent attitudes toward alcohol are reinforced in subtle ways. For example, look at the hard-drinking movie heroes. There's the guy who drinks and drinks and then calls for more, never gets drunk, outdrinks the bad guys, kills off the rustlers, and gets the girl in the end. Then there's Humphrey Bogart, who is a drunken mess wallowing in the suffering of mankind until the pure and beautiful heroine appears, at which point he washes up, shaves, gets a new suit, and they live happily ever after.

PORTRAIT OF A MAN WHO SWears HE will Never HAve another drink

Drunkenness versus alcoholism

It is important to see that alcoholism is not separate from alcohol. The alcoholic does not spring full-blown from some place in outer space. In general it is a problem that develops over time. Alcohol is available everywhere. A person really has to make a choice *not* to drink in our society. In some sets of circumstances one could drink for the better part of a day and never seem out of place at all. Some brunches have wine punch, Bloody Marys, or café brulet as their accompaniment. Sherry, beer, or a mixed drink is quite appropriate at lunchtime. Helping a friend with an afternoon painting project or even raking your own lawn is a reasonable time to have a beer. Then, after a long day comes the predinner cocktail, maybe some wine with the meal. Later, at cards with friends, drinks are offered. And surely, some romantic candlelight and a nightcap go hand in hand. For most people this combination of events would not be their daily or even weekend fare. The point is that none of the above would cause most people to raise an eyebrow. The accepted times of drinking can be all the time, anywhere. Given enough of the kind of days we described, the person who chooses to drink may develop problems. Alcohol is a drug and does have effects on the body.

When you ask one friend to dine,
Give him your best wine!
When you ask two,
The second best will do!

LONGFELLOW

Is alcoholism a purely modern phenomenon, a product of our times? There are no references to alcoholics as such in historical writing. The word itself is a modern one. But there are vague references, as far back in time as the third century, that distinguish between being merely intoxicated and being a drunkard. In a commentary on imperial law, a Roman jurist of that era suggests that inveterate drunkenness be considered a medical matter rather than a legal one. In the thirteenth century, James I of Aragon issued an edict providing for hospitalization of conspicuously active drunks. In 1655 a man named Younge, an English journalist, wrote a pamphlet in which he seemed to discern the difference between one who drinks and one who has a chronic condition related to alcohol. He says, "He that will be drawn to drink when he hath neither need of it nor mind to it is a drunkard."

History of alcohol treatment efforts

The first serious considerations of the problem of inebriety, as it was called, came in the eighteenth and nineteenth centuries. Two famous writings addressed the problem in what seemed to be a new light. Although their work on the physical aspects of alcohol became fodder for the temperance zealots, both Dr. Benjamin Rush and Dr.

Wine is a bad thing.
It makes you quarrel with your neighbor,
It makes you shoot at your landlord,
It makes you–miss him.

Thomas Trotter seriously considered the effects of alcohol in a scientific way. Rush, a signer of the Declaration of Independence and a Surgeon General of the Army, wrote a lengthy treatise with an equally lengthy title, "An Inquiry into the Effects of Ardent Spirits on the Human Body and Mind, with an Account of the Means of Preventing and the Remedies of Curing Them." Rush's book is a compendium of the attitudes of the time, given weight by scholarly treatment. The more important of the two, and the first scientific formulation of drunkenness on record, is the classic work of Trotter, an Edinburgh physician. In 1804 he wrote "An Essay, Medical, Philosophical, and Chemical, on Drunkenness and Its Effects on the Human Body." He states " . . . in the writings of medicine, we find drunkenness only cursorily mentioned among the powers that injure health. . . . The priesthood hath poured forth its anathemas from the pulpit; and the moralist, no less severe, hath declaimed against it as a vice degrading to our nature." He then gets down to the nitty-gritty of the matter: "In medical language, I consider drunkenness, strictly speaking, to be a disease, produced by a remote cause, and giving birth to actions and movements in the living body that disorder the functions of health."

Trotter did not gain many adherents to his position, but small efforts were also being made in the United States at the time. Around the 1830s, in Massachusetts, Connecticut, and New York, small groups were forming to reform "intemperate persons" by hospitalizing them, instead of sending them to jail or the workhouse. The new groups, started by the medical superintendent of Worcester, Massachusetts, Dr. Samuel Woodward, and a Dr. Eli Todd, did not see inebriates in the same class with criminals, the indigent, or the insane. Between 1841 and 1874 eleven nonprofit hospitals and houses were set up. In 1876 the *Journal of Inebriety* started publication to advance their views and findings. These efforts were taking place against the background of the temperance movement. Naturally, there was tremendous popular opposition from both the church and the legislative halls. The *Journal* was not prestigious by the standards of the medical journals of that time, and before Prohibition the hospitals were closed and the *Journal* had folded.

There was also another group that briefly flourished.

The Washington Temperance Society began in Chase's Tavern in Baltimore in 1840. Six drinking buddies were the founders, and they each agreed to bring a friend to the next meeting. In a few months parades and public meetings were being held to spread the message: "Drunkard! Come up here! You can reform. We don't slight the drunkard. We love him!" At the peak of its success in 1844, the membership consisted of 100,000 "reformed common drunkards" and 300,000 "common tipplers." A women's auxiliary group, the Martha Washington Society, was dedicated to feeding and clothing the poor. Based on the promise of religious salvation, the Washington Temperance Society was organized in much the same way as the ordinary temperance groups. There was this difference, however. It was founded on the basis of one drunkard helping another, of drunks telling their story in public. The society prospered all over the East Coast as far north as New Hampshire. A hospital, the Home for the Fallen, was established in Boston and still exists under a different name. There are many similarities between the Washington Society and Alcoholics Anonymous: alcoholics helping each other, regular meetings, sharing experiences, fellowship, reliance on a Higher Power, and total abstention from alcohol. The Society was, however, caught up in the frenzies of the total temperance movement: the controversies, power struggles, religious fights, and ego trips of the leaders. By 1848, eight short years after its founding, it was absorbed into the total prohibition movement. The treatment of the alcoholic became unimportant in the heat of the argument.

Recognition of the alcoholic as a sick person did not reemerge until very recently. The gathering of a group of scientists at Yale's Laboratory of Applied Psychology (later the Laboratory of Applied Biodynamics) and the Fellowship of Alcoholics Anonymous, both begun in the 1930s, were instrumental in bringing this about. It was also in the 1930s that a recovered Bostonian alcoholic, Richard Peabody, first began to apply psychological methods to the cure of alcoholics. He replaced the terms drunk and drunkenness with the more scientific and less judgmental alcoholic and alcoholism. At Yale, Yandell Henderson, Howard Haggard, Leon Greenberg, and later E. M. Jellinek founded the *Quarterly Journal of Studies on Alcohol*. Unlike the earlier *Journal of Inebriety*, the *QJSA* had a sound scientific footing and became the mouthpiece for alcohol information. Starting with Haggard's work on alcohol metabolism, these efforts marked the first attempt to put the study of alcohol and alcohol problems in a respectable up-to-date framework. Jellinek's masterwork, *The Disease Concept of Alcoholism*, was a product of the Yale experience. The Yale Center of Alcohol Studies and the Classified Abstract Archive of Alcohol Literature were established. The Yale Plan Clinic was also set up to diagnose and treat alcoholism. The Yale Summer School of Alcohol Studies, now the Rutgers School, educated professionals and laymen from all walks of life. Yale's prestigious influence had far-reaching effects. The National Council on Alcoholism, a volunteer organization, also grew out of the Yale School. It was founded in 1944 by the joint efforts of Jellinek and Marty Mann, a recovered alcoholic and the NCA's first president, to provide public information and education about alcohol.

On the other side of the coin, the Fellowship of Alcoholics Anonymous was having more success in treating alcoholics than any other group. AA grew, and in 1974 it estimated a membership of 700,000 in both America and abroad. Its members became influential in removing the stigma that had been so long attached to the alcoholic. Lawyers, businessmen, teachers, people from every sector of society began to recover. They could be seen leading useful, normal lives without alcohol. (More will be said later on the origins and program of AA itself.) The successful recoveries of its members have unquestionably influenced the course of recent developments.

New attitudes

The new attitudes toward alcoholism have become the foundation for public policy. Since 1960 alcoholism has been gaining recognition by the federal government as a major public health problem. At the center of the federal efforts is the National Institute of Alcohol Abuse and Alcoholism, the NIAAA, established in 1971. The NIAAA sponsors research, training, public education, and treatment programs. The legislation creating NIAAA is a landmark in the history of society's responses to alcoholism. The Comprehensive Alcohol Abuse and Alcoholism Prevention, Treatment, and Rehabilitation Act of 1970 is also known as the Hughes Act. Its sponsor was former Senator Harold Hughes, himself a recovering alcoholic. It establishes what might be called a Bill of Rights for alcoholic individuals. It recognizes that they suffer from a "disease that requires treatment"; it provides protection against discrimination in hiring former alcoholic patients. In a similar vein, the Uniform Alcoholism and Intoxication Treatment Act has been recommended for enactment by the states. This act mandates treatment rather than punishment. These acts incorporate the new attitudes emerging toward alcoholics and alcohol abuse: it is a problem; it is treatable.

PAYING THE PIPER

In the United States, statistics on who drinks, what, where, and when have been kept since 1850. However, making comparisons between different historical periods is difficult. One reason is that statistics have only been gathered methodically and impartially since 1950. Another reason is that there have been changes in the way the basic information is organized and reported. A century ago, reports included numbers of "inebriates" or "drunkards." In the 1940s through the 1960s, "alcoholics" were often a designated subgroup. Then came the 1970s and another change. "Heavy drinkers" or "heavy drinkers with a high problem index" (!) has begun to replace "alcoholics" as a category in reporting statistical information. So the task of identifying changes in drinking practices is not an easy one.

Who drinks what, when, and where

Nonetheless, out of the maze of statistics available on how much Americans drink, where they drink it, and with what consequences, some are important to note. It is estimated that over three fourths, or 77%, of men and 60% of women drink alcohol. They comprise 68% of the adult population. On the average they spend over 5% of their annual budget on alcohol. The per capita consumption is on the rise. During the decade of the 1960s, it increased 32%. In a year's time the statistically average American drinks 2.6 gallons of liquor, 2.16 gallons of wine, and 26.6 gallons of beer. Since the alcohol content of each varies, in terms of absolute alcohol, 42% of this alcohol comes from hard stuff, 12% from wine, and 46% from beer.

How does alcohol use in the United States compare to

There were roughly 100 beer cans per man, woman, and child manufactured in the United States in 1972.

that of other countries? *The President's Task Force Report: Drunkenness for 1967* reported that the United States had the second highest rate of alcoholism in the world. (France ranked first.) Among industrial countries, the United States currently ranks eighth in per capita consumption for all categories of alcohol, but we're number two in distilled spirits.

It is estimated that alcoholics make up 4% of the U.S. population 20 years or older, although some estimates are higher. The usual figure is 9,000,000 alcoholics in a population of 200,000,000. There are no specific figures on the nonalcoholics who abuse alcohol. These nonalcoholic drinkers include the one-time drunken traffic offender who appears in court; the person who, when drunk for the one and only time in his life, puts his foot through a window and ends up in a hospital emergency room; and those who miss work after a particularly festive New Year's Eve. The alcohol abuser, though costly and troublesome, is not usually a habitual offender. The alcoholic tends to be.

In the alcoholic population itself only 5% are on skid row. At least 95% of problem drinkers are employed or employable; they make up 5% of the nation's work force and perhaps 10% of the executives. Most of them are living with their families. The vast majority live in respectable neighborhoods, are housewives, bankers, doctors, sales people, farmers, teachers, clergymen, and so forth. They try to raise decent children, go to football games, shop for their groceries, go to work, and rake the leaves. According to a 1974 survey, the highest percentage of problem drinkers live in either the northeast, Middle Atlantic, or Pacific Coast states. They are mostly males. However, the percentage of women problem drinkers is on the rise. This is frequently attributed to increased drinking among women and to less protection of the woman alcoholic. A high proportion of problem drinkers are unmarried or divorced, live in large cities, and are both the least and the most educated part of the population.

Economic costs

Although they are only a small portion of the drinking population, both the alcohol abuser and the alcoholic cost the United States a huge amount of time and money each year. Following is a breakdown of the economic costs of alcohol misuse and alcoholism for 1971.

	Billions of dollars
Lost production	$ 9.35
Health and medical	8.29
Motor vehicle accidents	6.44
Alcohol programs and research	0.64
Criminal justice system	0.51
Social welfare system	0.14
TOTAL	$25.37

Personal costs

The personal cost of alcoholism is tremendous. Alcoholics' life expectancy is shortened by 10 to 12 years. Their mortality rate is two and a half times greater than that of nonalcoholics. They have a higher rate of violent deaths. In 1968, alcoholism accounted for 7% of all deaths. Alcoholism is listed as the reason for death on 13,000 death certificates yearly. This is an amazingly high figure considering the sus-

pected, undetected, unreported cases. Some 36 million Americans are affected by their relationships to an active alcoholic. According to the *1968 Alcohol and Highway Safety Report,* alcohol plays a role in about half the 60,000 highway deaths each year. In other words, more Americans were killed on the roads as a result of alcohol than were killed in the Vietnam War. According to *Accident Facts,* from the Indiana University Institute for Research in Public Safety, in 1971, out of 111 million drivers, 80 million drink, 13 million are heavy drinkers, 5 to 7 million are alcoholics. Chronic drinkers, as opposed to one-time of-

fenders, were responsible for two thirds of the fatalities. Disabilities as a result of highway accidents are estimated at 500,000 people yearly. In accidents involving pedestrians, 40% of pedestrians in fatal accidents had been drinking; 32% of pedestrians and 53% of the drivers had blood alcohol levels of more than 0.10%, the legal evidence for intoxication.

Crime and alcohol

Alcohol is also reflected in the crime statistics in the United States. One half of all homicides and one third of all suicides are alcohol related, resulting in 11,700 deaths a year. Two thirds of all assaults and felonies are committed by persons under the influence of alcohol. Almost half of the 5.5 million yearly arrests are related to the misuse of alcohol. In cases of child abuse, alcohol is a contributing factor in over half the cases. The role alcohol plays in sexual assaults is just now being studied. In one southwestern state, 50% of all the convicted rapists had been drinking prior to the rape, and 35% were considered alcoholic. Another study of men involved with child molesting found half were drunk when the crime was committed and one third were alcoholics. One half of all North American policemen killed while on duty are killed in the course of investigating family disputes. Alcohol is virtually a universal element in any family squabble reported to the police. Drunkenness accounts for 1,400,000 arrests; disorderly conduct and vagrancy, often euphemisms for drunkenness, account for 665,000. These crimes and misdemeanors cost the taxpayers around $100 million a year in arrest, trial, and jail fees. As the states adopt the Uniform Alcoholism and Intoxication Treatment Act, these arrests will go down. Instead, the alcoholic will be placed in appropriate treatment centers.

Health care and alcohol

Alcohol has an impact on the health care systems also. Of new admissions to state hospitals, alcoholism is the most common diagnosis (33%) for men. It ranks third for women (13%). In general hospitals, several years ago, over one in twenty admissions was an alcoholic. Studies have shown 20% of all hospitalized persons have a significant alcohol problem whatever the presenting problem is. The Vet-

The habit of using ardent spirits, by men in office, has occasioned more injury to the public and more trouble to me than all other causes.

THOMAS JEFFERSON

eran's Administration estimates 50% of all VA hospital beds are filled by veterans with alcohol problems.

• • •

Television, radio, billboard, and magazine campaigns by the NIAAA and the National Council on Alcoholism are designed to persuade Americans to examine the effects of drinking practices. A government survey of American attitudes toward alcohol was done in 1973. It showed that 11% more persons questioned knew that alcohol is a drug in 1973 than in 1971, representing an 18% change; 13% more in 1973 than in 1971 felt that heavy drinking is a very serious problem in the country today, representing a 22% change. People are becoming aware of the toll that alcoholism and alcohol abuse can take in our public and private lives. What people will individually and collectively do with this knowledge is the question. Statistics ten years hence will reflect the answer.

RESOURCES AND FURTHER READING
History and overview

Alcoholics Anonymous comes of age. New York: A.A. World Service, 1955.

Bacon, Seldon. The classical temperance movement in the U.S.A. *British Journal of Addiction,* 1967, *62,* 5-18.

Chafetz, Morris. *Liquor, the servant of man.* Boston: Little, Brown & Co., 1965.

D.P. The Washingtonians. *A.A. Grapevine,* 1971, 27(9), 16-22.

Paredes, Alfonso. The history of the concept of alcoholism. In Ralph Tarter and A. Arthur Sugerman (Eds.), *Alcoholism: interdisciplinary approaches to an enduring problem.* Reading, Mass.: Addison-Wesley Publishing Co., 1976.

Pittman, D. J., and Snyder, S. R. (Eds.). *Society, culture, and drinking patterns.* New York: John Wiley & Sons, Inc., 1962.

Rouche, Berton. *Alcohol: the neutral spirit.* New York: Berkley & Medallion Paperbacks, 1960.

Why people drink

Horton, Donald. Primitive societies. In R. McCarthy (Ed.), *Drinking and intoxication.* New Haven, Conn.: College & University Press, 1959.

MacAndrew, C., and Edgerton, R. *Drunken comportment.* Chicago: Aldine Publishing Co., 1969.

McClelland, D., et al. *The drinking man.* New York: The Free Press, 1972.

Weil, Andrew. Man's innate need: getting high. In *Dealing with drug abuse.* Ford Foundation Report, 1972.

Social costs

Keller, Mark, et al. *Alcohol and health.* Rockville, Md.: Department of Health, Education, and Welfare, 1971.

Keller, Mark, et al. *Alcohol and health, new knowledge.* Rockville, Md.: Department of Health, Education, and Welfare, 1974.

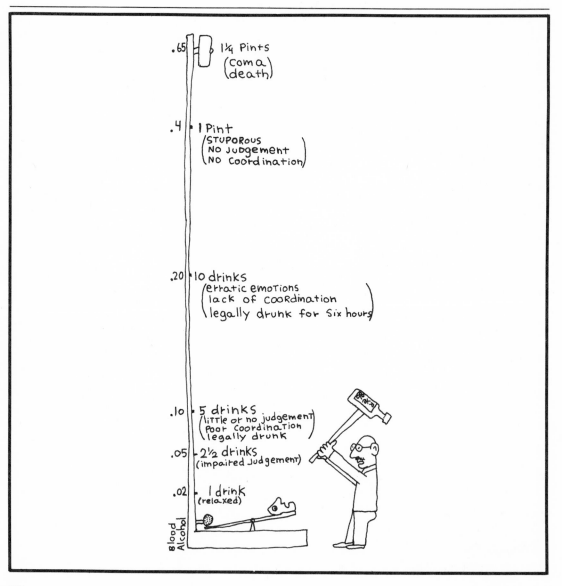

Alcohol is a drug. When it is ingested, there are predictable, specific physiological effects on the body. Any body. Every body. Alcoholic and nonalcoholic. This is all too often overlooked. Instead, attention is paid to the physical impact of chronic use or what happens with excessive use. What gets lost is the normal, routine effects on *anyone* who uses alcohol. Let's examine what happens to alcohol in the body, how it is taken up, broken down, and thereby alters the normal functions of the body.

DIGESTION

The human body is well engineered to take the foods ingested and change them into substances the organism needs to maintain life and to provide energy. Despite occasional upsets from too much spice or too much food, this process goes on without a hitch. The first part of this transformation is called digestion. A comparison might be made to the carpenter who dismantles an old building, salvages the materials, and later uses them in new construction. Digestion is the body's way of dismantling food to get the raw materials required by the body. Whether alcohol is properly termed a food was at one time a big point of controversy. Alcohol does have calories. One ounce of pure alcohol would contain 210 calories. To translate that into drinks, there are 75 calories in an ounce of whiskey or 150 calories in a 12-ounce can of beer. But alcohol's usefulness as a food is limited. Sometimes alcohol is described as providing "empty calories." It does not contain vitamins, minerals, or other essential substances. Also when alcohol is present, it interferes with the body's ability to use other sources of energy. As a food, alcohol is unique. It requires no digestion. Since alcohol is a liquid, no mechanical action by the teeth is required to break it down. And no digestive juices need be added to transform it into a form that can be absorbed by the bloodstream and transported to all parts of the body.

ABSORPTION

So what happens to alcohol in the body? Surprisingly, absorption of the alcohol begins almost immediately, with a very small amount being taken up into the bloodstream through the tiny capillaries in the mouth. But the majority goes the route of all food when swallowed: into the stom-

Calories	
Beer, 12 oz. can	173
Martini, 3 oz. 3:1	145
olive, 1 large	20
Rum, 1 oz.	73
Sherry, sweet, 3 oz.	150
Fortified wines	120-160
Scotch, 1 oz.	73
cola, 8 oz.	105
pretzels, 5 small sticks	20

THE JOY OF COOKING

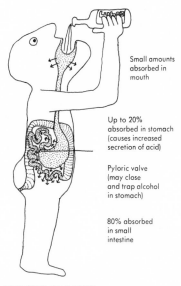

Small amounts absorbed in mouth

Up to 20% absorbed in stomach (causes increased secretion of acid)

Pyloric valve (may close and trap alcohol in stomach)

80% absorbed in small intestine

ABSORPTION OF ALCOHOL

ach. If other food is present in the stomach, the alcohol mixes with it. Here, too, some alcohol will seep into the bloodstream. Up to 20% can be absorbed directly from the stomach. The remainder passes into the small intestine to be absorbed.

The amount of food in the stomach when drinking takes place has important ramifications. Alcohol is an irritant. It increases the flow of hydrochloric acid, a digestive juice secreted by the stomach lining. Anyone who has an ulcer and takes a drink can readily confirm this. This phenomenon likewise explains the feeling of warmth in the tummy as the drink goes down. The presence of food acts to dilute the alcohol and therefore diminishes the irritant properties. The amount of food in the stomach is a big factor in determining the speed with which the alcohol is absorbed by the bloodstream. It is the rate of absorption that is largely responsible for the feelings of intoxication. In addition to the impact of food in the stomach, the rate of absorption will vary with the type of beverage. The higher the concentration of alcohol (up to 40%, or 80 proof), the more quickly it is absorbed. This partially explains why distilled spirits have more apparent "kick" than wine or beer. Plus, beer has some food substances that slow absorption. Carbon dioxide, which hastens the passage of alcohol from the stomach, has the effect of increasing the speed of absorption. Champagne, sparkling wines, or drinks mixed with carbonated soda give a sense of "bubbles in the head."

Meanwhile, on from the stomach to the pylorus valve. This valve controls the passage of the stomach's contents into the small intestine. It is sensitive to the presence of alcohol. With large concentrations of alcohol, it tends to get "stuck" in the closed position. When this pylorospasm happens, the alcohol trapped in the stomach may cause sufficient irritation and distress to induce vomiting. This phenomenon accounts for the nausea and vomiting that may accompany too much drinking. This "stuck" pylorus also may serve as a self-protective mechanism by preventing the passage of what might be life-threatening doses of alcohol.

BLOOD ALCOHOL CONCENTRATION

In considering the effects of alcohol, several questions come to mind. How much alcohol in how much person? How fast did the alcohol get there? And is the blood alcohol level rising or declining? Let's take each of these in turn. The concentration of alcohol in the blood is the first. One tablespoon of sugar mixed in a cup of water yields a much sweeter solution than a tablespoon diluted in a gallon of water. Similarly, a drink with one ounce of alcohol will give a higher blood alcohol level in a 100-pound woman than in a 200-pound man. In fact, it will be virtually twice as high. Her body contains less water than his.

The second factor is rate of absorption. The faster alcohol is absorbed, the more rapidly the blood alcohol level rises, and the greater the impairment that results. So quickly drink a scotch and soda on an empty stomach, and you will probably be more giddy than if you drink more alcohol more slowly, say in the form of beer after a meal. Even with the same blood alcohol levels, there is greater impairment with faster rates of absorption. Impairment is based on both the amount absorbed and the rate of absorption. Finally, for any drinking occasion, there are different effects depending on whether the blood alcohol level is going up or coming down.

Once in the small intestine, the remainder of the alcohol (at least 80%) is absorbed by the bloodstream. The bloodstream is the body's transportation system. It delivers nutrients the cells require for energy and picks up the wastes produced by cell metabolism. Thus alcohol diluted in the bloodstream is carried to all parts of the body.

While *blood* alcohol levels are almost universally used as the measure of alcohol in the body, this isn't to imply alcohol merely rides around in the bloodstream until the liver is able to break it down. Alcohol is soluble in water. It is able to pass through cell walls. Therefore it is distributed uniformly throughout the water of all body tissues. The blood alcohol concentration represents the alcohol content of any body tissues composed of water. The tissues' alcohol content varies in proportion to their amount of water. The alcohol content of liver tissue is 64% of that in the blood; of muscle, 84%; and that of the brain, 88%. It takes very little time for the tissues to absorb the alcohol circulating in the blood. For example, within two minutes, brain tissues reflect accurately the blood alcohol level.

Now that we have explained how alcohol is taken up by the body and distributed to the body tissues, what are the effects, and how is it broken down and removed?

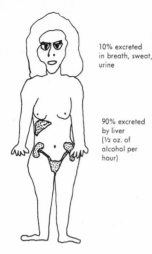

10% excreted
in breath, sweat,
urine

90% excreted
by liver
(½ oz. of
alcohol per
hour)

EXCRETION OF ALCOHOL

BREAKDOWN AND REMOVAL

The removal of alcohol from the body begins as soon as the alcohol is absorbed by the bloodstream. Small amounts leave unmetabolized through sweat, urine, or the breath. At most, this accounts for only 10% of the alcohol consumed. The rest has to be changed chemically, metabolized. The first step in the metabolism of alcohol is its change to acetaldehyde. A liver enzyme, alcohol dehydrogenase, or ADH in chemical shorthand, accomplishes this. The acetaldehyde that is formed is acted on by yet another liver enzyme, acetaldehyde dehydrogenase. Very rapidly the acetaldehyde breaks down to form acetic acid. The acetic acid then leaves the liver and is dispersed throughout the body, where it is oxidized to carbon dioxide and water. In summary, the chain of events is:

alcohol → acetaldehyde* → acetic acid → carbon dioxide + water

As you can see, the liver holds the key position in this process. Almost any organ can break down the acetic acid. But only the liver can handle the first steps. Generally the rate at which food is metabolized depends on the energy requirements of the body. Experience will confirm this, especially for anyone who has taken a stab at dieting. Chopping wood burns up more calories than watching the tube. Too much food, and a storehouse of fat begins to accumulate around the middle. By balancing calories taken in our meals and exercise, we can avoid accumulating a fat roll. Again, as a food, alcohol is unique. It is metabolized at a constant rate. The liver does not have a "piece rate" workset when it comes to alcohol. The presence of large amounts does not prompt the liver to work faster. Despite alcohol's seeming potential as a fine source of calories, increased exercise (and hence raising the body's need for calories)

---

*It is at this point that disulfiram (Antabuse), a drug used in alcoholism treatment, acts. Antabuse stops the breakdown of acetaldehyde by blocking acetaldehyde dehydrogenase. Thus, acetaldehyde starts to accumulate in the system. It is very toxic, and its effects are those associated with an Antabuse reaction. A better term would be an acetaldehyde reaction. The toxicity of acetaldehyde usually isn't a problem. It breaks down faster than it is formed. But Antabuse does not allow this to take place so rapidly. Thus the nausea, flushing, and heart palpitations. It has been observed that Orientals often have such symptoms when drinking. These are probably based on biochemical differences resulting from genetic differences. In effect, they have a built-in Antabuse-like response.

does not increase the speed of metabolism. This is probably not news to anyone who's tried to sober up a drunk. It's simply a matter of time. Exercise may only mean you've a wide-awake drunk, rather than a sleeping one, to contend with. But he's still drunk. The rate alcohol is metabolized by the liver may vary a little between people. It will also increase after an extended drinking career. Yet the average rate is around ½ ounce of *pure* alcohol per hour. That is roughly equivalent to one mixed drink of 86-proof whiskey. The unmetabolized alcohol remains circulating in the bloodstream, "waiting in line." The concentration of alcohol in the blood, and hence in the brain, is responsible for the intoxicating effects of alcohol.

A drunken night makes a cloudy morning.

SIR WILLIAM CORNWALLIS

ALCOHOL'S EFFECTS ON THE BODY

What is the immediate effect of alcohol on the various body organs and functions?

Digestive system. As already noted, alcohol is an irritant. This explains the burning sensation as it goes down. Alcohol in the stomach promotes the flow of gastric juices. A glass of wine before dinner may thereby promote digestion by "priming" the stomach for food. But with intoxicating amounts, alcohol impedes or stops digestion.

Circulatory system. Alcohol has only minor effects on the circulatory system. Heartbeat and blood pressure are little affected. In moderate amounts, alcohol is a vasodilator of the surface blood vessels. These vessels expand near the skin surface. This accounts for the sensation of warmth and a flush to the skin that accompanies drinking. Despite the feeling of warmth, body heat is being lost. Thus, whoever sends out the St. Bernard with a brandy cask to the aid of the snow-stranded traveler is misguided. Despite the illusion of warmth, a good belt of alcohol will further cool off the body.

Kidneys. Anyone who has had a couple of drinks may well spend some time traipsing back and forth to the wc. This increased urine output is not caused by alcohol's direct action on the kidneys and is not simply due to the amount of liquid consumed. This phenomenon is related to the effect of alcohol on the pituitary gland housed in the brain. The pituitary secretes a hormone regulating the amount of urine produced. As the pituitary is screwed up by alcohol, too little of the hormone is released, and the

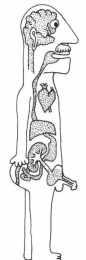

Interferes with brain activity, affecting first judgment, then muscular coordination, then sensory perception

Has few effects on heart or lungs except in high amounts, then may cause death

Interferes with liver's ability to maintain stable blood sugar

Leads to increased production of urine by kidneys

Irritates intestinal system; increases acid secretion by stomach

EFFECTS OF ALCOHOL

kidneys form too much urine. This effect is most pronounced on a rising blood alcohol level, as the alcohol is still being absorbed.

Liver. The liver has an incredible number of different functions. A very important one is its role in maintaining a proper blood sugar level. Sugar (the body's variety, not table sugar) is the only source of energy the brain cells can use. Since the brain is the master control center of the body, an inadequate supply of food has far-reaching consequences. When alcohol is present in the system, the liver throws its whole attention, so to speak, to metabolizing the alcohol. When taking care of the alcohol, it does *not* manufacture and release glucose (sugar) into the bloodstream. This doesn't really matter when other sources of glucose are available, for example, when digestion of a meal is taking place. But at other times, between meals, the body counts on the liver to keep the blood glucose level up to snuff. If alcohol is present then, a drop in blood sugar is likely. This is a hypoglycemic state, a below normal concentration of blood sugar. The brain is deprived of its proper nourishment. Symptoms include hunger, weakness, nervousness, sweating, headache, tremor. If the level is sufficiently depressed, coma can occur.

This effect of alcohol has been little understood. Hypoglycemia is sometimes touted as one of the causes of alcoholism. That's getting it backward. Alcohol ingestion can induce a hypoglycemic state. Despite the fact that alcohol is made from sugar and is high in calories, it is not available to the body as a sugar. Actually, it interferes with the standard means of maintaining an adequate sugar level. Drinking on an empty stomach or drinking for lengthy periods so that alcohol is still around long after a meal has been digested are two situations likely to produce a hypoglycemic state. This phenomenon may also explain some of the discomfort of the hangover. Beware lengthy cocktail parties on both accounts.

Central nervous system. The central nervous system (CNS), particularly the brain, is the organ most sensitive to the presence of alcohol. This sensitivity is what being high, drunk, or intoxicated is all about. The intensity of the effect is directly related to the concentration of alcohol in the blood. The drug alcohol is a CNS depressant. It interferes with or lowers the activity of the brain.

Not all parts of the brain are uniformly affected. If they were, the same amount required to release inhibitions would also be lethal by simultaneously hitting the parts controlling breathing. Watch, or recall, someone becoming intoxicated and see the progression of effects. The following examples refer to CNS effects in men.

One drink. (The "drinks" here are a little under ½ ounce of pure alcohol, the equivalent of a 12-ounce beer or an ounce of 86-proof whiskey. Many generous hosts and hostesses mix drinks with more than 1 ounce of booze. So, as you read on, don't shrug off the "10-drink" section as an impossibility. Five generous ones could easily have as much alcohol!) With one drink, the drinker will be a bit more relaxed, possibly loosened up a little. Unless he chugged it rapidly, thus getting a rapid rise in blood alcohol, his behavior will be little changed. Being of average height, weighing 160 pounds, by the end of an hour his blood alcohol level will be 0.02. Before two hours all traces of alcohol will be gone.

Two and a half drinks. With two and a half drinks in an hour's time, your party goer will have a 0.05 blood alcohol level. He's high. The "newer" parts of the brain, those controlling judgment, have been affected. That our friend has been drinking is apparent. He may be loud, boisterous, making passes; saying and doing things he might usually censor. These are the effects that mistakenly cause people to think of alcohol as a stimulant. The system isn't hyped up; the inhibitions have been suspended. At this time our friend is entering the danger zone for driving. With two and a half drinks in an hour, two and a half hours will be required to completely metabolize the alcohol.

And this is our new antialcoholic whiskey bottle. Preliminary testing suggests that at a blood alcohol level of .03 people can no longer figure out how to pour themselves a drink.

Five drinks. With five drinks in an hour, there's no question you've a drunk on your hands. The law would agree. A blood alcohol level of 0.10 is sufficient in most states to convict of driving while intoxicated. By this time judgment is nil. "Off coursh I can drive!" In addition to the parts of the brain controlling judgment, the centers controlling muscle coordination are depressed. There's a stagger to the walk and a slur to the speech. Even though the loss of dexterity can be measured, the drinker, now with altered judgment, will claim he's never functioned better. Five hours will be required for all traces of alcohol to disappear from the system.

Ten drinks. This quantity of alcohol in the system yields a blood alcohol content of 0.20, and even more of the brain is affected besides the motor centers. Emotions are probably very erratic—from laughter to tears to rage. Even if your guest could remember he had a coat, he'd never be able to put it on. Ten hours will be required for all the alcohol to be metabolized. Six hours, and he'll still be legally drunk.

One pint of whiskey. With this amount of booze, the drinker is stuporous. Though not passed out, nothing the senses take in actually registers. Judgment is gone, coordination wiped out, and sensory perception almost gone. With the liver handling 1 ounce of alcohol per hour, it will be sixteen hours, well into tomorrow, before all the alcohol is gone.

One and one-fourth pints of whiskey. At this point, the person is in a coma and dangerously close to death. The brain centers, which send out instructions to the heart and breathing apparatus, are partially anesthetized. At a blood alcohol level of 0.4 to 0.5, a person is in a coma; at 0.6 to 0.7, death occurs.

Differences in women

Substitute a 120-pound woman in these examples, and the weight differential would certainly speed up the process. With one drink in one hour, she would have a blood alcohol level of 0.03; two and a half drinks, she'd be up to 0.07. By five drinks, she'd have a 0.14 reading. Should she make it through a pint, she'd be in a coma with a level of 0.45. Tomorrow might not come as soon for her. Besides the differences in body weight, other factors can speed up or alter this process. Women and men differ in their relative amounts of body fat and water. Women have a higher proportion of fat and correspondingly lower amounts of water. Alcohol is not fat soluble. Therefore, a woman and a man of the same body weight, both drinking the same amounts of alcohol, will have different blood alcohol levels. Hers will be higher. She has less water than he has in which to dilute her alcohol.

There is another critical difference between men and women in regard to how they handle alcohol. A woman's menstrual cycle significantly influences her rate of absorption. This difference presumably relates to the changing balances of sex hormones and appears to be the result of several interacting factors. During the premenstrual phase of her cycle, a woman absorbs alcohol more rapidly. The absorption rate is significantly faster than in other phases of the menstrual cycle. So premenstrually a woman will get a higher blood alcohol level than she would get from drinking an equivalent amount at other times. In practical terms, a woman may find herself getting drunk faster right before her period. There is also evidence that women taking birth control pills also will absorb alcohol faster and thereby have higher blood alcohol levels.

Quite possibly other differences may exist between men and women in terms of alcohol's effects. Virtually all the physiological research has been conducted on men. The researchers have then blithely assumed the findings to be equally true for women. While the basic differences between absorption rates of men and women were reported as early as 1932, they were forgotten and/or ignored until the mid 1970s. Believe it or not, the impact of the menstrual cycle was first reported in 1976! With this failure to examine the effects of the primary and obvious difference between males and females, who knows what more subtle areas have not been looked at. End of sermon!

Alcohol as anesthetic

Alcohol is an anesthetic, just as it shows in all the old western movies. By modern standards, it is not a very good one. The dose required to produce a coma is very close to the lethal amount. When the vital centers begin to be affected, it only takes a wee bit more to permanently put them to sleep. Sadly, a couple of times a year almost any newspaper obituary column documents a death from alcohol. Usually it involves chugging a fifth of liquor on a dare, or as a prank, which very quickly yields a lethal dose of alcohol.

Despite differences between people, each and every human body basically reacts in the same way to alcohol. This uniform, well-documented response is what enables the law to set a specific blood alcohol level for defining drunkenness. This can be easily measured by blood samples or the breathalyzer. Computing the amount of unmetabolized alcohol that is exhaled corresponds to the amount circulating in the blood. Small capillaries in the lungs exchange carbon dioxide for oxygen as you breathe. The alcohol that escapes by this route can be measured on the breath.

CUMULATIVE EFFECTS

The immediate effects of the drug alcohol have been described. With continued drinking, changes take place. There are cumulative effects. Any drinker, not only the alcoholic, can testify to this. The first few times someone tries alcohol, with one drink they feel tipsy. With drinking experience, one drink no longer has that effect. In part this may reflect greater wisdom. The veteran drinker has learned "how to drink" to avoid feeling intoxicated, that is, by not chugging a drink or not drinking on an empty stomach. The other reason is that with repeated exposure, the CNS has adapted to the presence of alcohol. It can tolerate more alcohol and still maintain normal function. This is one of the properties which defines alcohol as an addictive drug. Over the long haul the body requires a larger dose to induce the effects earlier produced at smaller levels. Not only does this adaptation occur over time, there are also rapid adaptive changes in the CNS every time someone drinks. A drinker is more out of commission when the blood alcohol level is climbing than when it's falling. If someone is given alcohol to drink and then performs certain tasks, there are predictable results. Impairment is greater on the ascending climb, or absorption phase. As the blood alcohol level drops in the elimination phase, the individual will be able to function better with the same blood alcohol content. It is as if one learns to function better, after "practice" with the presence of alcohol. Here, too, there are differences between men and women. Both have more impairment as alcohol levels rise. There are differences in the *kinds* of impairment. With intoxication, women appear to have greater impairment than men for tasks that require motor coordination. They are superior to men on tasks that require attention. Since driving requires both skills, neither appears the better bet on the highway.

OTHER ALCOHOLS

In this discussion of alcohol, it is clear that we have been referring to "booze," "suds," "the sauce," "hooch," or any of the other colloquial terms for beverage alcohol. To be scientifically accurate, "our kind" of alcohol is called *ethanol, ethyl alcohol,* or *grain alcohol. Alcohol,* if one is precise, is a term used to refer to a family of substances. What all alcohols have in common is that each is composed of carbon, hydrogen, and oxygen atoms, linked up in the same way. How they differ is in the number of carbons. Each alcohol is named according to the number of carbons aboard. Ethanol has two carbon atoms.

The other kinds of alcohol with which everyone is familiar are wood alcohol (methyl alcohol) with one carbon and rubbing alcohol (isopropyl) with three carbons. With their different chemical makeup, they cause big problems if taken into the body. The difficulty lies in differences in rates of metabolism and the kinds of by-products formed. For example, it takes nine times longer for methanol to be eliminated than ethanol. When alcohol is present in the body that much longer, the chances for it to have direct toxic effects increase. To compound the problem, when alcohol dehydrogenese acts on methanol, formaldehyde instead of acetaldehyde is formed. The formaldehyde breaks down into formic acid, which is not as innocent as the acetic acid produced by ethanol metabolism. Ingestion of methyl alcohol can be fatal and requires prompt medical attention.

Poisonings from nonbeverage alcohols don't just happen to alcoholics, who in desperation will drink anything. There's the toddler who gets into the medicine cabinet, or maybe the teenager or adult who doesn't know that all alcohols are not the same and have different effects.

At present, it is becoming common knowledge that anything taken into the body (or breathed in for that matter) has effects on the body. And all too often we are discovering these effects to be more harmful than was thought. Chemical additives, fertilizers, and coloring agents are being found to be less benevolent than once supposed. Caution is urged in the use of all such agents, and the FDA has been outlawing some of them. Let us hope that this caution will begin to extend to the use of alcohol as well.

RESOURCES AND FURTHER READING

Greenberg, Leon. Alcohol in the body. In R. McCarthy (Ed.), *Drinking and intoxication*. New Haven, Conn.: College & University Press, 1959.

Keller, Mark, et al. *Alcohol and health*. Rockville, Md.: Department of Health, Education, and Welfare, 1971.

Levine, Louis. *Biology for a modern society*. St. Louis, The C. V. Mosby Co., 1977.

Lewis, Paul, and Rubenstein, David. *The human body*. New York: Bantam Books, 1972.

CHAPTER THREE Alcoholism

Drunkenness is nothing but voluntary madness.

SENECA

DEFINITIONS

The social problems associated with the use and misuse of alcohol have been described. Even if there were no such phenomenon as alcoholism, the mere presence of alcohol would lead to the disruption of the social order and considerable costs to society. Yet all statistics on dented fenders caused by inebriated drivers, or dollars lost by industry, or even percentage of alcohol-related hospital admissions have a limited gut-level impact. Most of us would judge them to be unfortunate or nuisances, but they would not strike us as a national tragedy. Our major concern and compassion usually flows toward people, not things. Not unexpectedly, the problem of alcohol that captures our attention is the person for whom alcohol is no longer servant, but master. It is the nine million plus alcoholics who come immediately to mind when we consider the human dimensions of alcohol problems. The chances are very good that this concern is particularized, with the faces of people we have known coming to mind.

What is alcoholism? Who is the alcoholic? These are the questions which will confront the alcohol counselor daily. A physician may request assistance in determining if an alcohol problem exists. A client may ask, or a spouse may challenge, "Why, he/she can't be an alcoholic because. . . ." Even in nonworking hours, the question may crop up during conversation with good friends or casual acquaintances. A number of definitions are available from a variety of sources. The word alcoholic itself can provide some clues. The suffix *ic* has a special meaning. According to *Webster's New Collegiate Dictionary:*

-ic n suffix: One having the character or nature of: one belonging to or associated with: one exhibiting or affected by.

Attaching *ic* to alcohol, this word means a person whom those around him link with alcohol. O.K., that's a start. Clearly not all drinkers are linked with alcohol, just as all baseball players are not linked with the Boston Red Sox. Why the link or association? The basis is probably frequency of use, pattern of use, quantity used, or frequency of signs that indicate the person has been tippling. "Belonging to" has several connotations, including an individual's being possessed by or under the control of. The Chinese have a saying that goes: "The man takes a drink, the drink takes a drink, and then the drink takes the man." This final step closely approximates what the word alcoho*lic* means. And the progression itself provides a good picture of the progression of alcoho*lism*.

It's worth noting that the discussion or debate on who is alcoholic and what is alcoholism is quite recent. This doesn't mean society has never noticed the alcoholic before. Certainly, persons in trouble with alcohol have been recognized for centuries. But their existence was accepted as a fact, without question. To the extent there was debate, it centered on why, and how the alcoholic should be handled. Essentially two basic approaches prevailed. One was that "obviously" the alcoholic was morally inferior. The evidence cited was the vast majority of people who drank moderately, without presenting problems for themselves or the community. The other view has been that "obviously" the alcoholic was possessed, since no one in his right mind would drink like that of his own volition.

With increasing scientific study and knowledge of "the drink taking the man" phenomenon, the more complicated the task of definition became. While still aware that these persons are distinctly different from the many who drink moderately, the other clear discovery is that all alcoholics are *not* alike. Not all develop DTs when withdrawn from alcohol. There are big differences in the quantity of alcohol consumed or the number of years drinking before family problems arise. Many alcoholics develop cirrhosis, but more do not. The more time spent on study, the less is known with certainty. What was previously seen as a single problem, alcoholism, is now discussed as alcoholisms.

Now that you are forewarned that there is no easy, single definition of alcoholism, we list a sample of the more recent formulations below.

Jellinek (1946). "Any use of alcoholic beverages that causes any damage to the individual or to society or both." Subclasses are alpha, beta, gamma, and delta. Phases are prealcoholic, symptomatic, prodromal, crucial, and chronic.

World Health Organization. The Alcoholism Sub-Committee (1951) defined alcoholism as "any form of drinking which in extent goes beyond the traditional and customary 'dietary' use, or the ordinary compliance with the social drinking customs of the community concerned, irrespective of etiological factors leading to such behavior, and irrespective also of the extent to which such etiological factors are dependent upon heredity, constitution, or acquired physio-pathological and metabolic influences."

American Psychiatric Association, Committee on Nomenclature and Statistics. Alcoholism is classified under the general category of addiction, and addiction is listed under the sociopathic personality disturbances. "Alcoholism: This category is for patients whose alcohol intake is great enough to damage their physical health, or their personal or social functioning, or when it has become a prerequisite to normal functioning. If the alcoholism is due to another mental disorder, both diagnoses should be made. The following types of alcoholism are recognized":

Episodic excessive drinking. If alcoholism is present and the individual becomes intoxicated as frequently as four times a year, the condition should be classified here. Intoxication is defined as a state in which the individual's coordination or speech is definitely impaired or his behavior is clearly altered.

Habitual excessive drinking. This diagnosis is given to persons who are alcoholic and who either become intoxicated more than twelve times a year or are recognizably under the influence of alcohol more than once a week, even though not intoxicated.

Alcohol addiction. This condition should be diagnosed when there is direct or strong presumptive evidence that the patient is dependent on alcohol. If available, the best directive evidence of such dependence is the appearance of withdrawal symptoms. The inability of the patient to go one day without drinking is presumptive evidence. When heavy drinking continues for three months or more it is reasonable to presume addiction to alcohol has been established.

Mark Keller. Keller, the editor of the *Quarterly Journal of Alcohol Studies*, Rutgers Center of Alcohol Studies, defines alcoholism as "a chronic disease manifested by repeated implicative drinking so as to cause injury to the drinker's health or to his social or economic functioning."

Marty Mann, National Council on Alcoholism. "An alcoholic is a very sick person, victim of an insidious, progressive disease, which all too often ends fatally. An alcoholic can be recognized, diagnosed, and treated successfully."

Alcoholics Anonymous. AA has no official definition, but the concept of Dr. William Silkworth, one of AA's friends, is sometimes cited by AA members: an obsession of the mind and an allergy of the body. The obsession or compulsion guarantees that the sufferer will drink against his own will and interest. The allergy guarantees that the sufferer will either die or go insane. An operative definition in use in AA is that "an alcoholic is a person who cannot *predict* with accuracy what will happen when he takes a drink."

• • •

In addition are all the definitions casually used by each of us and our neighbors. Here we find considerable variation, from "alcoholism is an illness," to "it's the number one drug problem," to "when someone's drunk all the time."

Although not necessarily conflicting, each of the expert definitions has a different focus or emphasis. Several concentrate on the unfortunate consequences associated with alcohol use. Others zero in on hallmark signs or symptoms, especially loss of control or frequency of intoxication. This is true of both expert and lay definitions. (Note laypeople seem to have more permissive criteria!) One other distinction between the available definitions is that some are descriptive and others attempt to handle the origins of the problem.

One swallow doesn't make a summer but too many swallows make a fall.

G. D. PRENTICE

Criteria for choosing a definition

Before supplying another definition, or examining those just listed, a little digression is in order. That is, how does one know the "true" definition or select the best one? There are guidelines used by physical scientists worth examining. When faced with a choice between two possible explanations, they judge on the basis of two criteria. The first is called the Law of Parsimony. This means that the better explanation is the one that adequately explains the data with the fewest number of factors. An example will help to illustrate this.

A worker in a mental health clinic has a client who is feeling down, isn't getting along at work, finds his wife is bitching at him, and his liver is acting up. One explanation is that by chance, his job is oppressive, his boss is obnoxious, by nature his wife has a nasty temperament, and furthermore, fate has conspired to give him a cirrhotic liver. Thus his feeling blue is a natural response to an unfortunate set of circumstances. An alternative explanation is that he is

I do Not drink
More Than
a Sponge. —Rabelais

an alcoholic. The simplest explanation that fits the facts is the best.

The second criterion the scientist uses when selecting between competing theories is heuristic value. This means taking into account the theory or explanation's usefulness as a guide to action. A car mechanic has an understanding of what makes an automobile tick. When it goes on the blink, he therefore has some sense of how to go about correcting the situation. The same is true for the counselor. Any definition of what alcoholism *is* should provide some clues about what *should be done*.

Applying these criteria to the many definitions available, which makes the most sense? This is going to depend on what the counselor is trying to do. The counselor will need to be acquainted with several definitions, but will probably latch on to one all-purpose definition as a starting point. The one selected should be readily understood by most people. It should be faithful to the facts. And finally, it should be watertight. By watertight we mean inclusive, applicable to persons in the early as well as the later stages of the disease. This is the major failing of most lay definitions. They are so specific and geared to the later stages that approximately 95%, or most alcoholics, cannot qualify.

A definition that has fit most of our purposes is a short one, closely following Jellinek or a simplified Keller. "Alcoholism is a disease in which the person's use of alcohol continues despite problems it causes in any area of life." Every definition has plusses and minuses. The utility of this one is its simplicity and its ability to cover people at various stages. The reference to disease suggests the potential for treatment and asserts the sufferer is entitled (as are all sick people) to care, not punishment or ostracism. Its weakness is the failure to address the issue of causes. Since the causes of alcoholism are not neat and clear-cut, ignoring that point may not be a bad idea.

The remainder of the chapter will be devoted to two major pieces of work that have led to our present understanding of what alcoholism is, its complexity, and how to recognize it. First is the work of Jellinek, who has been the father of alcohol studies in the United States and the world. Second are the guidelines established by a committee of the National Council on Alcoholism for diagnosing alcoholism, published in 1972.

A DISEASE?

Anyone who is sufficiently interested in alcoholism to have gotten this far is probably well accustomed to hearing alcoholism referred to as an illness, disease, or sickness. This has not always been the case. As discussed earlier, alcoholism has not always been distinguished from drunkenness. Or it has been seen as a lot of drunkenness and categorized as a sin or character defect. The work of Jellinek has largely been responsible for the shift to an illness model. In essence, through his research and writings, he said, "Hey, world, you guys mislabeled this thing. You put it in the sin bin, and it really belongs in the disease pile." How we label something is very important. It provides clues on how to feel and think, what to expect, and how to act. Whether a particular bulb is tagged as either a tulip or an onion is going to make a big difference (especially from the bulb's point of view). Depending on which I think it is, I'll either chop and sauté or plant and water. Very different behaviors are associated with each. An error may lead to strange-flavored spaghetti sauce and a less colorful flower bed next spring.

Implications of disease classification

Placing alcoholism in the category of disease has had a dramatic impact. Sick people are generally awarded sympathy. The accepted notion is that sick people do not choose to be sick, being sick is not pleasant, and care should be provided to restore health. During the period of sickness, the person will not be expected to fill his usual roles or meet his responsibilities. A special designation is given to people in this situation: patient. Furthermore, sick persons are not to be criticized for manifesting the symptoms of their illness. To tell a flu victim to stop "fevering" would be seen as pointless and unkind. With alcoholism an illness, the alcoholic is thought of as a sufferer and victim. Much of the bizarre behavior he displays is recognized as unwillful and a symptom of illness. No longer the object of scorn, the alcoholic is now seen to require care. The logical place to send the alcoholic is no longer jail, but a hospital, rehabilitation center, etc. There has been a gradual shifting in public attitudes since the 1940s. In a recent nationwide poll, over 80% of the respondents said they believed alcoholism to be an illness. While Jellinek's efforts may have triggered this shift, a number of other events added impetus. The National Council on Alcoholism put its efforts into lobbying and public education. The American Medical Association and American Hospital Association published various committee reports. State agencies developed programs for treating alcoholics. Probably the biggest push came from the presence of recovering alcoholics, especially through the work of AA. Virtually everyone today has personal knowledge of an apparently hopeless alcoholic who has gone off the sauce and seems a new, different person.

The formulation of alcoholism as a disease has opened up possibilities for treatment that were nonexistent. It has brought into the helping area the resources of medicine, nursing, social work, and others, who before had no mandate to help alcoholics. Also it is removing the stigma associated with alcoholism. This improves the likelihood that individuals and families will seek help rather than cover up. Finally, the resources of the federal government have been focused on alcoholism as a major public health problem. A host of treatment and educational programs have been brought into being.

The early sales pitch for selling alcoholism as a disease was probably the slogan: "Alcoholism is an illness, just like any other." With a little imagination, you can picture folks going around the radio talk show circuit flashing this phrase. Now that the notion has gained acceptance, the time may be approaching for a new, or refined, formulation. For there have been some disadvantages or limitations to the disease concept.

Disadvantages of disease classification

For one thing, the disease notion has possibly put too much emphasis on the physician as the major helper. The doctor certainly has a role to play in diagnosis and physical treatment. But medical training has not necessarily prepared physicians to do counseling. Even if it has, a physician's time might be used more efficiently in other areas and counseling left to others. Yet the disease concept implies the doctor alone is qualified to provide or direct treatment. Criticism is frequently leveled at doctors for being uninterested or unconcerned with the problems of alcoholism. The use of the disease concept may often foster unrealistic expectations and place undue burdens on the doctor.

In a similar vein, the disease concept may create the idea that alcoholism can be treated with a pill and that the alcoholic does not have to do anything. This notion is a mistake and an oversimplification of what the art of medicine is. This age has been an age of wonder drugs—penicillin, polio vaccines, measles vaccines, etc. Were a cancer vaccine to be developed, all would be delighted, but few shocked. Television commercials constantly push "wonder drugs" to instantly relieve headaches, insomnia, muscle pains, the blahs. We expect quick results. The side of the picture we neglect, since it isn't so spectacular, is the field of rehabilitative medicine. For instance, with physical therapy, accident victims learn to walk again. In these cases, patients are required to take active part in their recovery. To be successful, an alcoholic must also take an active part.

The other important distinction the layman usually does *not* make is between acute and chronic disease. Acute disease means you get sick, get treated, become better, and that's the end of it. Chronic diseases are different: once you have it, you have it. Chronic diseases may be amenable to treatment and arrested. A person might be able to get along as well as before. But there is always a possibility of relapse. Treatment is intended to help you live around the illness, in spite of it. Diabetes falls into this category as do some forms of bronchitis, arthritis, and alcoholism.

The other major criticism of the disease concept is that it can be used by alcoholics as a cop-out. "Don't look at me, I'm not responsible. I'm sick. Poor me (sigh, sigh)." Expect a drinking alcoholic to try shooting holes into any definition. Those who criticize the disease concept on this basis are possibly those who have been victims of the alcoholic's con game. Our sympathy goes out to them. Alcoholics do have a knack for immobilizing those around them, so that their drinking can continue undisturbed. As you acquire more information about alcoholism, you'll be better able to see these ploys coming and effectively counter them. A one-liner that seems to handle the situation fairly well comes from a billboard on the Boston skyline. "There's nothing wrong with being an alcoholic, if you're doing something about it."

PHASES A LA JELLINEK

How did Jellinek arrive at his disease formulation of alcoholism? A biostatistician by training, he was logically fascinated by statistics, the pictures they portray, and the questions they raise. Much of his work has been descriptive, defining the turf of alcoholism. Who, when, where. One of his first studies charted the signs and symptoms associated with alcohol addiction. This work was based on a survey of over 2,000 members of Alcoholics Anonymous. Although differences certainly existed between persons, the similarities were more remarkable. There was a definite pattern to the appearance of the symptoms. There was also a progression of the disease in terms of increasing dysfunction. The symptoms and signs tended to go together in clusters. Thus Jellinek developed the idea of four different phases of alcohol addiction: the prealcoholic, prodromal, crucial, and chronic phases. These have been widely used in alcohol treatment circles. The four phases are often portrayed graphically on a chart.

In the *prealcoholic phase*, the individual's use of alcohol is socially motivated. However, the prospective alcoholic soon experiences psychological relief in the drinking situation. Possibly his tensions are greater than other persons', or possibly he has no other way of handling his tensions. It does not matter. Either way, he learns to seek out occasions where drinking will occur. At some point the connection becomes conscious. Drinking then becomes his standard means of handling stress. But the drinking behavior will not look different to the outsider. This phase can extend from several months to two years or more. An increase in tolerance gradually develops.

Suddenly the prealcoholic will enter the *prodromal phase*. (Prodromal means warning or signaling disease.) According to Jellinek, the behavior that heralds the change is the occurrence of "alcoholic palimpsets," or blackouts. Blackouts are amnesia-like periods during drinking. The person seems to be functioning normally but later has no memory of what happened. Other behaviors emerge which give evidence that alcohol is no longer "just" a beverage, but a "need." Among these are sneaking extra drinks before or during parties, gulping the first drink or two, and guilt about the drinking behavior. Here consumption is heavy, yet not necessarily conspicuous. To look "okay" requires conscious effort by the drinker. This period can last from six months to four or five years, depending on the drinker's circumstances.

The third phase is the *crucial phase*. The key symptom that ushers in this phase is loss of control. Now taking a drink sets up a chain reaction. The drinker can no longer control the amount he will have once he takes a drink. But he can control whether or not he will take a drink. So it is possible to go on the wagon for a time. With loss of control, the drinker loses his cover-up. His drinking is now clearly different. This requires explanation, so rationalizations begin. Simultaneously, the alcoholic attempts a sequence of strategies to regain control. The thinking goes, "If I just _____ , then it will be okay." Common maneuvers attempted are periods of abstinence, changing drinking patterns, geographical escapes, changing jobs. These are doomed to failure. The alcoholic responds to these failures. He is alternately resentful, remorseful, and aggressive. Life has become alcohol centered. Family life and friendships deteriorate. The first alcohol-related hospitalization is likely. Morning drinking may begin to creep in, foreshadowing the next stage.

The final stage in the process is the *chronic phase*. In the preceding crucial phase, the drinker may have been somewhat successful in maintaining a job and his social footing. Now, as drinking begins earlier in the day, intoxication is an almost daily, day-long phenomenon. Benders are more frequent. He may also go to dives and drink with persons previously below his social class. Not unexpectedly the alcoholic finds himself on the fringes of society. When ethanol is unavailable, he'll drink poisonous substitutes. During this phase, marked physical changes occur. Tolerance for alcohol drops sharply. No longer able to hold his liquor, the alcoholic is stuporous after a few drinks. Tremors develop. Many simple tasks are impossible in the sober state. The alcoholic is beset by indefinable fears. Finally, the rationalization system fails. The long-used excuses are revealed as just that, excuses. The alcoholic is spontaneously open to treatment. Often, drinking is likely to continue because the alcoholic can imagine no way out of his dilemma. Jellinek did emphasize that alcoholics are not destined to go through all four stages before treatment can be successful.

SPECIES

The pattern on pp. 48 and 49 describes the stages of alcohol addiction. Jellinek continued his studies on alcoholics, focusing on alcohol problems in other countries. The differences he found could not be accounted for simply by the phases of alcohol addiction. These differences seemed more of kind than degree of addiction. This led to his formulation of species, or categories, of alcoholism. Each of these types he named with a Greek letter.

Alpha alcoholism. A purely psychological dependence on alcohol. There is neither loss of control nor an inability to abstain. What is evident is the reliance on alcohol to weather any, or all, discomforts or problems in life. This use may lead to interpersonal, family, or work problems. A progression is not inevitable. Jellinek notes that other writers may term this species *problem drinking*.

Beta alcoholism. Present when the various physical problems resulting from alcohol use develop, such as cirrhosis or gastritis, but the individual is not psychologically or physically dependent. This species is likely to occur in persons from cultures where there is widespread heavy drinking and inadequate diet.

Gamma alcoholism. Marked by a change in tolerance, physiological changes leading to withdrawal symptoms, and a loss of control. In this species there is a progression from psychological to physical dependence. It is the most devastating species in terms of physical health and social disruption. This is the species Jellinek originally studied. It progresses in four phases: prealcoholic, prodromal, crucial, and chronic. The gamma alcoholic appears to be the most prominent type in the United States. This species is the most common among the members of AA. Characteristics of this species alone are often seen as synonymous with alcoholism.

Delta alcoholism. Very similar to the gamma variety. There is psychological and physical dependence, but there is no loss of control. On any particular occasion the drinker can control his intake. He cannot, however, go on the wagon for even a day without suffering withdrawal.

Epsilon alcoholism. Not studied in depth, but appeared to be significantly different from the others. Jellinek called this *periodic alcoholism*, marked by binge drinking. While not elaborating, he felt this was a species by itself, not to be confused with slips by gamma alcoholics.

Having described these various species, Jellinek concluded that possibly not all species are properly categorized as a disease. Maybe alpha and epsilon varieties are symptoms of other disorders. There is no question that gamma and delta, each involving physiological changes and progression, are diseases. By more adequately classifying and categorizing the phenomena of alcoholism, he brought scientific order to a field that before had been dominated by beliefs. That was no modest contribution.

GUIDES FOR DIAGNOSIS

The next major step taken was in 1972 with a paper entitled "Criteria for the Diagnosis of Alcoholism," published in two major medical journals. This article was prepared by a special committee of the National Council on Alcoholism. Their task was to establish guidelines to be used in diagnosing alcoholism. Physicians are thereby provided a firm set of standards to use in making a diagnosis.

Although a little cumbersome on first sight, it is worth the effort to wade through the criteria. The Committee collected all the signs and symptoms of alcohol use that can be discovered through a physical examination, medical history, social history, laboratory tests, and clinical observations. They then organized these signs and symptoms into two categories, or tracks, of data. The first track is the physiological and clinical data. Included there are the things a physician can discover through a physical examination, laboratory tests, or medical history. The second track is termed the behavioral, psychological, and attitudinal; it includes what the patient or the family report about the client's life situation, or a social history, or what the doctor may directly observe about the patient's involvement with alcohol.

Table 1. Criteria for diagnosis of alcoholism*

Physiological data	Diagnostic significance†	Behavioral data	Diagnostic significance†
Major criteria		*Major criteria*	
Physiological dependence, evidenced by withdrawal syndromes when alcohol is interrupted or decreased	1	Continued drinking, despite strong medical indications known to patient	1
Evidence of tolerance, by blood alcohol level of 0.15 without gross evidence of intoxication or consumption of equivalent of fifth of whiskey for more than one day by 180-lb. man	1	Drinking despite serious social problems	1
		Patient's complaint of loss of control	2
Alcoholic blackouts	2		
Major alcohol-related illnesses in person who drinks regularly			
Fatty liver	2		
Alcoholic hepatitis	1		
Cirrhosis	2		
Pancreatitis	2		
Chronic gastritis	3		
Minor criteria		*Minor criteria* (very similar to Jellinek's symptoms of phases of alcohol addiction)	
Laboratory tests			
Blood alcohol level of 0.3 or more at any time	1‡	Repeated attempts at abstinence	2
Blood alcohol level of 0.1 in routine examination	1‡	Unexplained changes in family, social, or business relationships	3
Odor of alcohol on breath at time of medical appointment	2	Spouse's complaints about drinking	2

*Modified from Criteria Committee, National Council on Alcoholism. Criteria for the diagnosis of alcoholism. *American Journal of Psychiatry,* August 1972, *129*(2), 41-49.
†1, must diagnose alcoholism; 2, probably indicates alcoholism; 3, possibly due to alcoholism.
‡There seems to be some discrepancy between 1, meaning *must* diagnose alcoholism, and the committee's statement that more than one of the minor criteria must be in evidence. We note this but have no explanation.

Within each of the two data tracks, the criteria are further divided into major and minor subgroups. That means exactly what you would expect. Major criteria are the "biggies"; only one must be present to diagnose alcoholism. However, several of the minor criteria from both tracks are required to make the diagnosis. Finally, each of the potential signposts is weighted as to whether it "definitely," "probably," or "possibly" indicates alcoholism.

Table 1 summarizes some of the key criteria set forth by the Criteria Committee.

There are many similarities between the symptoms of alcohol addiction developed by Jellinek and the criteria published in 1972. However, Jellinek composed his list based on the self-reports of recovered alcoholics. So the signs are from their point of view. A good number of the symptoms Jellinek included involve deception and the alcoholic's attempts to appear normal. This provides little assistance to the physician or helper interviewing a drinking alcoholic. The physician is unable to rely on the usual instincts to believe the patient. What further complicates diagnosis is that many of the behaviors included by Jellinek are not the kind of thing a physician can easily detect. What the criteria have accomplished is to pinpoint *objective* measures for the physician, who can use readily available information, thus cutting through the alcoholic's alibis. For example, "odor of alcohol on the breath at the time of medical appointment" is designated as a "possible" sign. A person displaying this behavior "is under strong suspicion of alcoholism." The physician is directed to look for additional supporting evidence.

In the criteria, alcoholism is further described as a chronic progressive disease. Although incurable, it is very treatable. Since it is a chronic disease, this means the diagnosis once made can *never* be dropped. An individual successfully involved in a treatment program would have the diagnosis amended to "alcoholism: arrested" or "alcoholism: in remission." Suggested criteria are provided for determining when this change in diagnosis is appropriate. The panel recommends that factors other than the length of sobriety be taken into account. Among the factors they list as signs of recovery are full, active participation in AA, active use of other treatments, use of Antabuse-like preparations, no substitution of other drugs, and resumption of work. The paper is primarily interested in diagnosis, not treatment. Yet implicit in the standards suggested for diagnosing "alcoholism: arrested" is a view that alcoholism requires a variety of treatment and rehabilitative efforts.

In his book *The Disease Concept of Alcoholism*, Jellinek notes that a disease is "simply anything the medical profession agrees to call a disease." Therefore, alcoholism is officially a disease. And, with the addition of the criteria, we finally have some clear direction for determining who's got it.

RESOURCES AND FURTHER READING

Chafetz, Morris, and Demone, Harold. *Alcoholism and society*. New York: Oxford Press, 1962.

Criteria Committee, National Council on Alcoholism. Criteria for the diagnosis of alcoholism. *American Journal of Psychiatry*, August 1972, *129*(2), 41-49.

Finn, Richard, and Clancy, John. Alcoholism, dilemma or disease: a recurring problem for the physician. *Comprehensive Psychiatry*. March 1972, *13*(2), 133-138.

Gitlow, Stanley. Alcoholism: a disease. In P. G. Bourne and R. Fox (Eds.), *Alcoholism: progress in research and treatment*. New York: Academic Press, Inc., 1973.

Jellinek, E. M. *The disease concept of alcoholism*. New Haven, Conn.: Hill House Press, 1960.

Jellinek, E. M. Phases of alcohol addiction. In D. J. Pittman and S. R. Snyder (Eds.), *Society, culture and drinking patterns*. New York: John Wiley & Sons, Inc., 1962.

CHAPTER FOUR

Etiology of alcoholism

WHY ALCOHOL?

What are the causes of alcoholism? As more knowledge is gained, the answers become more complex. It might be useful to make a comparison to the common cold. Once you have "it," there isn't much question. The sneezing, the runny nose, the stuffed-up feeling the cold tablet manufacturers describe so well leave little doubt. But why you? Because "it" was going around. Your resistance was down. Others in the family have "it." You became chilled when caught in the rain. You forgot your vitamin C. Everyone has a pet theory and usually chalks it up to a number of factors working in combination against one. There does seem to be some chance factor involved. There are times we do *not* catch colds that are going around. Explaining the phenomenon cannot be done with great precision. It's more a matter of figuring out the odds and probabilities, as the possible contributing factors are considered. The folks in the public health field have developed a systematic way of tackling this problem of disease, causes, and risks of contracting one. First, they look at the agent, the thing that causes the disease. Next they take a look at the host, the person who has the illness, to find characteristics that may have made him a likely target. Finally, the environment is examined, the setting in which the agent and host come together. A thorough look at these three areas ensures that no major influences will be overlooked.

PUBLIC HEALTH MODEL

Alcoholism certainly qualifies as a public health problem. It is the third leading cause of death in the United States. It affects one out of every twelve adults. If alcoholism were an infectious disease such as polio, it would constitute an epidemic. People would be clamoring for a place in line to get vaccine. The response to alcoholism is pale in comparison.

From the public health viewpoint, the first item to be examined as a possible cause of alcoholism is the agent. For alcoholism, the agent is the substance, alcohol. This is such an obvious fact that it might seem silly to dwell on it. No one can be alcoholic without being exposed to alcohol. The substance must be used before the possibility of alcoholism exists. Alcohol is an addictive substance. With sufficient quantities over a long enough period, the organism will undergo physiological changes. When this has occurred and the substance is withdrawn, there is a physiological response, withdrawal. For alcohol there is a well-defined set of symptoms that may accompany cessation of alcohol use in an addicted person. An individual can be addicted to alcohol. To use this fact alone to explain alcoholism represents untidy thinking. That alcohol is addicting does not explain why anyone would drink enough to reach the point of addiction. Temperance literature tries to paint a picture of an evil demon in the bottle. Take a sip, and he's got you. This may appear humorous to those comfortable with drinking alcoholic beverages. It is obvious that drinking need not inevitably lead to a life of drunkenness. Let's look at the action of the drug itself. What invites its use and makes it a candidate for sufficient use to cause addiction?

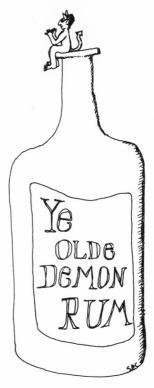

The agent

We humans take any number of substances into our bodies—from meats to sweets, as solids or liquids. Although everyone overeats occasionally, abusing these substances is extremely unlikely. The notion of being addicted to cornflakes sounds ridiculous to our ear. Part of the humor of the Frito Bandito on the tube is that you *know* you can't be addicted to the product. So the notion is amusing, not terrifying. There is simply nothing which cornflakes or Hershey bars or soda pop can do for us *so* good, that we're likely to overdo. Alcohol does do that something. It's a depressant drug. One of its first effects is on the central nervous system, the "higher" centers related to judgment, inhibition, and the like. What is more important is what this feels like, how it is experienced. With mild intoxication comes relaxation, a more carefree feeling. It is generally experienced as a plus, a high. Pre-existing tensions are relieved. A good mood can be accentuated. Alcohol is experienced as a mood changer, in a good direction. This capacity of alcohol is one factor to remember in trying to understand use sufficient for addiction.

A common expression is "I sure could use a drink *now*." It may be said after a hard day at work, after a round of good physical exercise, or after a period of chaos and emotional stress, when the wobbly knees are setting in. This expression certainly includes the recognition that alcohol can be a mood changer. Equally as important is the word *now*.

Candy is dandy
But liquor is quicker.
OGDEN NASH

The peculiar charm of alcohol lies in the sense of careless well-being and bodily comfort which it creates. It unburdens the individual of his cares and fears. . . . Under such conditions it is easy to laugh or to weep, to love or to hate, not wisely but too well.

DR. HAVEN EMERSON, *ALCOHOL AND MAN*

There is a recognition that the effects are immediate. Not only does alcohol make a difference, it does so very rapidly. If alcohol had a delayed reaction time, say three days, or three weeks, or even three hours, it wouldn't be a useful method for changing one's mood. Most people's lives are sufficiently unpredictable, so that drinking now for what may happen later would seem silly. So the speed of the mood change is another characteristic of the drug alcohol that enhances its likelihood of abuse.

Alcohol has another characteristic common to all depressant drugs. With mild inebriation, behavior is less inhibited, there are feelings of relaxation. However, at the same time there is a gradual increase of psychomotor activity. The drinker is unaware of this while feeling the initial glow. As the warm glow subsides, the increased psychomotor activity will become apparent. He may feel wound up, edgy, very similar to the feelings caused by too much coffee, especially in combination with cigarettes. The increase in psychomotor activity builds up gradually and extends beyond the feeling of well-being. Since it is delayed and its onset masked, the drinker is not very likely to recognize it as a product of the alcohol use. Instead, he thinks the edginess is his "normal" self. In fact, it is more probable that the drinker is feeling less serene or calm than when he began. What would be the rational thing to do? Have another drink! It is quite possible that many people, including nonalcoholics, have a second or third to get rid of the very feelings created by earlier drinks. There is one nasty catch to this approach. The agitation phase, which accompanies alcohol consumption, extends considerably beyond the relaxed initial experience. A second drink will only temporarily cover the edginess of the first drink. The second drink, with its own edge coming on behind, will combine with the edge left over from the first. Were this to continue, a point would be reached when the accumulated tensions and increased psychomotor activity could no longer be masked by adding more alcohol. Normally, people are wholly unaware of this phenomenon because it is interrupted after two or three drinks. They've set their limit. They have dinner and go on to other activities. They go to bed.

These particular characteristics of alcohol do not alone account for the phenomena of alcoholism, but they are certainly responsible for the *possibility* of alcoholism. As other factors are examined, we can see how an interaction may work.

The host—genetic factors

The belief that alcoholism runs in families has long been a part of the folk wisdom. In your childhood, possibly, a great-aunt explained away the town drunk with "He's his father's son. . . ." No further comment was necessary. The obvious truth was so clear: that many of life's misfortunes are the result of "bad" genes. Just such an inadequate understanding of genetics, supported by warped theological views, led to statutes that authorized the sterilization of the feebleminded, hopelessly insane, and chronically drunk.

In the face of new knowledge, such an approach has fallen into disrepute. It is now clear that heredity isn't as simple as it seemed. Each individual, at the point of conception, receives a unique set of genetic material. This material is like a set of internal "instructions" which guide the individual's growth. In some respects, the genetic endowment simply sets down limits, or predispositions. The final outcome will depend on the life situation and environment in which the person finds (or places) himself. Thus, there are some people who tend to be slim, and some who tend to put on weight easily. Such a *tendency* is probably genetic. But whether the person is fat, thin, or just right depends on him.

Nature versus nurture. What are the facts about heredity in alcoholism? Actually, alcoholism does run in families. The child of an alcoholic parent *is* more likely to become alcoholic. One recent study tracing family trees has found that 50% of the descendents of alcoholics were also alcoholics. While that figure is a bit higher than other similar studies, it is simply a more dramatic example of the typical findings.

Something's running in families is not proof that it is inherited. After all, speaking French runs in families—in France. Recognizing the role of psychological factors influencing behavior, separating nature from nurture becomes a complex, but necessary, job. Certainly an alcoholic parent must have an impact on a growing child. It's not unreasonable to expect that inherent in the family lies the soil of

Drunkards beget drunkards.

PLUTARCH

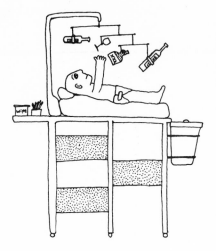

addiction. But again, simply because this sounds reasonable does not make it true. However, the most current hypothesis is that heredity does play a role in the development of alcoholism in some persons. Which persons, and by what mechanisms, has not been established. Considerable research is being done in this particular area of alcoholism. If heredity is a factor, there must be some basic biochemical differences between those who are alcoholism prone and those who are not.

The observations of people working in the area of alcohol rehabilitation and treatment would tend to support a constitutional vulnerability. Certain individuals develop alcoholism very early in their life, and it progresses very rapidly in the absence of any unique, identifiable, psychological stress. At AA meetings the remark may be heard, "I was an alcoholic from my first drink." Usually this means that for seemingly idiosyncratic reasons the speaker never drank "normally" as did his peers, but used, and was affected by, alcohol differently.

Twin and adoption studies. Scientific investigational methods using an experimental model are not possible in the task of separating nature and nurture. Human research requires locating persons with particular life experiences or characteristics and then comparing them to people with other backgrounds. Twin studies and adoption studies are the two classical methods for doing this. Goodwin, reviewing the work done on alcoholism and heredity, speaks of two excellent twin studies conducted in Scandinavia. These countries keep very complete records of marriages, births, etc., so tracing families is made easier. The research was based on a large sample of twins. In each set, *one* twin was alcoholic. The researchers determined if the twins were identical or fraternal. They then interviewed the twin of the known alcoholic. The prediction: if alcoholism has a hereditary base, the other twin of identical sets would then be more likely to also be alcoholic than if he was fraternal. This assumption was made because identical twins share the same genetic material. That proved to be the case. However, the hereditary endowment does *not* act to totally dictate the development of alcoholism because not all the identical twins were both alcoholic. It was further discovered that there exists an apparent predisposition toward having, or being spared, the social deterioration associated

with alcoholism. If both twins were alcoholic, the best predictor of the other twin's life situation was *not* how much,
or how long he had been drinking. The life situation of the
first twin was more reliable. So there appears to be both a
hereditary predisposition to alcoholism and also to the
social problems associated with it.

An adoption study conducted by Goodwin using Danish
subjects further supports the influence of heredity. He
traced children born of alcoholic parents. These children
had been adopted by age 6 weeks. He then compared them
to adopted children of nonalcoholic parents. The adoptive
families of both groups were essentially the same. He discovered that those whose natural parents were alcoholic
were in adulthood themselves more likely to be alcoholics.
Thus, the alcoholism cannot be attributed simply to the
home environment. In passing, Goodwin recalls Jellinek's
speculation that cases of "early onset" alcoholism may have
a hereditary base. The average age of the individuals in
Goodwin's study was 30 years. If the children of nonalcoholic parents were to be studied again in fifteen or twenty
years, possibly new cases of alcoholism would become apparent. Such a finding would lend support to Jellinek's
hypothesis.

Genetic marker studies. Finally, another group of studies are given the shorthand title of "genetic marker"
studies. In such investigations, attempts are made to link
alcoholism to any traits that are known to be inherited. This
would establish a genetic base for alcoholism. Some of the
possibilities that have been studied include blood types.
It's known that blood type is inherited and the genes
controlling this may also be responsible for other characteristics. Other leads that have been followed include other
blood substances; ability to taste or not taste phenylthio-
carbamide; and blue-yellow color blindness. Nothing
definite has resulted, although research continues.

Animal studies. Another avenue of investigation involves animal studies. These studies cannot be generalized
to humans. Work with chimps, baboons, or rats can shed
light on the promising areas for human investigation and
provide clues. Some of the more curious studies involve
rats. Different strains of rats were given a choice of water or
water spiked with alcohol of differing concentrations. Inevitably, they sampled each and usually opted for plain wa-

ter. If the only liquid available had alcohol added, they'd
drink it. Several strains of rats were important exceptions.
They preferred alcohol and water solutions of around 5%.
These "drinking rats" could be inbred and produce off-
spring who preferred even higher alcohol concentrations.
The tentative conclusion is that biochemically they are
different from their water-drinking counterparts. Interestingly, even "drinking rats" very rarely choose to drink to
intoxication. While a taste for alcohol may exist, they don't
go on to become alcoholic. Dogs are apparently different.
They will drink to intoxication more frequently. They'll
even indulge in several days of "heavy" drinking, but they
stop spontaneously. Despite the fact that the dogs seem to
experience what the experimenters interpret as a hangover
or mild withdrawal, the animals abstain. Unless the dogs
were binge drinkers, it would appear that alcoholism is a
human problem.

The host—psychological factors

Psychological theories attempt to explain alcoholism by
looking at the personalities of the people who become alcoholic. The question to be answered: "Is there anything in
the person's character, or personality makeup, that makes
him likely to become an alcoholic?" Many people drink, but
in proportion, few become alcoholic. Alcoholism is a
deviant behavior. It is not the normal, average state of affairs. What are the conditions within an individual that
render him a likely target, or host, for this abnormal situation?

The ways in which we look at behavior today are really
quite new, less than a hundred years old. The credit for the
revolution goes to Dr. Sigmund Freud. A testimony to his
influence is our common daily use of words such as "unconscious," "neurotic," "repressed," "anxious," "Freudian
slip," to describe behavior. Although Freud might not consider our usage proper, nonetheless, these words have
been added to our vocabularies.

Psychological needs. It is now generally recognized that
our behavior is at least partially determined by factors of
which we are unaware. What are these factors? Our grade
school geography classes usually focused on food, clothing,
and shelter as the three basic human needs. But there are
emotional needs, just as real and important, if people are to

survive healthy and happy. What do we need in this realm? Baruch, in her book *New Ways of Discipline: You and Your Child Today*, puts it this way:

What are the emotional foods that every human being must have regardless of age? What are the basic emotional requirements that must come to every small infant, to every growing child, to every adult?

In the first place, there must be affection and a lot of it. Real down-to-earth, sincere loving. The kind that carries the conviction through body warmth, through touch, through the good mellow ring of the voice, through the fond look that says as clearly as words, "I love you because you are you."

Closely allied with being loved should come the sure knowledge of belonging, of being wanted, the glow of knowing oneself to be a part of some bigger whole. *Our town, our school, our work, our family*—all bring the sound of togetherness, of being united with others, not isolated or alone.

Every human being needs also to have the nourishment of pleasure that comes through the senses. Color, balanced form and beauty to meet the eye, harmonious sounds to meet the ear. The hearty enjoyment of touch and taste and smell. And finally, the realization that the pleasurable sensations of sex can be right and fine and a part of the spirit as well as the body.

Everyone must feel that he is capable of achievement. He needs to develop the ultimate conviction, strong within him, that he can do things, that he is adequate to meet life's demands. He needs also the satisfaction of knowing that he can gain from others recognition for what he does.

And most important, each and every one of us must have acceptance and understanding. We need desperately to be able to share our thoughts and feelings with some other person, or several, who really understand. . . . We yearn for the deep relief of knowing that we can be ourselves with honest freedom, secure in the knowledge that says, "This person is with me. He accepts how I feel!"*

If these needs are not satisfactorily met, the adult is not whole. A useful notion to assess what has happened is to think of the unmet needs as "holes." Everybody has some "holes." They can vary in number, size, and pattern. What is true for all is that "holes" are experienced as painful. Attempts are made to cover up, patch over, or camouflage our holes. Thus we feel more whole, less vulnerable, and more presentable. The various psychological theories

MAybe we should put some "STOPleak" in his hext drink.

*From Baruch, Dorothy. *New ways of discipline: you and your child today*. New York: McGraw-Hill Book Co., 1949. Used with permission of McGraw-Hill Book Co.

essentially attempt to categorize the nature of the "holes," their origins, and the devices used to cover them up.

Psychoanalytic theories. The first family of personality theories is the *psychoanalytic*, based on the work of Freud. Freud himself never devoted attention to alcoholism. However, his followers have since applied aspects of his theory to this disease. It is impossible to briefly present the whole of Freud's work. He recognized that psychological development is related to physical growth. He identified stages of development, each with its particular, peculiar hurdles that a child must overcome on the way to being a healthy adult. Tripping over one of the hurdles, he felt, led to difficulties in adulthood. Some of the events of childhood are especially painful, difficult, and anxiety producing. The situation may persist unrelieved by the environment. This makes the child feel incompetent, resulting in a hole. He would seek his own ways to patch over the holes he feels. However, the existence of the hole shapes his future behavior. It may grow larger, requiring more patchwork. The hole may render him more vulnerable to future stress and lead to new ones.

The concept of *oral fixation* has been used in applying psychoanalytic theory to alcoholism. This means the holes began way back in earliest childhood. Observe infants and see how very pleasurable and satisfying nursing and sucking are. Almost any "dis-ease" or discomfort can be soothed this way. An individual whose most secure life experiences are associated with this period will tend to resort to similar behaviors in times of stress. These people will also, as adults, tend to have the psychological characteristics of that life period. The major psychological characteristics of the oral period are the infant's egocentricity and inability to delay having his needs met. He's hungry when he's hungry, be it a convenient time from mother's viewpoint or not. And he's oblivious to other persons except as they fit into his world. Thus the alcoholic, according to this theory, is likely to be an individual who never fully matured beyond infancy. He is stuck with childlike views of the world and childlike ways of dealing with it. He is easily frustrated, impatient, demanding, wants what he wants when he wants it. . . . He has little trust that people can help him meet his needs. He is anxious and feels very vulnerable to the world. Nursing a drink seems an appropriate way of handling his discomforts. Alcohol is doubly attractive, since it works quickly: bottled magic.

Another psychoanalytic concept applied to male alcoholics is that of *latent homosexuality*. Its origins are in the *Oedipal period*, which corresponds to the preschool, kindergarten age. According to Freud, an inevitable part of every little boy's growing up is a fantasy love affair with his mother. There is an accompanying desire to get Dad out of the picture. Given the reality of Dad's size, he has a clear advantage in the situation. The little boy eventually gives up and settles on being *like* Dad, rather than taking his place. Through this identification process, the little boy assumes a male role. There are several possible hitches that can occur. Maybe the father is absent, or the father is not a very attractive model. In such instances, the child will not grow to manhood with a sense of himself as a healthy, whole male. As an adult he may turn to alcohol to instill a sense of masculinity. Or he may like drinking because it provides a socially acceptable format for male companionship.

Feelings of dependency. Other personality theorists have focused on different characteristics. Adler latched onto the feelings of dependency. He saw the roots of alcoholism being planted in the first five years of life. He thought firstborn children were most likely to become either alcoholic or suicidal. In his view the dynamics of both are essentially the same. The firstborn is displaced or dethroned by the next child. He loses a position in which both parents pampered him and feels less important. If the parents are unable to reassure him, he has increased feelings of inferiority and pessimism. The feelings of inferiority or the longing for a sense of power require strong proofs of superiority for satisfaction. When new problems arise, arousing anxiety, the person seeks a sense of *feeling* superior rather than really overcoming difficulties. Theoretically, then, drinking as a solution is, to the alcoholic, intelligent. Alcohol does temporarily reduce the awareness of anxiety and gives relief from the inferiority feelings.

Alcoholic personality. Another psychological approach to alcoholism attempts to define the "alcoholic personality." The hope has been to identify common characteristics by looking at groups of alcoholics. So far these attempts have met with little success, and the search is largely being abandoned. Since active alcoholics were studied, what appeared to be the "alcoholic personality" was in fact a set of symptoms for alcoholism. Thus the behavior being studied was either drugged or behavior essential to continue the drugged state. Although an alcoholic personality exists, it is seemingly unrelated to the prealcoholic personality.

In 1960, William and Joan McCord published their *Origins of Alcoholism*. Their studies used quite extensive data. The data had been collected on 255 boys throughout their childhood. What they found negated many of the psychoanalytic theories. In brief, oral tendencies, latent homosexuality, and strong maternal encouragement of dependency were not, in fact, predictors of alcoholism. From their analysis, a consistent, statistically significant picture emerged. The typical alcoholic, as a child, underwent a variety of experiences that heightened inner stress. This stress produced the paradoxical effect of intensifying both his need for love and his strong desire to repress this need. The conflict produced a distorted self-image. McCord and McCord examined "the personality of alcoholics, both in childhood and in adulthood. In childhood, the alcoholics appeared to be highly masculine, extroverted, aggressive, 'lone-wolfish'—all manifestations . . . of their denial of the need to be loved. An analysis of the personality of adult alcoholics leads to the conclusion that the disorder itself produces some rather striking behavioral changes." Their contribution was significant. They highlighted the complexity of the social and psychological interactions.

In the past decade, there has been an emergence of what has been called the *human potential*, or *growth*, *movement*. In essence it has been devoted, not to "curing" mental illness, but to applying the expertise of psychology and psychiatry to assisting "normal" people to function better (whatever that means to them). Tied in with this has been the emergence of new psychological or personality theories. The primary question has become, "What is going on now, and how can the individual/client/patient change?" The previously important question, "Why, or how, did the sickness or screwed-up-ness originate?" is less important. Transactional analysis, popularly known as TA, and reality therapy are two of these recent arrivals. Both have made a big splash in lay circles as well as in the professional community. Both have addressed themselves to the problem of alcoholism.

Transactional analysis (TA). *Games Alcoholics Play* by Claude Steiner has applied TA to alcoholism and the alcoholic. According to this thesis, the origins of alcoholism lie in the alcoholic's childhood conditions and his responses to them. The child finds himself in a predicament with his parents. When he behaves in a way that feels good or makes sense to him, he runs into problems. He discovers the real him isn't O.K. To overcome this and become O.K., he adopts a life-style or script for himself. In the script, he attempts to respond so as to counterbalance the message that said, "You're not O.K." For the alcoholic, the dominant script theme, according to Steiner, is "Don't think." This originates in a home where there are clear disparities between what is going on and what the parents say is happening. An observant child picks this up. If he points it out, he gets a "You just do what I say," or "You just mind your own business," or "Don't get sassy." To survive, he needs to find mechanisms for tuning out, turning off. As an adult, being an alcoholic is a fine way to continue the "Don't think" script.

Reality therapy. William Glasser developed reality therapy. He believes that besides the obvious and inborn biological needs, all humans have two basic needs: to love and be loved, and to feel that we are worthwhile to ourselves and others. Failure to fill these needs leads to pain. A possible solution is the route to addiction; use of some substance or behavior that, while it continues, completely removes the pain.

Reinforcement of learning theories. The other major class of psychological theories used to explain alcoholism has come from a different branch of psychology. These are the reinforcement of learning theories, which look at behavior differently. They see behavior as a result of learning motivated by an individual's attempt to minimize unpleasantness and maximize pleasure. What is pleasant is a very individual thing. A child might misbehave and be "punished," but the punishment, for him, might be a reward and more pleasant than being ignored.

In applying reinforcement of learning theories to alcoholism, the idea is that alcoholic drinking has a reward system. Either alcohol, or its effects, are reinforcing enough for the individual to cause continuation of drinking. Behavior most easily learned is that with immediate, positive results. The warm glow and well-being associated with the first sips are more reinforcing than the negative morning-after hangover. This theory would hold that anyone could become alcoholic if the drinking were sufficiently reinforced. Vernon Johnson, director of a highly successful treatment program and author of a book, *I'll Quit Tomorrow*, gives great emphasis to the importance of learning in explaining drinking. He notes that users of alcohol learn from their first drink that alcohol is exceedingly trustworthy (it works every time) and that it does good things. This learning is highly successful, sufficient to set up a lifetime relationship with alcohol. The relationship may alter gradually over time, finally becoming a destructive one. But the original positive reinforcement keeps the person seeking the "good old days" and minimizing the destructive elements. Looked at in this light, alcoholism is not so far distant from people who remain in what are now unsatisfactory marriages, jobs, or living situations out of habit or some hope that the original zest will return.

A word should be said in reference to the aforementioned theories. Some were formulated in the "salad days" of psychology. No one is likely nowadays to rely on any one of them as a single definitive explanation of a person's actions.

Combination theories. Psychology is the study of behavior. Within the field of psychology, it is currently recognized that a number of different influences need to be considered in explaining behavior. This general approach is now being applied to alcoholism as a behavior. For lack of a better phrase, this may be termed the "slot-machine theory." To be alcoholic requires getting three cherries. An individual may be born with a physiological cherry. The environment and culture he is raised in may provide a second, or sociological, cherry. And his personality makeup, with its unique set of holes, may be the third cherry. Or it may be some variation: say two-thirds psychological and one-third sociological. But one lone cherry is not an accurate predictor of who becomes alcoholic.

Although not neatly fitting into either the sociological or psychological approaches to the etiology of alcoholism, some mention of the work of Gregory Bateson is in order. Bateson is an anthropologist-sociologist who has done a wide variety of work. He has most recently been involved in looking at how computers work, how people process information, and how a comparison can give us clues to understanding human behavior. An essay was published in 1972, "The Cybernetics of 'Self': A Theory of Alcoholism," which offers some intriguing ideas on why alcoholism may be reaching epidemic proportions. It certainly provides an interesting hypothesis on why abandoning alcohol is so difficult for the alcoholic.

Bateson points out that Western and Eastern cultures differ significantly in the way they view the world. Western societies focus on the individual. The tendency of Eastern cultures is to consider the individual in terms of the group or in terms of his relationships. To point out this difference, consider how you might respond to the question, "Who is that?" The "Western" way to answer is to respond with the person's name, "That's Joe Schmoe." The "Eastern" response might be, "That's my neighbor's oldest son." This latter answer highlights the relationship of several persons.

One of the results of Westerners' zeroing in on the individual is an inflation of the sense of "I." We think of ourselves as wholly separable and independent. Also we may not recognize the relationships of ourselves to other persons and things and the effects of our interactions. According to Bateson, this can lead to problems. One example he cites is the relationship of man to the physical environment. If nothing else, the ecology movement has taught us the old rallying cry of "man against nature" doesn't make sense. Man can't beat nature. We only win, i.e. survive, if we allow nature to win some rounds too. To put it differently, now we are starting to see man as a part of nature.

How does this fit in with alcohol? The same kind of thinking is evident. The individual who drinks expects, and is expected, to be the master of alcohol. If problems develop, you can count on hearing "control your drinking," "use willpower." The person is supposed to fight the booze and win. Now there's a challenge. Who can stand losing to a "thing?" So the person tries different tactics to gain the upper hand. Even if he quits drinking for awhile, the competition is on: me vs. it. To prove that he is in charge, sooner or later, he will have "just one." If disaster doesn't strike then, the challenge continues to "just one more." Sooner, or later. . . .

Bateson asserts that successful recovery requires a change of world views by the person in trouble with alcohol. The Western tendency to see the self (the I) as separate and distinct from, and often in combat with, alcohol (or anything else) has to be abandoned. The alcoholic has to learn the paradox of winning through losing, the limitations of the I and its interdependence with the rest of the world. He continues with examples of the numerous ways in which Alcoholics Anonymous fosters just this change of orientation.

The environment—sociological factors

Genetic and psychological approaches fall short of fully explaining the phenomenon of alcoholism. This is because they concentrate on why isolated individuals are, or become, alcoholic. Looking at the larger picture shows something else at work. The particular society or culture in which someone lives makes a big difference. All groups or cultures do not have similar difficulty with alcohol. Statistically, the odds on becoming alcoholic vary significantly from country to country. Through studies in epidemiology it is known that the Irish, French, Chileans, and Americans have a high incidence of alcoholism. The Italians, Jews, Chinese, and Portuguese have substantially lower rates. The difference seems to lie with the country's habits and customs. Indeed, whether someone drinks at all depends as much on culture as it does on individual characteristics.

Culture includes the unwritten rules and beliefs by which a group of people live. Social customs set the ground rules for behavior. The rules are learned from earliest childhood and are followed later, often without a thought. Many times it is such social customs that account for the things we do "just because. . . ." The specific expectations for behavior differ from nation to nation, and between separate groups within a nation. Differences can be tied to religion, sex, age, or social class. The ground rules apply to drinking habits as much as to other customs. Cultures vary in attitudes toward alcohol use just as they differ in the sports they like or what they eat for breakfast.

Cultural orientation's effects on alcoholism rates. Several distinctive drinking patterns and attitudes toward alcohol's use have been identified. Which orientation predominates in a culture is influential in determining that society's rate of alcoholism. One such attitude toward drinking is to-

tal abstinence, as with the Moslems or Mormons. With drinking forbidden, the chances of alcoholism are mighty slim. Expectedly, the group has a very low rate of alcoholism. Another cultural attitude toward alcohol promotes *ritual use.* The drinking is primarily connected to religious practice, ceremonies, and special occasions. Any heavy drinking in other contexts would be frowned upon. When drinking is tied to social occasions, with the emphasis on social solidarity and camaraderie, this is termed *convivial use.* Finally, there is *utilitarian use.* The society "allows" people to drink for their own personal reasons, to meet their own needs, for example, to relax, to forget, or to chase a hangover. Rates of alcoholism are highest where utilitarian use is dominant.

Differences among nations may be growing less marked with television, jet planes, increased travel, etc. Italy has adopted the cocktail party; America is on to France's wine kick. Nonetheless, a look at some of the differences between the *traditional* French and Italian drinking habits shows cultural attitudes toward the use of alcohol can influence the rate of alcoholism. Both France and Italy are wine-producing countries, France first in the world, Italy second; both earn a substantial part of their revenue from the production and distribution of wine. Yet the incidence of alcohol addiction in Italy in 1952 was less than one-fifth that of France.

In France there are no controls on excess drinking. Indeed, there is no such thing as excessive drinking. Wine is publicly advertised as good for the health, creating gaiety, optimism, and self-assurance. It is seen as a useful or indispensable part of daily life. Drinking in France, as in

Ireland, is a matter of social obligation; a refusal to drink is met with ridicule, suspicion, and contempt. It is not uncommon for a Frenchman to have a little wine with breakfast, to drink small amounts all morning, to have half a bottle with lunch, to sip all afternoon, to have another half bottle with dinner, and to nip until bedtime, consuming two liters or more a day. Frenchmen do get drunk. On this schedule, drunkenness does not always show up in drunken behavior. The body, however, is never entirely free of alcohol. Even people who have never shown open drunkenness have withdrawal symptoms and even delirium tremens when they abstain. The "habit," and the social atmosphere that permits it, are obviously facilitating factors in the high rate of alcoholism in France.

Italy, on the other hand, which has the second highest wine consumption in the world, consumes only half of what is consumed in France. Italy has a low rate of alcoholism on a world scale. The average Italian doesn't drink all day, but only with his noon and evening meals. One liter a day is the accepted amount, and anything over that is considered excessive. There is no social pressure for drinking as in France. As Jellinek said, "In France, drinking is a must. In Italy it is a matter of choice." Drunkenness, even mild intoxication, is considered a terrible thing, unacceptable even on holidays or festive occasions. A guy with a reputation for boozing would have a hard time getting along in Italy. He would have trouble finding a wife. Both she and her parents would hesitate to consent to a marriage with such a man. His social life would be hindered, his business put in jeopardy, he would be cut off from the social interaction necessary for advancement.

The Jews, in spite of their share of the world's misery, have a low rate of alcoholism. Jewish drinking patterns are similar to the Italians'. Plus there is the additional restraint of religion. The Irish are more like the French and have a high incidence of alcoholism for many of the same reasons. The Irish have many ambivalent feelings toward alcohol and drunkenness, which can produce tension and uneasiness. Drinking among the Irish (and other groups with high rates) is largely convivial on the surface; yet purely utilitarian drinking—often lonely, quick, and sneaky—is a tolerated pattern.

What, then, are the specific factors that account for the

differences? These are obviously not based on abstinence. Among the Italians and Jews, many use alcohol abundantly and yet they have a low incidence of alcoholism. In cultures with low rates of alcoholism, children are gradually introduced to alcohol in diluted small amounts, on special occasions, within a strong, well-integrated family group. Parents who drink a small or moderate amount with meals, who are consistent in their behavior and their attitudes set a healthy example. There is strong disapproval of intoxication. It is neither socially acceptable, stylish, funny, nor tolerated. A positive acceptance of moderate, nondisruptive drinking and a well-established consensus on when, where, and how to drink create freedom from anxiety. Drinking is not viewed as a sign of manhood and virility, and abstinence is socially acceptable. It is no more rude to say no to liquor than to coffee. Liquor is viewed as an ordinary thing. No moral importance is attached to drinking or not drinking; it is neither a virtue nor a sin. In addition, alcohol is not seen as the primary focus for an activity; it accompanies rather than dominates or controls.

Portrait of a woman who has never tasted alcohol.

Portrait of a man who never has more than one drink.

High rates of alcoholism tend to be associated with the reverse of the above patterns. Wherever there is little agreement on *how to* drink and *how not to* drink, alcoholism rates go up. In the absense of clear, widely agreed upon rules, whether one is behaving or misbehaving is uncertain. Ambivalence, confusion, and guilt can easily be associated with drinking. Those feelings further compound the problem. Persons who move from one culture to another are especially vulnerable. Their guidelines may be conflicting, and they are caught without standards to follow. Persons who belong to groups that promote abstinence similarly run a very high risk of alcoholism if they do drink.

The focus has been on the unwritten rules that govern drinking behavior and influence the rates of alcoholism. How about the rules incorporated into law, which govern use and availability? What impact do they have on the rates of alcoholism? While their impact is less than the factors just discussed, which permeate all of daily life, they do make a difference. Think back to the nation's experience of Prohibition, which can only be described as a fiasco. Few would maintain Prohibition was successful in significantly curtailing consumption or reducing alcoholism.

No nation is drunken where wine is cheap; and none sober where the dearness of wine substitutes ardent spirits as the common beverage.

THOMAS JEFFERSON

What is clear is that laws must, to a large degree, reflect how people want people to behave if they are to work.

Change our culture, change our drinking attitudes? Short of Prohibition, there are still significant ways society can influence the use of alcohol. Among these are cost of alcoholic beverages, regulations on advertising, and when and where alcohol may be sold. Evidence from other countries would suggest that the rate of alcoholism is related to per capita consumption. So banning advertising, increasing taxes, etc. to thereby reduce sales might achieve a lower rate of alcoholism. Discussion is hot and heavy on these issues. Many states are now busy either raising or lowering the legal drinking age as a way to handle alcohol problems. The governor of Alaska, in what he acknowledged was a drastic and probably unpopular move, proposed a legislative package to "combat the grim statistics" of alcohol abuse in the state. Among the proposals were allowing bush villages to establish possession limits on alcohol, adopt unlimited sales taxes on alcohol, and impose a two-week lag time between purchase and pickup.

It must be noted here that in the United States, the laws in reference to alcohol use are set by the states for the most part. The blood alcohol level used to define legal intoxication is not even universally the same in the United States. States may vary on when, where, and what a citizen may drink within its borders. And some states even vary from county to county (Texas for example). And these laws go from dry to beer only to anything at all but only in private clubs, to sitting down but not walking with drink in hand, ad infinitum.

As a society we are attempting to "have our booze and drink it too." We want alcohol without the associated problems. Since that is not possible, the question is what compromises are we willing to make. The Uniform Code, mentioned in Chapter 1, which promotes treatment, not punishment, of alcohol abusers is a step in the right direction. But what other inconveniences and costs is society willing to assume? Will we accept a ban on package sales after 10 P.M. on the assumption folks who want to buy alcohol at that hour don't need it? Will we allocate a reasonable share of the alcohol tax dollar to help the inevitable percentage who get into trouble with the drug?

America in the 1970s has no consensus on how, when,

"Man comes from dust and ends in dust" (Holy Day Musaf prayer)—and in between, let's have a drink.

YIDDISH PROVERB

and where to drink. Convivial and utilitarian drinking have largely replaced ritual use of alcohol. In some quarters, it is manly and sophisticated to drink. In others, drinking is felt to be unnecessary, if not outright decadent. The attitudes toward alcohol embodied in our liquor laws testify to this contradiction. The law implies minors should not drink, yet on the magical 21st (maybe 18th) birthday, they are treated as if they suddenly knew how to handle alcohol appropriately.

With alcohol everywhere, until agreement emerges on appropriate and inappropriate use, American society will continue to be a fertile breeding ground for alcoholism.

RESOURCES AND FURTHER READING

Bateson, Gregory. The cybernetics of "self": a theory of alcoholism. *Psychiatry*, February 1971, *34*, 1-18.

Blane, Howard. *The personality of the alcoholic: guises of dependency.* New York: Harper & Row, Publishers, Inc., 1968.

Goodwin, Donald. Is alcoholism hereditary? A review and critique. *Archives of General Psychiatry*, December 1971, *25*, 545-549.

McCord, William, and McCord, Joan. A longitudinal study of the personality of alcoholics. In D. J. Pitman and C. R. Snyder (Eds.), *Society, culture, and drinking patterns.* New York: John Wiley & Sons, Inc., 1962.

Roebuck, Julian, and Kessler, Raymond. *The etiology of alcoholism.* Springfield, Ill.: Charles C Thomas, Publisher, 1972.

Medical complications

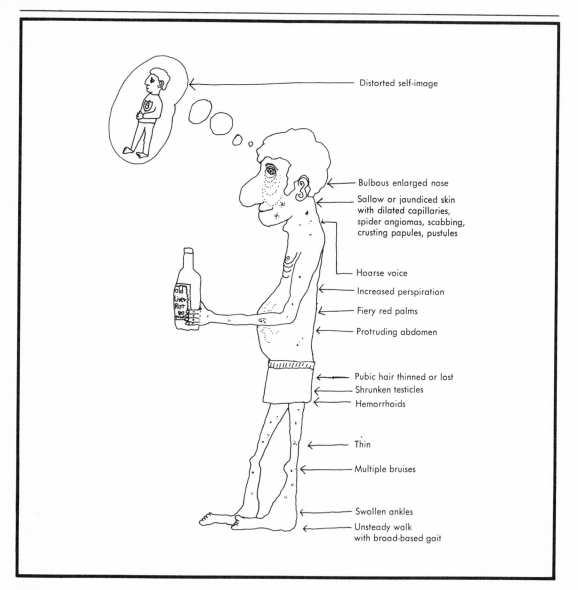

CHAPTER FIVE

Distorted self-image

Bulbous enlarged nose

Sallow or jaundiced skin with dilated capillaries, spider angiomas, scabbing, crusting papules, pustules

Hoarse voice

Increased perspiration

Fiery red palms

Protruding abdomen

Pubic hair thinned or lost

Shrunken testicles

Hemorrhoids

Thin

Multiple bruises

Swollen ankles

Unsteady walk with broad-based gait

COMPOSITE PHYSICAL PICTURE OF THE CHRONIC ALCOHOLIC

Alcoholism is a debilitating chronic disease. It involves a multitude of organ systems and leads to a variety of specific pathological and functional consequences. It has a host of physical signs and symptoms. An acquaintance with the multitude of medical complications of chronic alcoholism is equivalent to familiarity with an exceedingly broad cross section of physical disease. In this section we will touch briefly, in a systems-oriented fashion, on most of the major alcohol-related problems. First, let's examine a composite picture of a person afflicted with the stigmata of chronic alcoholism.

Statistically, the typical alcoholic is male; thus we will say he. However, women alcoholics can and do show virtually all the same symptoms of chronic alcohol use, except those involving the reproductive organs. So, on to an examination of a composite picture of the chronic drinker.

There are more old drunkards than old physicians.

RABELAIS

He is a typically thin, but occasionally somewhat bloated-appearing, middle-aged individual. Hyperpigmented, sallow, or jaundiced skin accentuates his wasted, chronically fatigued, and weakened overall appearance. He walks haltingly and unsteadily with a broad-based gait (ataxia); multiple bruises are evident. He perspires heavily. His voice is hoarse, punctuated by occasional hiccups, and he carries an odor of alcohol. The abdomen protrudes.

Closer examination reveals *caput medusae* (a prominent superficial abdominal vein pattern). There is marked ankle swelling, and he has hemorrhoids. His breasts may be enlarged, his testicles shrunken, and his chest, axillary, and/or pubic hair entirely lost or thinned. Inspection of the skin reveals dilated capillaries, acne-like lesions, and maybe a bulbous enlarged nose. There is scabbing and crusting secondary to generalized itching. He has spider angiomas on the upper half of the body. These are small red lesions that blanch with light pressure to their centers and spread into a spidery pattern with release of pressure. His palms are fiery red (liver palms), and he may have "paper money" skin. In colder climates, there is evidence of repeated frostbite. Even the fingers and the nails are likely affected. They may have either transverse white-colored bands (Muehrcke's lines) or transverse furrows, or may be totally opaque without moons showing at the base of the nail. He may well have difficulty fully extending the third, fourth, and fifth fingers (a flexion deformity). A swelling of the glands in the cheeks, giving him the appearance of having the mumps, is known as "chipmunk facies." Finally, a close look at the whites of the eyes reveals blood vessels with a corkscrew shape.

Now, with this as a general picture, let us look more closely at the underlying diseased organ systems and see how they account for it.

GASTROINTESTINAL SYSTEM

Alcohol affects the gastrointestinal system in a variety of ways. This is the route by which alcohol enters the body and is absorbed. It's where the first steps of metabolism take place. Moderate amounts of alcohol can disturb and alter the normal functioning of this system. And chronic use of alcohol can raise havoc. Alcohol can have both direct and indirect effects. Direct effects are any changes that occur in response to the presence of alcohol. Indirect effects would be whatever occurs next, as a consequence of the initial, direct impact.

Many a man keeps on drinking till he hasn't a coat to either his back or his stomach.

GEORGE D. PRENTICE

Irritation and bleeding

Chronic use of alcohol, as does any use, stimulates the stomach lining's secretion of hydrochloric acid and irritates the gut's lining. It also inhibits the muscular contractions that pass food along the intestines. In combination, these effects can lead to a generalized irritation of the mucous membrane lining the gut, especially in the stomach. Occasionally intestinal standstill (atony) can occur; this means the peristaltic movements slow to a halt. When this happens, the abdomen can become distended; this condition can mimic peritonitis or intestinal perforation. There may also be belching, loss of appetite, alternating diarrhea and constipation, morning nausea, and vomiting.

Irritation, rather than being found throughout the gastrointestinal system, can be localized to particular portions. If the esophagus is irritated, this is experienced as midchest pain and pain on swallowing. Acute stomach irritation involves inflammation, abdominal pain, and maybe even bleeding. Chronic alcohol use, if not indeed causing, can certainly aggravate ulcers of the stomach or duodenum (the first section of the small intestine). Bleeding can occur at

Pouring to achieve a large "head" on the beer enhances the bouquet and allows less carbonation to reach the stomach.

any of the irritated sites. This represents a very serious medical problem. Bleeding along the gastrointestinal system can either be slow or massive. Either way, it's serious. It is not unlikely that the alcoholic's blood clots less rapidly. So the body's built-in defenses to reduce bleeding are weakened. Surgery may be required to stop the bleeding.

Alcohol is frequently the culprit in causing acute inflammation of the pancreas. The pancreas is a gland tucked between the stomach and small intestine. It makes digestive juices, which are needed to break down starches, fats, and proteins. These juices are secreted into the duodenum through the pancreatic duct, in response to alcohol as well as other foodstuffs. They are alkaline and thus are important in neutralizing the acid contents of the stomach, thereby helping to protect the intestinal lining. The pancreas also houses the islets of Langerhans, which secrete the hormone insulin, needed to regulate sugar levels in the blood. The pancreatic duct, opening into the duodenum, can become swollen if the small intestine is irritated. Alcohol is one of the most frequent causes of such irritation. As it swells, digestive juices cannot pass through it freely. The pancreas itself, "stopped up," becomes inflamed. The symptoms include nausea, vomiting, occasional diarrhea, and severe upper abdominal pain radiating to the back. Chronic inflammation of the pancreas can lead to calcification, visible on abdominal x-ray films. This is almost always associated with long-standing alcohol abuse. Diabetes can result from the decreased capacity of the pancreas to produce and release insulin.

A drunkard is like a whiskey bottle, all neck and belly and no head.
AUSTIN O'MALLEY

In addition to the causes of gastrointestinal bleeding mentioned earlier, there are several other causes. The irritation of the stomach lining, not unexpectedly, upsets the stomach. With that can come prolonged violent nausea, vomiting, and retching. This may be so severe as to cause mechanical tears in the esophageal lining and bring on massive bleeding. Another cause of massive, and often fatal upper gastrointestinal bleeding is ruptured dilated veins along the esophagus (esophageal varices). The distention and dilation of these veins occurs as the result of chronic liver disease and cirrhosis. Although there are no specific diseases of the large intestine caused by alcohol abuse, diarrhea frequently occurs. Hemorrhoids, also a by-product of liver disease, and cirrhosis are common.

Liver disease

The liver is a most fascinating organ. You recall that it is the liver enzyme, alcohol dehydrogenase, which begins the breakdown process of alcohol. The liver is also responsible for a host of other tasks. It breaks down wastes and toxic substances. It manufactures essential blood components, including clotting factors. It stores certain vitamins, such as B_{12}, which is essential for red blood cells. It helps regulate the blood sugar level, a very critical task, since that's the only food the brain can use. Liver disease occurs because the presence of alcohol disturbs the metabolic machinery of the liver. Metabolizing alcohol is always a priority liver function. Therefore, whenever alcohol is present, the liver is "distracted" from other normal and necessary functions. For the chronic alcoholic, this can be a goodly part of the time.

As you may know, liver disease is one of the physical illnesses most commonly associated with alcoholism. There are three major forms of liver disease associated with alcohol abuse. The first is acute *fatty liver*. Fatty liver gets its name from the deposits of fat that build up in the normal liver cells. There is an increase in fat synthesis by the liver, plus the transport of fat from stores in other parts of the body. Acute fatty liver occurs whenever 30% or more of the dietary calories are in the form of alcohol. This is true even if the diet is otherwise adequate. Acute fatty liver is a reversible condition if alcohol use is stopped.

Alcoholic hepatitis is a more serious form of liver disease. It often follows a severe or prolonged bout of drinking. There is actual inflammation of the liver and some damage to liver cells. Liver metabolism is even more seriously disturbed. Jaundice is a usual sign of hepatitis. Jaundice refers to the yellowish cast of the skin and the whites of the eyes. The yellow color comes from the pigment found in bile, a digestive juice made by the liver. The bile is being handled improperly and is therefore circulating in the bloodstream. Other symptoms of alcoholic hepatitis include weakness, easy fatigability, loss of appetite, occasional nausea and vomiting, low-grade fever, mild weight loss, and increasing ascites. Some of the changes associated with alcoholic hepatitis are reversible if the person stops drinking. If drinking continues, a portion (perhaps 10%) of such cases develop into *alcoholic cirrhosis*. But

cirrhosis can appear without the prior occurrence of alcoholic hepatitis.

Approximately 8% of chronic alcohol abusers develop cirrhosis; but among cases of cirrhosis, alcohol abuse is the cause of the vast majority. The word cirrhosis simply means scarring. In cirrhotic livers there is widespread destruction of liver cells. They have been replaced by scars. Consequently, there are very serious and often relatively irreversible metabolic and physiological abnormalities. That is very bad news. The liver is simply unable to perform its work properly. Toxic substances, normally removed by the liver, circulate in the bloodstream, creating problems elsewhere in the body. The liver normally handles the majority of the blood from the gut or intestinal tract as it returns to the heart. The cirrhotic liver, now a mass of scar tissue, is unable to handle the usual blood flow. The blood, unable to move through the portal vein (the route from the blood vessels around the intestines to the liver), is forced to seek alternative return routes to the heart. This leads to pressure and "back up" in these alternative vessels. It is this pressure which causes the veins in the esophagus to become distended, producing esophageal varices and inviting hemorrhaging. The same pressure accounts for hemorrhoids. Another phenomenon associated with cirrhosis is ascites. Here the liver "weeps" fluid directly into the abdominal cavity. This would normally be taken up by the bloodstream. Large amounts of liquid can collect and distend the abdomen, and a woman, for example, would look very pregnant. If you were to gently tap the side of a person with ascites, you would see a wavelike motion in response, as fluid sloshes around. Another result of alcoholic liver disease is diminished ability of the liver to manufacture and store glycogen, the body's storage form of sugar. This can lead to low blood sugar levels, as well as improper handling of sugar from the diet. This is an important fact when it comes to treating an alcoholic diabetic. Insulin also lowers the blood sugar. Another situation in which this is important is in treating apparent coma in any alcoholic. Insufficient amounts of blood sugar may cause coma, essentially because the brain is without enough of a fuel supply to function. Intravenous glucose may be necessary to prevent irreversible brain damage.

The prognosis for treatment of cirrhosis is not good.

I know what the doctor said about my cirrhosis, but I can't imagine that a chateau margaux, 1969, could hurt my liver.

Hepatic coma (hepatic encephalopathy) can be one result of cirrhosis. In this case, the damage comes from toxins circulating in the bloodstream. In essence, the brain is "poisoned" by these wastes and its ability to function seriously impaired, leading to coma. Cancer of the liver is another complication of long-standing cirrhosis. Another source of bad news is that, of people who get cirrhosis, as many as 50% will also have developed pancreatitis. So these persons have two major serious medical conditions.

The different forms of alcohol-related liver disease result from specific changes in liver cells. Unfortunately, there is no neat and consistent relationship between a specific liver abnormality and the particular constellation of symptoms that develop. Although laboratory tests indicate liver damage, they cannot pinpoint the kind of alcohol-related liver disease. Therefore, some authorities believe a liver biopsy, which involves direct examination of a liver tissue sample, is essential to properly evaluate the situation.

Until fairly recently, it was believed that liver damage common to alcoholism was *not* a direct effect of the alcohol. Rather, it was believed the damage was caused by poor nutrition. It has since been learned that alcohol itself plays a major direct role. Liver damage can occur even in the presence of adequate nutrition.

HEMATOLOGICAL SYSTEM

The blood, known as the hematological system, is the body's major transportation network. The blood carries oxygen to the tissues. It takes up waste products of cell metabolism and carts them off to the lungs and kidneys for removal. It carries nutrients, minerals, and hormones to the cells. The blood also protects the body through the anti-infection agents it carries. Although the blood looks like a liquid, it contains formed elements (solid components). These formed elements include red blood cells, white blood cells, and platelets. They are all suspended in the serum, the fluid or liquid part of the blood. Each of the formed elements of the blood is profoundly affected by alcohol abuse. Whenever there is a disturbance of these essential blood ingredients, problems arise.

Red cells

Let's begin with the red blood cells. The most common problem here is anemia, too few red blood cells. Anemia is

a general term like fever. It simply means insufficient function or amounts. Logically, one can imagine this result
coming about in a number of ways. Too few can be manufactured if there's a shortage of nutrients to produce them.
If they are produced, they can be defective. They can be
lost, for example, through bleeding. Or they can actually
be destroyed. In fact, alcohol contributes to anemia in each
of these ways.

How does alcohol abuse relate to the first situation,
inadequate production? The most likely culprit here is
inadequate nutrition. Red blood cells can't be manufactured if the bone marrow does not have the necessary
ingredients. Iron is a key ingredient. Alcohol is thought to
inhibit the bone marrow's ability to use iron in making
hemoglobin, the oxygen-carrying part of the blood. Even if
there is enough iron in the system, it "just passes on by."
Or, because of a poor diet, not uncommon in the alcoholic,
the iron intake may be insufficient. There may also be
chronic gastrointestinal bleeding as a result of chronic alcohol abuse. If so, the iron is lost and not available for recy-
cling. This type of anemia is called *iron deficiency anemia.*
Another variety is *sideroblastic anemia.* It, too, is related to
nutritional deficiencies, too little vitamin B_6, pyridoxine.
This vitamin is also needed by the bone marrow cells to
produce hemoglobin.

These first two varieties account for the inadequate production of red blood cells. Another variety, *megaloblastic
anemia,* is also related to nutritional deficiencies. There is
too little B_{12} and folate. This happens because it's not in the
diet, and/or the small intestine is unable to absorb it properly because of other effects of chronic alcohol abuse.
What results then is defective red blood cell production.
Without these vitamins, red blood cells cannot mature.
They are released in primitive, less functional forms from
the bone marrow.

Chronic loss of blood from the gut, gastrointestinal
bleeding, can result in anemia. Here the bone marrow
simply cannot make enough new cells to keep up with those
which are lost. The body can also destroy red blood cells.
This is called *hemolysis.* One cause of hemolysis is hypersplenism, which results from chronic liver disease. The
spleen, enlarged and not working properly, destroys perfectly good red blood cells as well as the old worn-out ones.
Toxic factors in the serum of the blood are also thought to

THE DOCTOR SAID
Alcohol WAS MAKING
MY blood too thin—
So Now I add a little
CORN STARCH TO each
drink to help thicken
it up.

be responsible for three other varieties of hemolysis. *Stomatocytosis* is a transient anemia related to binge drinking and unrelated to severe alcoholic liver disease. *Spur cell anemia* is associated with severe, often end-stage, chronic alcoholic liver disease. The name comes from the shape of the red cell, which, when seen under the microscope, has jagged protrusions. *Zieve's syndrome* is a rare occurrence of jaundice, hemolytic anemia, elevated cholesterol levels, severe liver disease, and hypersplenism in an alcoholic patient.

In France, and maybe elsewhere, other changes in red blood cells have been reported in persons who drink at least 2 to 3 quarts of wine each day. The changes are typically associated with lead poisoning. (Lead, even in low concentrations, can mean trouble.) Excessive intake of wine in France is thought to be a significant source of dietary lead. In the United States, there are periodically reports of lead poisoning connected with alcohol use. However, the circumstances are different; the beverage has not been wine, but moonshine! In these cases, old car radiators were used in the distilling process.

White cells

On to the effects of alcohol on white blood cells. These cells are one of the body's main defenses against infection. The chronic use of alcohol affects white cells. This contributes to the increased susceptibility to and frequency of severe infections, especially respiratory tract infections. Alcohol has a direct toxic effect on the white blood cell reserves (bone marrow granulocytes), which produces a relative lack of white cells to fight infection. Chemotaxis, or white cell mobilization, is diminished by alcohol. In other words, although the white cells' ability to actually take in and kill the bacteria is not affected, they have difficulty reaching the site of infection. Alcohol also interferes with white cell adherence to bacteria, which is one of the body's defensive inflammatory reactions. The ability of serum (the unformed elements of the blood) to kill gram-negative bacteria is also impaired by alcohol. This may be related to the diseased liver's lowered ability to produce complement. Many immune and defensive responses depend on its presence.

Platelets

Alcoholics are frequently subject to bleeding disorders. They bruise easily. Bleeding can occur in the gastrointestinal tract, the nose, and the gums. This is largely explained by the effect of alcohol in decreasing the number of platelets. Platelets are a major component of the body's clotting system and act like putty on a leak. Alcohol has a direct toxic effect on bone marrow production of platelets. It can also cause hypersplenism, which destroys platelets as well as red blood cells. When the liver's metabolic processes are disrupted by the effects of chronic alcohol abuse, there is a decrease in the production of some of the necessary serum clotting factors. One thing to bear in mind is that there are thirteen to fifteen different reactions needed to make a clot. Of these, five are liver produced; ergo, liver disease may lead to bleeding problems in alcoholics.

Another area of current research is examining other ways the immune system may be altered by alcohol. Actually, there are two different immune systems. One is associated with the serum proteins, called *immunoglobulins*, in the blood system. The other is based in the individual cells. It appears that the alcohol-induced changes in some white cells together with changes in the cell-based immune system may lead to an increased production of proteins used to build fibrous tissues. It is these fibrous tissues that are characteristic of cirrhosis. A current $64 question is whether the scar tissue of cirrhosis can be attributed to white cell changes and alterations in the cells' immune response.

CARDIOVASCULAR SYSTEM

Alcohol is thought to be directly responsible for a specific but not too common form of heart disease, *alcoholic cardiomyopathy*. This is a severe condition with heart failure, shortness of breath at the least exertion, and dramatic enlargement of the heart. It responds well to discontinuation of alcohol plus long-term bed rest. Another form of heart disease with congestive heart failure known as *beriberi heart disease* may be seen in chronic alcoholism. This is caused by impaired dietary intake and thiamine, or vitamin B_1, deficiency and may respond dramatically to replacement of thiamine in the diet.

As an aside, a rather unusual and specific type of severe

cardiac disease was noted to occur a few years ago among drinkers of a particular type of Canadian beer. It was found to be due not to alcohol per se, but rather to the noxious effects of cobalt, which had been added to the beer to maintain its "head." These cases occurred in the late 1960s with a mortality rate of 50% to 60%. Fortunately, the cause has been eliminated, and this will hopefully no longer happen.

A variety of *abnormalities in cardiac rhythm* have been associated with alcohol. The upper chambers (atria) of the heart are like the primers to the lower (ventricular) part that acts as the pump. Thus ventricular irregularities tend to be more serious. Atrial fibrillation occurs in the upper heart muscles and produces an ineffective atrial beat. This condition is often associated with withdrawal. Paroxysmal atrial tachycardia is an irregular beat in the upper part of the heart producing a different and more rapid than usual beat. Alcohol also causes an increase in the frequency of premature ventricular contractions. These are irregular or in-between contractions of the lower part of the heart. It can be a very dangerous condition, and if the irregular contractions occur in a particular pattern, they can cause death. A fourth effect is sinus tachycardia with palpitations secondary to postulated vagus nerve neuritis. The sinus node is the normal pacemaker of the heart, in part regulated by the vagus nerve. If the nerve is irritated by alcohol, a speeding up of the normal rhythm can occur.

Alcohol, even in moderate amounts, exacerbates certain pre-existing abnormalities of blood fats, especially *Type IV hyperlipoproteinemia*. This is an elevated fat level of a particular kind that has been suggested to increase the rate of development of arteriosclerosis, or hardening of the arteries. The coronary arteries become increasingly occluded or blocked, hence making premature heart attacks more likely. Even a small amount of alcohol can badly affect this disorder.

In work recently reported, a definite link was shown between heavy drinking and *hypertension*. Heavy drinkers had both elevated systolic and diastolic blood pressures. This was true even when weight, age, serum cholesterol, and smoking were controlled for. Although this relationship is clear, the role alcohol plays in the development of atherosclerosis is not. (Atherosclerosis has a similar relationship to high blood pressure.)

Alcohol is well known to cause dilation of peripheral superficial blood vessels and capillaries. It does not have this same effect on the coronary blood vessels. Therefore, despite its use in the past, it is not helpful in treating angina.

There are reports of a new alcohol-related syndrome. It goes by the name *holiday heart*. As you might expect with that name, it occurs after heavy alcohol intake, around holidays and on Mondays after weekend binges. The syndrome includes palpitations and arrhythmias, but no evidence of cardiomyopathy or congestive heart failure. The signs and symptoms clear completely after a few days of abstinence.

Somewhat surprisingly, some recent experimental evidence suggests that alcohol may possibly provide some protective effect against the occurrence of heart attacks in people without blood fat abnormalities. Such reports suggest that one cocktail a day has roughly the same effect on serum cholesterol as the average lipid-lowering diet. It causes increased levels of HDL cholesterol and decreased levels of LDL cholesterol. High and low levels of these substances, respectively, are associated with lower risks of heart attacks. So take your pick, liver disease or heart attack!

Wine is at the head of all medicines.

TALMUD: BABA BATHRA, 58b

GENITOURINARY SYSTEM
Urinary tract

The kidneys, almost uniquely, are not directly affected by alcohol. What happens in the kidneys is the result of disordered function elsewhere in the body. For example, alcohol promotes the production of urine through its ability to inhibit the production and output of antidiuretic hormone by the hypothalamic region of the brain. The blood goes to the kidney for filtering, and water and wastes are separated from it and excreted through the bladder. Normally, in this process, the antidiuretic hormone allows water to be reabsorbed by the kidney to meet the body's needs. When the hormone levels are suppressed, the kidney's capacity to reabsorb water is diminished. It is therefore excreted from the body. Alcohol only inhibits this hormone's production when the blood alcohol level is rising. This is so with as little as 2 ounces of pure alcohol. When the blood alcohol level is steady, or falling, there is no such effect. In fact, the opposite may be true. There may be a retention of fluids by the body. This makes the use of intravenous fluids as a standard practice not only often useless, but possibly hazardous.

Alcohol can lead to acute urinary retention and recurrence and exacerbation of urinary tract infections and/or prostatitis. This is due to its ability to cause spasm and/or congestion in diseased prostate glands and in the area of previously existing urethral strictures.

A nearly uniformly fatal, but fortunately uncommon, consequence of chronic alcohol abuse is the so-called *hepatorenal syndrome*. This is thought to be caused by a toxic serum factor, or factors, secondary to severe liver disease. These factors cause shifts in kidney blood flow and diminish effective perfusion (filtering through) of the kidney. Unless the underlying liver disease is somehow reversed, irreversible kidney failure can occur. One reason for *not* giving diuretics to relieve ascites is that they can precipitate this disorder. Interestingly, there is nothing intrinsically wrong with the kidneys themselves. They can be transplanted into a patient without underlying liver disease and perform normally.

Reproductive system

Heavy alcohol use affects the reproductive system. In women there may be skipped menstrual periods; in men, sterility. In addition to its many other functions, the liver plays an important role in the balance of sex hormones. So when the liver is impaired, an imbalance of sex hormones results. Both male and female sex hormones are present in both sexes, only in different proportions. The increased levels of female hormones in alcoholic men can also lead to "feminization" of features. Breasts can enlarge, testicles shrink, and a loss or thinning of body hair can occur. Sex hormone changes in males also result from alcohol's direct action on the testes, which decreases the production of testosterone, a male sex hormone. Testosterone levels may be lowered as well by alcohol's effect on various brain centers, such as the hypothalamus and pituitary gland, which produces luteinizing hormone (LH), which in turn prompts the release of testosterone. This is currently under investigation. These latter hormonal effects are the direct results of alcohol. They are independent of any liver or nutritional problems. The situation in women in terms of sex hormone changes is not as completely understood. The female reproductive system, located within the body, is less accessible for research. Also, women and alcohol as a distinct area of inquiry is a very recent development.

Finally, although sexual interests and pursuits may be heightened by alcohol's release of inhibitions, ability to perform sexually can be impaired. For example, in men there may be either relative or absolute impotency.

ALCOHOL AND PREGNANCY
Fetal alcohol syndrome

Since 1971, there has been renewed attention given to the effects of chronic alcohol use during pregnancy. At that time, a researcher reported his observations of infants born to alcoholic mothers. The constellation of features observed have since been termed the *fetal alcohol syndrome*. Alcohol can pass through the placenta to the developing fetus and interfere with prenatal development. At birth, infants with fetal alcohol syndrome are smaller, both in weight and length. There is a decrease in head size, probably related to a decrease in brain growth. These infants also have a "dysmorphic appearance," that is, they are strange looking, just appear "different," although the difference is not easily described. At birth the infants are jittery and tremulous. Whether this jitteriness is the result of nervous system impairment from the long-term exposure to alcohol and/or miniwithdrawal is unclear. There have been reports of newborn infants having the scent of alcohol on their breath. Cardiac problems and retardation are also associated with the fetal alcohol syndrome. This syndrome is now being seen as the third leading cause of mental retardation. (See Chapter 7 for further discussion of the effects of maternal alcoholism on children.)

Other dangers to the fetus

Perhaps even more worrisome than the fetal alcohol syndrome are recent reports on the effects of as little as two drinks (1 ounce of pure alcohol) on the unborn baby. As little as two drinks a day may lead to increased risk of abnormalities. This two-drink figure is *not* a numerical average. It refers to the amount of alcohol consumed on any one day. As the amount of alcohol consumed on any given day rises, the risk also increases:

Less than two drinks	Very little risk
Two to four drinks	10% risk of abnormalities
Ten drinks	50% risk of abnormalities
Over ten drinks ·	75% risk of abnormalities

Based on this information, in the summer of 1977 the National Institute on Alcohol Abuse and Alcoholism issued a health warning, advising expectant mothers not to have more than two drinks a day.

How alcohol interferes with normal prenatal growth is not fully understood. Nor is it known if there are critical periods during pregnancy when alcohol is especially hazardous. Research with animals suggests the alcohol level of some of the fetus' tissues may be ten times higher than that of the mother. If this is the case, the mechanisms have not been identified. One would guess that the alcohol, since it can pass through the placenta to the fetus, could exit as easily. Therefore both would have equivalent blood alcohol levels.

However, *if* there is this difference in alcohol levels, if the fetus' is ten times greater than the mother's, consider the following possibility. A 140-pound expectant mother has two highballs, consuming 1 ounce of pure alcohol. Her blood alcohol level would be 0.045 and that of certain organs in the baby would be 0.45. The fetal alcohol concentration is reaching the level that produces coma in an adult. Although the fetus doesn't have to breathe on its own, that's still a whopping amount of alcohol.

What is clear from case reports of women who drank alcohol during delivery, and in whom blood alcohol level studies were done, is that the newborn baby's blood alcohol level did not drop as fast as the mother's. The reason presumably is that the infant has an immature liver. Newborns don't have the fully developed enzyme systems (alcohol dehydrogenase) necessary to metabolize alcohol.

RESPIRATORY SYSTEM

Alcohol affects the respiration rate. Low to moderate doses of alcohol increase the respiration rate, presumably by direct action on the medullary respiration center in the brain. In larger, anesthetic, and/or toxic doses the respiration rate is decreased. The lungs, however, are not directly damaged by alcohol. They are susceptible to its noxious effects in an indirect fashion. The combination of stuporousness, or unconsciousness, and vomiting from alcohol abuse can lead to aspiration of mouth and nose secretions or gastric contents. On the one hand, the mouth and nose contents can lead to bacterial aspiration pneumonias and anaerobic pulmonary infections with lung abscesses. On the other, aspiration of gastric contents can lead to chemical pneumonias with secondary bacterial infection. With the alcoholic's diminished defenses against infection, pulmonary infections, especially with pneumococci, seem to occur more frequently than in nonalcoholics. Also, with decreases in defenses the incidence of reactivated tuberculosis is increased in alcoholics. Thus, any alcoholic with a newly positive skin test for tuberculosis should be considered for treatment to prevent possible reactivation of the dormant tuberculosis bacteria.

ENDOCRINE SYSTEM

The endocrine system is composed of the glands of the body and their secretions, the hormones. Hormones can be thought of as chemical messengers, released by the glands into the bloodstream. They are vital in regulating countless body processes. There is a very complex and involved interaction between hormonal activity and body functioning.

Alcohol can affect the endocrine system in three major ways. Although there are many glands, the pituitary gland, located in the brain, can be thought of as the "master gland." Many of its hormonal secretions are involved in regulating other glands. So one way that alcohol can affect the endocrine system is by altering the function of the pituitary. If this happens, then other glands are unable to function properly because they are not receiving the proper hormonal instructions. Alcohol can also affect other glands directly. Despite their receiving the correct instructions from the pituitary, alcohol can impede their ability to respond. Finally, interference with the endocrine system can develop as a result of liver damage. One of the functions of the liver is to break down and metabolize hormones, thereby removing them from the system. With liver disease, this capacity is diminished and hormonal imbalances can result.

Several hormonal changes have already been mentioned. The level of testosterone, the male sex hormone, is lowered by alcohol, possibly in two ways. The first is the direct action of alcohol on the testes. The other may be by its inhibition of the portion of the pituitary gland that secretes luteinizing hormone (LH), the hormone necessary to regulate the testes' secretion of testosterone.

Serious liver disease reduces the liver's ability to break down another of the pituitary's hormones, melanocyte-stimulating hormone (MSH). This results in increased levels of MSH, which lead to the "dirty tan" skin color.

The adrenal glands are also affected by alcohol. The adrenals produce several hormones and thus serve multiple functions. One function known to us all comes from the release of adrenaline when we are frightened or fearful. The effects of this charge of adrenaline, rapid heartbeat and sweating, comprise "the fight or flight response." Heavy intake or withdrawal of alcohol prompts increased discharge of catecholamines by the adrenals. This may be partly responsible for the rapid heartbeat and hypertension during withdrawal. Another adrenal hormone, aldosterone, is increased with both heavy use or withdrawal. This often leads to significant and potentially serious salt and water imbalances due to the kidney changes in reabsorption in the face of altered hormone levels. Secondarily, increased aldosterone levels are a frequent accompaniment of cirrhosis and ascites. In response to alcohol's action on the pituitary, the adrenals secrete excess cortisol.

Animal research is raising several interesting questions about alcohol's effects on the endocrine system. In animals, heavy drinking increases the levels of norepinephrine in the heart. So the question is asked whether this may contribute to the development of alcoholic cardiomyopathy.

Another area of research is whether alcohol's effect on the endocrine system can lead to several kinds of cancer. Heavy drinkers have a higher incidence of skin, thyroid, and breast cancer. Recall that the pituitary gland is a master control. It influences the activity of the tissues through the hormones it releases. Alcohol inhibits the breakdown of MSH. It also stimulates the release of hormones that promote thyroid activity and milk production by the breast. These three hormones have one thing in common: they affect their target tissues, the skin, thyroid gland, and breast, by prompting these tissues to increase the speed with which cells divide to form new tissue. Aha, so the pieces may be falling into place. Cancer, simply put, is when there is uncontrolled excessive cell growth. Is it possible that alcohol's presence produces so many hormonal "speed-up-cell-production" messages to the skin, thyroid, and breast tissues that tumors can form? Maybe.

NERVOUS SYSTEM

The nervous system is perhaps the most widely and profoundly damaged by the effects of both acute and chronic alcohol abuse. The major acute effect of alcohol on the central nervous system is that of a depressant. The common misconception that alcohol is a stimulant comes from the fact that the depressant action disinhibits many higher cortical functions. Thus, parts of the brain are released from their usual inhibitory restraints. Acute alcohol intoxication, in fact, induces a mild delirium. Thinking becomes fuzzy, time sense is altered. An EEG done when someone is high would show a slowing of normal brain waves, associated with mild delirium. This is completely reversible.

Physical dependence

Chronic alcohol use can lead to physical dependence and addiction. This state is marked by the development of tolerance and withdrawal symptoms. What is tolerance? This refers to changes which occur as a result of repeated exposure to alcohol. There are changes in how the body handles the alcohol (metabolic tolerance) and changes in alcohol's impact on the nervous system (functional or behavioral tolerance). There is both an increased rate of metabolism of alcohol and a decrease in impairment for a particular blood alcohol level. The nontolerant individual will have a relatively constant and predictable amount of impairment for a given dose of alcohol. As tolerance develops, the person requires increasing amounts of alcohol to get the effects he previously had at lower doses. Tolerance represents the nervous system's ability to adapt and function more or less normally despite the presence of alcohol. This adaptation occurs rapidly. For example, if the blood alcohol levels are raised slowly, virtually no signs of intoxication may be seen. The reason(s) are unclear. The best guess is that there are subtle shifts or adjustments in nerve metabolism. Furthermore, if the dose of alcohol leading initially to high blood alcohol levels is held constant, nonetheless the blood alcohol levels fall and clinical evidence of intoxication may decrease. The basis for this metabolic tolerance has not been established. Chronic alcoholics well along in their drinking careers often experience a sharp drop in tolerance. Rather than being able to drink more, with only a drink or two they are intoxicated. This phenomenon is referred to as *reverse tolerance*. The reasons for this drop in tolerance are thought to be related, in part, to the diseased liver's decreased ability to catabolize alcohol.

Withdrawal

In chronic alcohol users, the most dramatic effects on the nervous system are those associated with an *acute lack* of alcohol. An individual who has regularly abused alcohol, that is, developed tolerance, will have withdrawal symptoms whenever there is a relative absence of alcohol. These can include intention tremors (the shakes when he tries to do something), which are rapid and coarse, involving the head, tongue, and limbs. Most likely this will be worse in the morning, assuming the last drink was the night before and the blood alcohol level has dropped since. Another manifestation of alcohol withdrawal in the early stages is the all too familiar "hangover headache." This is most likely related to vascular change and actually has nothing to do with the brain. The brain itself has no pain receptors. So any pain would be from the nerves of the surrounding lining, skin, vessels, or muscles.

If the chronic alcohol abuser does not take more alcohol, he is likely to develop other symptoms of withdrawal. The withdrawal syndrome is the nervous system's response to the lack of alcohol. The severity of the symptoms of withdrawal can vary widely, depending on the length of time of heavy drinking and the amount of alcohol consumed, plus individual differences in people. Symptoms of withdrawal can include tremulousness, agitation, seizures, and hallucinations. This will be discussed later in detail.

Pathological intoxication

Aside from withdrawal symptoms, there are other important nervous system disorders related to alcohol use. A relatively unusual manifestation is a condition called *pathological intoxication*. Some persons, for reasons unknown, have a dramatic change of personality when they drink even small amounts of alcohol. It is a transient psychotic state, with a very rapid onset. The individual is confused and disoriented and may have visual hallucinations and be very aggressive, anxious, impulsive, and enraged. This can last for only a few minutes or several hours. Then he lapses into a profound sleep and has amnesia for the episode. Were he to be interviewed later, he might be very docile, not at all the madman he was during the episode. Most likely he'd report: "I don't know what happened, I just went bananas."

Organic brain disease

Chronic alcohol use can also lead to varying degrees of dementia and organic brain disease. The particular type of brain disease, its name and associated impairment, is determined by the portion of the brain that is involved. *Wernicke's syndrome* and *Korsakoff's psychosis* are two such syndromes closely tied to alcoholism. Sometimes they are discussed as two separate disorders. Other times people lump them together as Wernicke-Korsakoff's syndrome. Both are caused by nutritional deficiencies, especially thiamine, a B vitamin, in combination with whatever toxic effects alcohol has on nerve tissue. The difference, pathologically, is that Wernicke's syndrome involves injury to the brain stem and areas near the third and fourth ventricle of the brain; Korsakoff's psychosis results from damage to the cortex and peripheral nerve tissue. Prognostically, Wernicke's syndrome has a brighter picture, many times responding very rapidly to vitamins. Korsakoff's psychosis is much less likely to improve. Someone with Korsakoff's psychosis will probably require chronic nursing home care.

Clinically, a person with Wernicke's syndrome is apt to be confused, delirious, and apprehensive. There is a characteristic dysfunction called *nystagmus* and/or paralysis of the eye muscles that control eye movements. Nystagmus is often one of the first symptoms to appear. Also, the development of ataxia, difficulty in walking due to peripheral and/or cerebellar nerve damage, is likely.

Korsakoff's psychosis presents a somewhat different picture. There is severe disorientation, delirium, memory loss, and confabulation. Confabulation is the hallmark sign. Because of the severe brain damage, the person simply cannot process and store information. In order to fill in the memory gaps, he makes up stories. These aren't deliberate lies. Trickery would require more memory and intent than someone with Korsakoff's psychosis could muster. For example, were you to ask someone with this disorder if he had met you before, his response might be a long, involved story about the last time you'd been together. It would be pure fantasy. This phenomenon is confabulation. However, memory for things that happened long ago is relatively intact. The impairment is in the *recent* memory function, all recent memory. Things simply aren't stored for recall, and the person can't remember things even five minutes later. With Korsakoff's psychosis, ataxia is also possible. There is a characteristic awkward walk, with the feet spread apart to assist in walking. Korsakoff's and Wernicke's diseases can both have a sudden, rapid onset. However, it's often the case that Korsakoff's psychosis follows a bout of the DTs. Cerebral atrophy (shriveling up) can occur in some severely impaired persons with the Wernicke-Korsakoff disorder. The cause is unknown.

Treatment of these diseases includes administration of thiamine and discontinuation of alcohol. This is more successful in reversing the signs and symptoms of Wernicke's syndrome. Only about 20% of persons with Korsakoff's psychosis recover completely. The recovery process is slow. It may take from six months to a year. The mortality rate of the combined disorder is around 15%.

Alcoholic cerebellar degeneration is a late complication of chronic alcohol abuse. It is more likely to occur in men, usually only after ten to twenty years of heavy drinking. In such cases patients gradually develop a slow, broad-based, lurching gait, as if they were about to fall over. This results from the fact that the cerebellum, the area of the brain that is damaged, is what coordinates complex motor activity. There is *no* cognitive or mental dysfunction, since the portions of the brain governing such activities are not affected.

Another brain syndrome associated with alcoholism is *chronic hepatocerebral disease*. This is a complication of long-standing liver disease, when the brain is adversely affected by toxins circulating in the bloodstream. The brain becomes scarred (astrocytic). There is a corresponding loss of function, with dementia, ataxia, impairment of speech (dysarthria), and strange movements. Brain tissue cannot be repaired. Any such loss is permanent. Such patients require chronic care facilities.

Two final organic brain diseases, which are quite obscure but potentially serious, are related to nutritional deficiencies. *Central pontine myelinosis* involves a part of the brain stem known as the pons. This disease can vary in intensity from being inapparent to rapidly causing death over a two- to three-week period. The pons controls respiration. As it degenerates, coma and finally death occur from respiratory paralysis. Second, *Marchiafava-Bignami disease*, also exceedingly uncommon, involves the frontal areas of the brain. Their degeneration leads to diminished language and motor skills, gait disorders, incontinence, seizures, dementia, and hallucinations.

IT'S A MARTINI SANDWICH - A 5th of gin and an empty vermouth bottle. His doctor told him to eat more and drink less.

In the field of alcoholism, you are likely to come across the term "wet brain." A physician would most likely look blank if you were to use this term in discussion. There is *no* specific medical condition that goes by this name. Probably it developed colloquially among nonmedical alcoholic workers to encompass nonreversible organic brain syndromes other than Korsakoff's psychosis. The confabulation of Korsakoff's psychosis is so distinctive that it probably is recognized as different. From our experience, "wet brain" seems to be used to describe patients who have significant mental impairment and diminished physical capacity requiring nursing home care.

Nerve and muscle tissue damage

Nerve tissue other than the brain can also be damaged by chronic alcohol use. The most common disturbance is *alcoholic polyneuropathy* from nutritional deficiencies. This has a gradual onset and progresses slowly. Recovery is equally slow, taking weeks to months with discontinuation of alcohol, plus appropriate vitamins. Most commonly the distal nerves are affected (those farthest from the body trunk). The damage to these nerves seemingly is caused directly by toxic properties of alcohol. Typically, someone with polyneuropathy will have a painful burning of the soles of the feet, yet an absence of normal sensation. Since there is sensory impairment, the individual isn't getting feedback to the brain to tell him how his body is positioned. This loss of position sense leads to a slapping style of walk because he's unsure of where his feet and legs are in relation to the ground.

Muscle damage can go hand in hand with nerve damage. There is often a wasting of muscle tissue in the areas affected by nerve damage because in some fashion muscles are improperly nourished if there is surrounding nerve damage. Other forms of muscle damage and degeneration have been reported even in the absence of neuropathy. The condition is termed *alcoholic myopathy* and involves the proximal muscles (those nearer the body trunk). Another form of muscle damage may result when a person is intoxicated and passes out, lying in the same position for a long time with constant pressure of body weight on the same muscles. Muscle degeneration means certain muscle proteins are released into the bloodstream. If these protein (myoglobin) levels are too high, kidney damage can occur. Potassium is also a product of muscle tissue breakdown. An increase in the level of potassium can disturb mineral balance throughout the body. For reasons that are entirely unclear, alcoholics are known to be very prone to muscle cramps.

Finally, an entity known as *tobacco-alcohol amblyopia* (dimness of vision) is another nervous system disorder. As the name implies, it is associated with chronic, excessive smoking and drinking. It is characterized by slow onset of blurred, dim vision with pain behind the eye. There is difficulty reading, intolerance of bright light, and loss of central color vision. Although eventually blind spots can occur, total blindness is uncommon. The cause is thought to be a vitamin deficiency coupled with the toxic effects of alcohol. Treatment includes B complex vitamins, plus abstinence, and is usually effective in reversing the eye symptoms.

Subdural hematoma

An indirect result of chronic alcoholism is the increased frequency of *subdural hematomas*. These occur as the result of falling down and striking the head. A blow on the head can cause bleeding of the vessels of the brain lining, the dura. The skull is a rigid box, so any bleeding inside this closed space exerts pressure on the brain. This can be very serious and is often overlooked. The typical appearance is an atypical presentation. Signs can vary widely, although fluctuating states of consciousness (i.e., drifting in and out of consciousness) are often associated with this. Treatment involves removal of the blood clot.

NEUROPSYCHOLOGICAL IMPAIRMENT

Personality change has long been regarded as an aspect of chronic alcohol abuse. Historically this was chalked up to serious underlying psychological problems. Then the emphasis shifted to viewing the "alcoholic personality" as a life-style the alcoholic developed to rationalize his alcohol problems and/or to protect his right to drink. There was little systematic research to explore a physiological basis, if any, and to correlate it to personality changes. This is now changing. Neuropsychological research, using psychometric tests, has uncovered specific impairments associated with alcohol abuse.

Overall intellectual deterioration is not seen until very late in the course of alcoholism. The IQ of most alcoholics remains relatively intact and normal. Nonetheless, there are other specific deficits, including decreased ability to solve problems, a lessened ability to perform complex psychomotor tasks, and a decreased ability to use abstract concepts. Drinking history is the major factor determining the severity of the impairments. How much alcohol, for how long? These deficits improve with abstinence. The first two to three weeks bring the most dramatic improvement. After that, improvement is gradual for the next six months to a year. It is important to realize that the improvement, while considerable, is not complete.

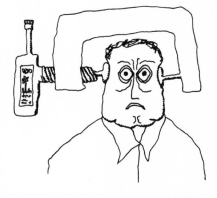

The portions of the brain implicated in the deficits just described are the frontal lobes. This may help explain the profound personality changes associated with chronic alcohol abuse. In fact, some of the behaviors accompanying alcoholism, such as "inability to abstain" and "loss of control," may partially be a product of organic brain dysfunctions. Most of the impaired functioning being discussed is subtle. It is not readily apparent. In fact, many of the patients in the clinical studies documenting neuropsychological impairment seemed "normal." They could be described as "young, intelligent, and looking much like any other citizen." That should alert us to the possibility that such alcohol-related brain damage may be more widespread than previously thought.

OTHER MISCELLANEOUS EFFECTS

Alcohol is also related to a variety of other signs, symptoms, and conditions that do not fit neatly into a discussion of a particular organ system.

Hodgkin's disease is a form of cancer, which, although certainly very serious, is becoming more and more treatable. Any person with Hodgkin's disease who drinks alcohol may well experience a pain in the regions involved in the disease.

Alcohol abuse is also associated with *Dercum's disease*, which is characterized by symmetrical and painful deposits of fat around the body and limbs.

Alcoholism has for a long time been thought to occur more frequently than would be expected by chance in persons who have manic-depressive illness, although some recent work has brought this association into question.

An interesting property of alcohol is its ability to relieve tremors in persons with familial tremor. As suggested by the name, this condition runs in families. The cause is unknown. It is hypothesized that such persons might medicate themselves by drinking and thereby invite alcoholism.

Alcohol abuse is associated with a variety of metabolic disorders:

• Gout, a painful joint swelling caused by increased levels of uric acid due to overproduction by the body or inadequate excretion by the kidneys. This kidney problem can result from the alcohol-damaged liver's failure to function normally. Elevated levels of blood ketones and lactate accumulate because of liver dysfunction and exert their effect on the kidneys' handling of uric acid.

• Potassium levels can be diminished because of excess mineral-regulating hormone associated with cirrhosis and ascites. Serum magnesium levels can go down, probably a direct effect of alcohol on the kidneys' handling of magnesium.

• Lactic acidosis, which can result from alterations in the liver's metabolic functioning, may be seen in some alcoholics. This can be a life-threatening situation and requires prompt and vigorous treatment.

• Calcium is lost from bones. This is probably the result of increased levels of adrenal steroids caused by excessive alcohol use.

What have been described here are the many physical illnesses frequently associated with alcoholism. But it is important to realize that health problems can arise from alcohol use, period. One does not have to be an alcoholic first. We predict it will become increasingly popular to discuss alcohol use as a risk factor for the development of a variety of illnesses, rather than to limit the focus to alcoholism and major diseases. The current general notion is that

'Tis pity wine should be so deleterious,
For tea and coffee leave us much more
serious.

LORD BYRON

alcohol poses a health hazard "only if you really drink a lot." Evidence indicates this isn't so. For some people, in some circumstances, what is usually considered a moderate amount of alcohol is too much. Remember the two-drink limit during pregnancy. And 15% of American men have the Type IV blood fats; alcohol use dramatically increases their chances of heart disease. Then there are the folks with ulcers or diabetes. Their use of alcohol invites additional problems. Certainly the list can be extended. Public education is warranted to increase the awareness that alcohol-related medical problems are not reserved for the alcoholic. They are potentially faced by any drinker. Alcohol, even in moderation, is simply not as benign a substance as has long been assumed.

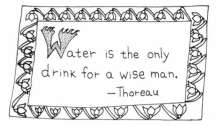

Water is the only drink for a wise man.
—Thoreau

SLEEP AND SLEEP DISTURBANCES IN ALCOHOLICS

Many people say they can't sleep unless they have a drink or two before bedtime, "to relax." On the other hand, alcohol actually interferes with sound sleep. To understand this paradox, we will take a look at how people sleep, how alcohol affects normal sleep, and what can be done for clients who cannot sleep after they have stopped drinking.

Scientists have studied sleep by recording brain waves of sleeping subjects on the electroencephalograph (EEG). It is known that everyone sleeps basically in the same way. There are four stages of sleep. Each stage has characteristic brain wave patterns. These occur in a fairly regular pattern throughout the night.

Sleep patterns

Before we can fall asleep, however, we need to relax and cut down on stimulation to the arousal centers in the brain. This is a fairly individualized affair—one man's relaxant is another man's tension! Some relax best in a dark, quiet bedroom; others need a loudspeaker blasting rock music before they can let go. In either case, as soon as one can become drowsy, the brain will show alpha waves.

Next comes the transition period, a time when one is half asleep and half awake. This is called *stage 1* and is characterized by theta waves. One still feels awake, but does not attend to input from the environment. Little dreamlets or pictures may appear in front of the mind's eye. Stage 1 sleep lasts anywhere from two to ten minutes.

Finally, there comes the real thing—sleep! The average, nondreaming sleep is called *stage 2,* and we spend about 60% to 80% of our sleep in this stage. Stage 2 is a medium deep and restful sleep, and the first episode of it will last about twenty to forty-five minutes.

Gradually, after that time, bigger and slower brain waves start to appear on the EEG. When these slow delta waves take over, we are in the soundest sleep of the night: *delta sleep.* The length of time one spends in delta sleep depends on age. This type of sleep lasts only a few minutes for older people, but up to two hours for children. Delta sleep is mainly concentrated into the early part of the night; there is rarely any left after about the first three hours of sleep.

After delta, we return to stage 2 sleep for awhile. Then, about sixty to ninety minutes after falling asleep, the most exciting sleep begins. This is *r*apid *e*ye *m*ovement sleep, REM sleep. The brain waves now resemble a waking pattern. The eyes are moving rapidly under closed eyelids, but the body is completely relaxed and asleep. During REM sleep we dream. The first dream of the night lasts about five minutes. Following it, there is a return to stage 2 and then, possibly, some delta sleep again, but it is not quite as deep as the first time. After the few minutes more delta, we return again to stage 2. The second dream of the night occurs about three hours after sleep onset and lasts about ten minutes.

The cycle of alternating nondreaming (stage 2) and dreaming (REM) sleep then continues throughout the night. Dreams occur about every ninety minutes. As the night goes on, nondreaming sleep becomes shorter, and dreaming (REM) sleep becomes longer.

From the above, you can see you are guaranteed about four dreams in six hours of sleep. In fact, you dream for about 20% of an average night. During dreaming, part of the brain is awake, part is not. For example, the long-range memory part of the brain does not function during dreaming. So, in order to remember a dream, you have to wake up from it and think about the dream immediately after you awaken. (Since dreaming is a light state of sleep, one often wakes up from it.) If someone reports he dreams a lot, it means one of two things: either he is not sleeping very well, and therefore wakes up a lot, or he thinks about his dreams a lot just after he does awaken. Someone who says he never dreams is probably a reasonably sound sleeper, with few awakenings. He is probably also one who jumps right out of bed when he wakes up and therefore forgets his dreams. Someone who tells you he is dreaming "more" lately has either become more interested in himself and thinks more about his dreams, or he is waking up more because he has developed poorer sleep.

Sleep seems to be good for both body and mind. Stages 2 and delta are thought to be mainly body-recovery sleep. When this sleep functions well, the body feels refreshed on awakening in the morning. Delta sleep appears to be more efficient than stage 2 in refreshing the body. Dreaming sleep, on the other hand, has something to do with our psychological processes. People do not go crazy if they are deprived of dreams, as was originally believed, but they lose some psychological stability. Someone who is usually very reliable, stable, and punctual may become irresponsible, irritable, and impulsive if deprived of REM sleep. As to the amount of sleep someone needs, the old 7 to 8 hours rule is useless. It depends on the individual. Two or three hours are enough for some of us; twelve hours are necessary for others.

Sleep disturbances

Why do we need sleep? Take it away and see what happens! Despite what most of us think, an occasional sleepless night is not all that important. Although you might feel awful and irritable, *loss of sleep for one or two nights has surprisingly little effect on normal performance and functioning.* There are two exceptions: very boring tasks, such as watching radar blips, or very creative tasks, such as writing an essay, are affected by even one night of very little sleep. On the other hand, for most jobs of average interest and difficulty, one can draw upon one's reserves and "rally" to the task even after two to four totally sleepless nights if one really tries to do so.

There are three brain systems regulating our existence: the awake or arousal system (the reticular activating system), the sleep system, and the REM (dreaming) system. There is a continual struggle between the three, each trying to dominate the other two. The three different systems have different anatomical places in the brain and apparently run on different neurochemicals. If you influence these neurochemicals, then you disturb the balance between the three systems.

It is not too difficult to disturb the balance between the waking and the sleeping systems for a few days. Stimulants (coffee, Dexedrine) will strengthen the waking system; sleeping pills will help the sleeping system. However, after just a few days or weeks, the brain chemistry compensates for the imbalance, and the chemicals become ineffective.

After a month on sleeping pills, one's sleep will be as lousy as ever. There is even some evidence that the continued use of sleeping pills causes poor sleep in itself. Furthermore, when the sleeping pill is withdrawn, sleep will become extremely poor for a few days or weeks because the balance is now disturbed in the opposite direction. Many people stay on sleeping pills for decades even though the pills do not really help them because of this "rebound insomnia" when they try to sleep without drugs.

Because one sleeps so poorly for awhile when withdrawing from the chronic use of sleeping pills, caution should be used. Go slow, cutting down the use of drugs in very gradual doses over a period of weeks. Abrupt withdrawal from some sleeping pills can be dangerous and even cause seizures. In addition, practically all sleeping pills, contrary to advertising, suppress dreaming sleep. After stopping the pills, the dreaming sleep increases in proportion to its former suppression. It can then occupy from 40% to 50%, in some cases even 90%, of the night. Dreaming sleep, too, takes ten days or so to get back to normal. During these days there is very little time for deep sleep, as dreaming is taking up most of the night. You feel exhausted in the morning because you had very little time for body recovery. Nevertheless, people who have taken heavy doses of sleeping pills for a long time often sleep better after being withdrawn than they did while taking them. It is all right to take a sleeping pill on *rare* occasions, say before an important interview, or after three to four nights of very poor sleep. However, it does not make any sense to take sleeping pills regularly for more than a week.

Insomnia

Insomnia can be based on either an overly active waking system or on a weak sleeping system. On rare occasions, this can have an organic or genetic basis. Some people have a defective sleep system from birth. However, most insomnias are based on psychological factors. Any stress, depression, or tension will naturally arouse the waking system. That is how the human brain is built. If that is the problem, the cure obviously involves helping the person deal with the psychological stress.

Surprisingly, poor sleep is often little more than a bad habit! Say a person went through a stressful life situation a few years back and, quite naturally, couldn't sleep for a few nights because of it. Being very tired during the day after a few poor nights, he then needed sleep more and more. So the person tried harder and harder to get to sleep, but the harder one tries, the less one can fall asleep. Soon a vicious cycle develops. Everything surrounding sleep becomes emotionally charged with immense frustration, and the frustration alone keeps you awake.

How do you break this habit? The rules for its treatment are simple, and treatment is effective, provided the client has enough willpower. Simply tell him he is misusing the bed if he lies in it awake and frustrated! The specific rules for treatment are as follows: (1) Whenever you can't fall asleep relatively quickly, get up because you are misusing the bed. You can do your "frustrating" somewhere else, but *not* in the bedroom! (2) As soon as you are tired enough and think you might fall asleep quickly, you are to go to bed. If you can't fall asleep quickly, you are to get up again. This step is to be repeated as often as necessary, until you fall asleep quickly. (3) No matter how little sleep you get on a given night, you have to get up in the morning at the usual time. (4) No daytime naps! If, with a counselor's help and support, a client sticks to this regimen for a few weeks, the body again becomes used to falling asleep quickly.

Shortening the time spent in bed is also crucial to many insomniacs. Because they haven't slept during the night, many insomniacs stay in bed for half the morning. They want to catch a few daytime naps, or they feel too tired and sick after not sleeping to get up. Pretty soon they lie in bed routinely for twelve, fourteen, even twenty hours. They sleep their days away, while complaining of insomnia. It is important that one maintain a regular day/night rhythm, with at least fourteen to sixteen hours out of bed, even if the nights are marred by insomnia.

Alcohol's effects on sleep

What does alcohol do to all this? Many find that a night-cap "fogs up" an overly tense and aroused waking system. Therefore, people can fall asleep faster with a drink. *However, alcohol depresses REM (dreaming) sleep, as well as delta (deep) sleep, and it causes many more awakenings.* A small drink is metabolized relatively fast. The dreaming and the deep sleep that are lost in the beginning of the night can be made up later during the same night. More alcohol, however, suppresses REM and delta sleep for the entire night, and the drinker frequently awakens through-out the night, leading to a lack of recovery during sleep.

These effects continue in chronic drinkers. In addition, the pressure to dream becomes stronger the longer it is suppressed. The dreaming sleep system will finally demand its due. Thus, after a binge, there is a tremendous recovery need for dreaming. It is thought that part of the DTs and the hallucinations of alcohol withdrawal can be explained by this pressure to dream. The dreaming system has been suppressed so long that it now invades the waking state!

The great fragmentation of sleep and the lack of delta and REM sleep in chronic alcoholics is a serious problem. Even though they think they sleep well, there is little or no recovery value in it. Some alcoholics stay only in stage 1. This very poor sleep makes people want to sleep longer in the morning and during the day. This adds to the usual problems of coping.

What happens to sleep when the booze is taken away from a chronic alcoholic! First, there is the rebound of dreaming. Increased dreaming can last up to ten days be-fore subsiding. Often there are nightmares because dream-ing is so intensive. The sleep fragmentation lasts longer. The suppression of delta sleep can go on for as long as two years after stopping drinking! In sober alcoholics as a group, there are still many more sleep disturbances than in nonalcoholics. We don't know why. It could be due to some chronic damage to the nervous system, as has been produced in alcoholic rats, or it could be that some alcohol-ics were lousy sleepers to start with. In any case, it appears that the longer one can stay on the wagon, the more sleep starts to normalize and approximate the sleep one had before getting hooked on booze.

Sweet dreams!

BLACKOUTS

Having covered a multitude of physical disorders associated with alcohol abuse, it would seem that there is nothing left to go wrong! Yet there remains one more phenomenon associated with alcohol use. It is highly distinctive: the blackout. Contrary to what the name may imply, it does *not* mean passing out or losing consciousness. Nor does it mean psychological blocking out of events, or repression. A blackout is an amnesia-like period that is associated with drinking. Someone who is drinking may appear to be perfectly normal, whatever passes for normal drinking behavior. Yet later, the person has no memory of what has transpired. A better term might be *blank-out*. The blank spaces in the memory may be total or partial. A person who has been drinking and who experiences a blank-out will not be able to recall how he got home, or how the party ended, or the decisions made at a business lunch. As you can imagine, this spotty memory can cause some severe distress and anxiety.

What causes blackouts? The mechanisms are not fully understood. Blackouts are not related to the amount of alcohol consumed at the time they occur. Nor are they related to the previous drinking history. Some alcoholics experience blackouts early in their drinking careers, others much later. Some alcoholics have never had a blackout. Some persons have blackouts frequently, others only on occasion. So the relationship of blackouts and alcoholism is less clear-cut than originally supposed by Jellinek thirty years ago. He saw the blackout as heralding the progression of the addictive form of alcoholism from the prealcoholic to the prodromal stage. It is now being suggested by some that blackouts may not be restricted to alcoholics. In fact, they may be fairly common in the general population. The difference between alcoholics and other persons is that the latter sharply curtail their use of alcohol after one blackout. In distinction, the alcoholic accepts blackouts as one of the psychological costs of drinking.

What is evident, despite the scanty research, is that for

some reason, in some persons, alcohol interferes with the process of memory. Memory is one of the many functions of the brain. It is a complex process. We can recall and report what happened to us five minutes ago. Similarly, many events of yesterday or a week ago can be recalled. In some cases, our memories can extend back ten years or more. Psychological and neuropsychological research has distinguished between different types of memory. Immediate, recent, and long-term memory is one classification system. Memory of whatever type involves the brain's capacity to handle and store information. It is thought that the brain has at least two different kinds of "filing systems" for information. Recent memory is stored electrically. Long-term memory involves a chemical storage system. For short-term memory to be stored over the long haul, its conversion from electrical impulses to a chemical format is required. This is the point at which, it is hypothesized, alcohol interferes. The presence of alcohol inhibits the brain's ability to move short-term memory into long-term storage. Part of the reason for believing that immediate and recent memory are not altered is on the basis of behavior. Were these *not* intact, a person in a blackout would be forgetting things from moment to moment. This would be readily observable to persons around him. Experimental evidence also supports the idea that for the time periods involved, the amnesia state is total, although a person can slip into and out of a blackout. It is as if alcohol throws a switch to an off position, as opposed to just dimming it.

In conclusion, it might be added that there has been recent discussion of blackouts being employed as a defense in criminal proceedings. To our knowledge, no such cases have yet been resolved. Although a novel approach, it would appear that there is no support to any contention that a blackout alters judgment or behavior at the time. The only deficiency is in memory of what has occurred. Of course, having no recollection would make it difficult to prepare a case or decide from one's own knowledge whether to plead guilty or innocent.

It is hoped that more can be learned of blackouts in the future. Research is difficult, since it depends almost entirely on self-report. So far, no one has found a way to know that an alcoholic blackout is occurring and to study it with EEGs and other tests at the time it is happening. Other types of brain research may eventually lead to the key to this phenomenon.

WITHDRAWAL

Alcohol is an addictive drug. Thus, taken in sufficient quantities, the body becomes adapted or accustomed to its presence. Drinking a quart of liquor daily for one week can create physical dependence. After physical dependence is established, if consumption is curtailed, there will be symptoms of withdrawal. These symptoms can also be termed as abstinence syndrome. One sure way to terminate an abstinence syndrome is to administer more of the addictive drug. Another facet of addiction is that tolerance develops. Over the long haul, increasing amounts of the drug are necessary to continue warding off withdrawal. The withdrawal symptoms for any drug are generally the mirror images of the effects induced by the drug itself. Alcohol is a depressant. The alcohol abstinence syndrome has symptoms that are indicative of a stimulated state. A hangover, a kind of miniwithdrawal, testifies to these stimulated qualities. Jumpy, edgy, irritable, hyped-up—these well-known symptoms are the exact opposite of alcohol's depressant qualities.

The basis of withdrawal is related to alcohol's depressant effects on the central nervous system. With regular chronic use of alcohol, the central nervous system is being chronically depressed. With abstinence, this chronic depressant effect is removed. There is a "rebound" hyperactivity. An area of the central nervous system particularly affected is the reticular activating system that oversees the general arousal level and CNS activity. The duration of the withdrawal syndrome is determined by the time required for the "rebound" to be played out and a normal baseline level of functioning to be reestablished. Studies of CNS activity with EEGs during heavy drinking, abstinence, and withdrawal support this.

Not everyone physically dependent on alcohol who stops drinking has the same identical set of symptoms. In part, the severity of the withdrawal state will be a function of how long someone has been drinking and how much. Another big factor is going to be the person's physical health plus his unique physiological characteristics. Therefore, accurately predicting the difficulties of withdrawal is impossible. Despite the phrase abstinence syndrome, with-drawal can occur even while someone continues to drink. The key factor is a *lowering* of the blood alcohol level. *Relative abstinence* is the condition that triggers withdrawal. It is this phenomenon that often prompts the alcoholic's morning drink. He is treating his withdrawal symptoms.

Withdrawal syndromes

Five different withdrawal syndromes have been de-scribed in conjunction with alcohol. Although they can be distinguished for the purposes of discussion, clinically the distinctions are not so neat. In real life, these different syndromes blend together.

The most common syndrome of alcohol withdrawal is *tremulousness*. It is this shakiness which prompts the ac-tively drinking alcoholic to have a morning or midday drink. Recall that increasing amounts of an addictive drug are necessary to ward off withdrawal, and a lowered BAL is sufficient to induce withdrawal. An alcoholic who is used to drinking heavily in the evenings is eventually going to find himself feeling shaky the next morning. A drink will take this discomfort and edge away. With time, further boosts of booze may be necessary to maintain a BAL suffi-cient to prevent the shakes.

If the physically dependent person abstains completely, there would be a marked increase of tremulousness. The appearance is one of stimulation. The alcoholic startles easily, feels irritable, and in general is "revved up" in a very unpleasant way. There's a fast pulse, sweating, dilated pupils, and a flushed face. Sleeping will be difficult. Usual-ly these symptoms subside in two or three days. The shakes will go away, and the temperature returns to normal. Feel-ing awful, irritability, and sleep difficulties can persist two to three weeks. This syndrome by itself does not require medical treatment. It is important that the person not be alone and that an evaluation be made about the likelihood of DTs. As this acute stage passes, the probability of DTs is greatly lowered. But if the jitteriness does not subside, be-ware. Be sure the person is evaluated by a physician.

Another syndrome of alcoholic withdrawal is *alcohol hallucinosis*. This occurs in some 25% of persons withdraw-ing from alcohol. This syndrome does not include true hal-lucinations. Rather, the person misperceives existing stimuli. The individual is oriented, knowing who he is, where he is, and the time. Very bad nightmares often accompany this withdrawal syndrome. It is believed the nightmares may result from the suppressing of dreaming sleep for so long by alcohol. Hence, there is a rebound effect. Hallucinosis is not important of itself and does not require specific medical treatment. It is very important, however, to accurately distinguish it from other withdrawal phenomena, especially hallucinations.

Auditory hallucinations accompanying alcohol withdrawal are a separate syndrome. Usually the hallucinations are of voices familiar to the patient, probably family and friends. Often they are threatening, demeaning, or invoke guilt. Since they are true hallucinations, the person thinks they are real and acts as if they are. This can lead to the person doing harm to himself or others. In contrast to hallucinosis, anyone with withdrawal hallucinations *must* have medical treatment. Alcoholic hallucinations do not indicate any underlying psychiatric problem. They are simply a response to the body's lack of alcohol. Appropriate treatment means placing someone in an environment in which he will be safe, plus possible use of mild sedation.

Another phenomenon of alcohol withdrawal is *convulsive seizures*, referred to often as "rum fits." These seizures are major motor seizures; the eyes roll back in the head, the body muscles contract and extend rhythmically, and there is loss of consciousness. After the seizure, which lasts a minute or two, the person is stuporous and groggy for six to eight hours. Although very frightening to watch, seizures of themselves are not dangerous. Any treatment during a seizure is limited to preventing injury, such as inserting a gag in the client's mouth to avoid biting the tongue or placing a pillow under the head. A very uncommon, though serious outcome is the development of *status epilepticus*, in which seizures follow one another with virtually no inter-

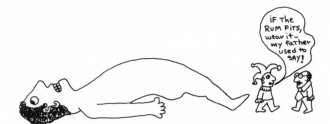

vening periods of consciousness. Most typically, only one or two seizures occur with rum fits. The only long-term treatment of alcohol withdrawal seizures is abstinence. Anticonvulsants would not be routinely prescribed, since further seizures are not expected after withdrawal. It is critical, though, to rule out any other possible sources of seizures and not merely to assume alcohol is responsible. Infections or falls to which the alcoholic is prone can be causes. Seizures are most likely to occur between twelve and forty-eight hours after stopping alcohol. But they can occur up to one week after the last drink. Alcohol withdrawal seizures indicate a moderate to severe withdrawal problem. One third of all persons who have seizures go on to have delirium tremens, DTs, which are serious business.

Withdrawal seizures are thought to be caused by the "rebound," CNS hyperexcitability. Alcohol has an anticonvulsant effect; it raises the seizure threshold. But with abstinence, the seizure threshold is correspondingly lowered. (This has been postulated as the basis for the increased seizures in epileptics who drink, since these seizures occur the morning after, while sobering up.)

Delirium tremens is the most serious form of alcohol withdrawal syndrome. Despite the availability of good medical care, there is a mortality rate of 20%. One out of every five persons who goes into DTs dies. The name indicates the two major components of this withdrawal state. Either of these components can predominate. Delirium refers to hallucinations, confusion, and disorientation. Tremens refers to the heightened autonomic nervous activity, the agitation, fast pulse, and fever. Someone who develops the DTs will have all the symptoms first described with tremulousness. Instead of clearing by the second or third day, the symptoms continue and get worse. In addition to a real shakiness, profuse sweating, fast pulse, and fever, there are mounting periods of confusion and attacks of anxiety. In full-blown DTs there are delusions and hallucinations, generally visual and tactile. The terrifying nature of the hallucinations and delusions is captured by the slang phrase for DTs, "the horrors." Seeing bugs on the walls and feeling insects crawling all over the body naturally heighten the anxiety and emotional responses. In this physical and emotional state, infections, respiratory problems, fluid loss, and physical exhaustion create further difficul-

ties. These complications hike the mortality rate. The acute phase of DTs can last from two days to a week. Eighty percent are over in twenty-five hours. The person will then fall into a profound sleep and, on awakening, feel better with possibly little memory of what has happened.

Treatment of DTs is aimed at providing supports during the medical crisis. Vital signs are monitored closely to spot any developing problems. Efforts are made to reduce the agitation, conserve energy, and prevent exhaustion. This involves medication to achieve some sedation. Despite arguments to the contrary, there simply is no clear-cut single regimen obviously superior to all others. Amounts and type of medication will be determined by the patient's physical condition. One of the concerns will be liver function. The liver, possibly damaged by alcohol, is the organ that is needed to metabolize virtually any drug given. If the liver is not up to the task, the drugs will not be as speedily removed from the body, a situation that can introduce further problems. The benzodiazepines (Librium, Valium, Serax) are often the first choice because they seem at least as effective as other agents, they have a wider margin of safety and less toxicity than other drugs, plus they have a significant anticonvulsant effect as well. Their dose is decreased by 25% as symptoms abate and to avoid cumulative unwanted sedation. Paraldehyde, an old, time-tested, and effective agent, has become less popular. It is metabolized by the liver and consequently must be used with care when there is significant liver disease. It must also be carefully stored in sealed brown bottles to prevent its breakdown into acetaldehyde. Last, it has an objectionable odor that is unavoidable, since it is excreted to a significant degree by the lungs. The major tranquilizers, or antipsychotic agents, are also less preferred. Although they have sedative properties, they also lower the seizure threshold, which is already a problem for withdrawing alcoholics. Whatever medication is used, the intent is to ease the medical crisis of DTs, not to introduce long-term drug treatment for the alcoholism.

Although predictions cannot be made about who will have DTs, persons who fit the following description are the most likely candidates. A daily drinker who has consumed over a fifth a day for the last week and who has been a heavy drinker for ten years is very susceptible. If he abstained

before and had convulsions, extreme agitation, marked confusion, disorientation, or DTs, he is more vulnerable. Another ominous sign is recent abuse of other sedatives, especially barbiturates, which also have withdrawal syndromes. Abuse of multiple drugs complicates withdrawal management. If it is anticipated that there is a physical dependence on more than one drug, generally they will not be withdrawn simultaneously, but first one, then the next, and so on.

Some cautions

Not all persons who experience withdrawal symptoms intend to do so by design! Withdrawal occurs by itself whenever a drug is reduced or terminated in physically dependent persons. So circumstances may play their part and catch persons unaware. Addicted persons who enter hospitals for surgery, curtailing their usual consumption, may to their surgeon's (and even their own) amazement develop DTs. Another possibility is the family vacation, when the secretly drinking housewife, who has been denying a problem, intends to just sweat it out. She can wind up with more than she bargained for.

Any counselor working with active alcoholics is going to work with people who do want to loosen their grip. Giving up alcohol can be tough on the body as well as the emotions. In making any assessment, the counselor will have to be concerned about the real possibility of physical dependence. Planning has to include arrangements for care during this physical withdrawal. No person should be alone. Family members need to know what to be alert to so that medical treatment can be provided. A simple rule of thumb is that if there is likelihood of DTs, seek hospitalization. Virtually every alcoholic has stopped drinking for a day or so, so he has some sense of what happened then. If there has been any kind of difficulty previously during withdrawal, seek medical evaluation and management. If in the absence of previous problems, this time is *worse*, seek medical treatment immediately. At every step along the way it is imperative that the alcoholic receive lots of TLC. He needs reassurance and support. He needs procedures explained. Anything that can be done to reduce the anxiety and fear is vitally important.

RESOURCES AND FURTHER READING

Fisher, Arthur. Sober—yet drinking too much. *New York Times Magazine*, May 18, 1975, p. 18.

Iber, Frank. In alcoholism, the liver sets the pace. *Nutrition Today*, January/February, 1971, p. 2.

Keller, Mark. *Alcohol and health*. Rockville, Md.: Department of Health, Education, and Welfare, 1971.

Manual on alcoholism. Chicago: American Medical Association, 1968.

Martin, James. The fetal alcohol syndrome: recent findings. *Alcohol Health and Research World*, 1977, *1*(3), 8-12.

Victor, Maurice, and Wolfe, Sidney. Causation of the alcohol withdrawal syndrome. In P. G. Bourne and R. Fox (Eds.), *Alcoholism progress in research and treatment*. New York: Academic Press, Inc., 1973.

Effects of alcohol on behavior

Leaving aside theories about alcoholic personalities and behavioral or psychological causes, there are some striking similarities in the behavioral "look" of alcoholics. From these, a general profile could be drawn. Although *not* applying totally to *all* alcoholics, this profile would cause signal bells to ring when seen by someone familiar with the disease.

THE COMPOSITE ALCOHOLIC

Our composite alcoholic would be most confusing to be around. He is always sending mixed messages. "Come closer, understand/Don't you *dare* question me!" Jubilant, expansive/secretive, angry, suspicious; laughing/crying. Tense, worried, confused/relaxed, "Everything's fine." Uptight over bills/financially irresponsible (He'll buy expensive toys for the kids, while the rent goes unpaid.) He's easygoing/fighting like a caged tiger over a "slight." Telling unnecessary lies and having them come to light is not uncommon behavior. He might also spend considerable, if not most, of his time justifying and explaining why he does things. He is hard to keep on the track. He always has a list of complaints about a number of people, places, and things. (If only . . .) He considers himself the victim of fate and of a large number of people who are "out to get" him. He has thousands of reasons why he *really* needs/deserves a drink. He will come in exuberant over a minor success and decline rapidly into an "I'm a failure because of . . ." routine. He's elusive. Almost never where he said he'd be when he said he'd be there, or he's absolutely *rigid* about his schedule, especially his drinking times.

His mood swings are phenomenal! His circular arguments never quite make sense to a sober person, and a lot of hand-throwing-up results. The thought that he might be crazy is not at all unusual from either side because of the terrible communication problems. Perfectionistic at some times and a slob at others. While occasionally cooperative, he's often a stone wall. His life is full of broken commitments, promises, and dates that he often doesn't remember making. Most of all, his behavior denotes guilt. He is extremely defensive. This seems to be one of the key behaviors that is picked up early and seen, but not understood, by others. "Wonder why A _____ 's so touchy? He sure has a short fuse!" Certainly at times a drunken slob is much in evidence, but often the really heavy drinking is secretive and carefully hidden. It would be easier to pin down the alcoholism if the behaviors described only occurred with a drink in hand. This is often not the case. The behaviors are sometimes *more* pronounced when the alcoholic is going through an "on the wagon," or controlled drinking, phase. The confusion, anger, frustration, and depression are omnipresent unless a radical change in his attitude toward the drinking takes place.

HOW, IF NOT WHY

Woe unto them that rise up early in the morning, that they may follow strong drink.

ISAIAH 5:11

The profile on p. 117 is a fair description of alcoholic behavior. This kind of behavior is part of the disease syndrome. Unfortunately, this behavior pattern develops slowly, and the many changes of personality occur gradually, making them less discernable to the alcoholic himself, and his family. So the slow, insidious change of personality is almost immune to recognition as it is happening. Despite the fact that the alcoholic is vulnerable to a host of physical problems, these behavioral changes cannot simply be chalked up to an alcohol-damaged brain. Neurological and physiological data cannot shed light on this phenomenon. Yet, despite the inability to provide a simple answer, *how* the transformation occurs can be described. Johnson, in *I'll Quit Tomorrow*, has developed a four-step process that neatly sets forth the personality changes which occur in the alcohol-dependent person. Becoming familiar with these stages will be helpful in dealing with alcoholics and problem drinkers.

Alcohol dependence requires the use of alcohol, an obvious fact. Another obvious fact: for whatever reasons, drinking becomes an important activity in the life of the problem drinker or alcoholic. The alcoholic develops a *relationship* with alcohol. The relationship, with all it implies, is as real and important a bond as with friends, a spouse, or a faithful dog. Accordingly, energy is expended to maintain the relationship. The bond with the bottle may be thought of as an illicit love affair. Long after the thrill, pleasure, and fun are gone, all kinds of mental gymnastics are gone through to act as if it's still great.

The first step Johnson describes is quite simple. The drinker *learns the mood swing*. The learning has a physiological basis. Alcohol is a drug; it has acute effects. It makes us feel good. Someone's mood could be plotted at any time on a graph, on which one end represents pain and the other end euphoria. If someone is feeling "normal" and then has a drink, his mood shifts toward the euphoric end. Then after the effects of the alcohol wear off, he's back where he started.

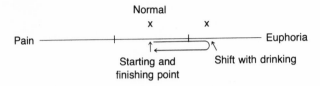

Anyone who drinks learns this pharmacological effect of alcohol and learns that it happens consistently. Alcohol can be depended on.

The second stage in the developmental process is *seeking the mood swing*. This happens *after* someone learns that alcohol can be counted on to enhance or improve mood. Drinking now has this particular purpose. Anyone who drinks occasionally does so to make things better. Whatever the occasion—an especially hard day at work, a family reunion, celebrating a promotion, or recovery from a trying day of hassling kids—the expectation is that alcohol will help. In essence, the person is entering into a contract with alcohol. True to its promise, alcohol keeps its side of the bargain. By altering the dose, the person can control the mood swing. Still there are no problems.

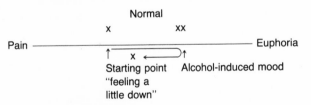

According to Johnson, only a thin line separates the second and third phases. The third phase is *harmful dependence*, in which, suddenly, alcohol demonstrates a boomerang effect. Alcohol, which previously had only a beneficial, positive effect, now has some negative consequences. These can include such things as a hangover or feelings of embarrassment over last evening's antics. *Emotional costs* are going to be exacted to continue drinking in that fashion. Many people will say: "Forget it, no more nights like last night for me." They really mean it. What's

Wine in excess keeps neither secrets nor promises.

CERVANTES, Don Quixote

more, there is no problem for them in sticking with that decision. In the future, they are more cautious about drinking. But there are a significant minority of people who react differently. These are the people bound for trouble with alcohol. Unwilling to discontinue their use of alcohol to alter their moods, they are willing to pay the price. In a sense, they remain "loyal" to their relationship with booze. This decision to pay the price isn't a conscious decision, logically thought out. It's based on how the person is feeling. In the pain-euphoria chart, the mood shift initially heads in the right direction, achieves the drinker's purpose, but in swinging back, drops the person off in a less comfortable place than where he began.

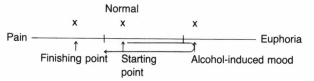

The costs are psychological. The person's drinking behavior and its consequences are inconsistent with his values and self-image. To continue drinking requires revamping the personality. The normal psychological devices will be used to twist reality just enough to explain away the costs. Every person does this every day to some degree. If I'm walking down the street, say hello to a friend and get no response, my feelings are momentarily hurt. Almost automatically, I tell myself, "He must not have seen or heard me." So I shut off the hurt feelings with an explanation which may or may not be true. I pick the "reality" that makes me comfortable. Or another time, if I'm particularly ill-tempered and nasty, acting in a way I don't really like, I become uncomfortable with myself. I could say to myself: "Yep, I sure have been a grouch." More likely it will come out: "I've not been myself. It must be the pressure of work that's gotten to me." In this fashion, each of us attempts to control our discomfort and maintain psychic harmony. This is what the budding problem drinker does to keep harmony in his relationship with alcohol. One thing he does to twist reality to explain away the costs is to suppress his emotions. When he feels some negative emotions arising, he tries to push this away. "I just won't think about it." So, the fellow who made an ass of himself at last night's party tries to ignore the whole thing. "Heavens, these things happen sometimes. There's no sense in worrying about it." However, pretending your emotions aren't there doesn't make them disappear. They simply crop up somewhere else. Since suppression doesn't work totally, other psychological gymnastics are used. Rationalization is a favorite device—coming up with a reason that inevitably stays clear of alcohol itself. "I really got bombed last night because Harry was mixing such stiff ones." Here we see projection at work as well. The reason for getting bombed was that the drinks were *stiff*, and it's *Harry's* fault! No responsibility is laid on the drinker or on alcohol.

Now there might not be any problems if these instances of distortion are only occasional. But they aren't. And what's worse, with continued heavy drinking, the discrepancy between what is expected to happen and what *does* happen gets larger and larger. Proportionately, so does the need for further distortion to explain it. Drinking is supposed to improve the mood, but the budding alcoholic keeps being dropped off further down on the pain side.

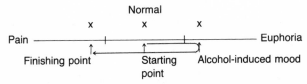

A vicious cycle is developing. The mental gymnastics used to minimize the discomfort are also preventing the alcoholic from discovering what's really happening. None of the defenses, even in combination, are completely foolproof. At times, the alcoholic feels real remorse about his behavior. At those times it doesn't matter where the blame lies—on Harry, on himself, on alcohol—anyway you cut it, he regrets what's happening. So a negative self-image is developing.

For the most part, the drinker truly believes the reality of his projections and rationalizations. Understandably, this begins to screw up his relationships with others. There are continual hassles over whose version of reality is accurate. This introduces additional tensions as problems arise with friends, family, co-workers. The alcoholic's self-esteem keeps shrinking. The load of negative feelings expands. Ironically, the alcoholic relies more and more heavily on the old relationship with alcohol. Drinking is deliberately

Boundless intemperance
In nature is a tyranny; it hath been
Th' untimely emptying of the happy
  throne
And fall of many kings.

SHAKESPEARE, Macbeth

structured into life patterns. Drinking is anticipated. The possibilities of drinking may well determine which invitations are accepted, where business lunches are held, and other life activities. Gradually, *all* of his leisure time is set up to include drinking.

The stage is now set for the last developmental phase of the alcoholic personality. The alcoholic now *drinks to feel normal.* By now the alcoholic is in chronic pain, beset by a load of negative feelings, constantly at the negative end of the mood scale. Drinking is now done to enhance the mood, to achieve a *normal* feeling state.

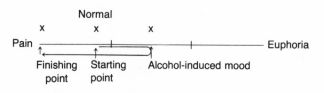

In addition to achieving this normal feeling state, alcohol may assist "normal" functioning in other respects. Psychologists have documented the phenomenon of "state-dependent learning." Things learned in a particular context are most readily recalled under similar circumstances. Thus, things learned when sober are best recalled later when sober. Similarly, learning that occurs while intoxicated will also be more available for recall later when the person is again (or still) intoxicated. Thus, the heavy drinker may have a repertoire of behavior, coping mechanisms, social skills, even information that, if learned during drinking, is less accessible when he's sober. In fact, drinking may be necessary to tap a reservoir of knowledge. This fact is what sometimes explains the alcoholic's inability to find liquor stashes he has hidden when drunk. Another way in which alcohol may be essential to "normalize" function is to ward off withdrawal symptoms if he has become physically dependent.

Other memory distortions are not uncommon at this point. Blackouts may mean the absence of memory for some events. Repression is a psychological mechanism that also blocks out memory. Further havoc is raised by the alcoholic's euphoric recall. The alcoholic remembers only good times, and/or the sense of relief he associates with drinking. The problems and difficulties seemingly don't penetrate.

DETERIORATING FUNCTIONING

Given the transformation of thinking, the distorted view of reality, and the ebbing self-esteem, the alcoholic's functioning deteriorates. Each of us is expected to fulfill various roles in life. For each slot we find ourselves in, there is an accompanying set of expectations about what is appropriate behavior. Some of the typical roles are parent, spouse, worker, citizen, friend. Other roles may be more transient, such as scout leader, committee chairman, patient, or Sunday school teacher. No matter what the role, the alcoholic's performance suffers. There are expectations that others have of someone in a position. The alcoholic does not meet them. His behavior is inconsistent. He cannot be depended upon. Sometimes he does what is expected, and does it beautifully. Yet the next time, no show, followed later by the flimsiest excuse. To add insult to injury, he gets furious at you for being disappointed, or annoyed, or not understanding. This has a profound impact on the people around the alcoholic. Being filled with the normal insecurities of all humans, those around the alcoholic think it might/must be their fault. Unwittingly others accept the alcoholic's rationalizations and projections. People around the alcoholic are confused. Often they feel left out. They sense and fear the loss of an important relationship, one which has been nourishing to them. In turn, their usual behavior is kinked out of shape. Now, in addition to whatever problems the alcoholic has directly with alcohol, interpersonal relationships are impaired. This adds more tension.

FAMILY AND FRIENDS

Let's focus on the family and friends of the alcoholic for a moment. Applying behavioral learning terms, the alcoholic has those around him on a variable-interval reinforcement schedule. There they are, busily trying to accommodate him. The family feels that somehow if they behave differently, do the "right thing," the alcoholic will respond. One time they're harsh, the next time they try an "understanding" tack. Then another time they might try to ignore him. But nothing works. The alcoholic's behavior doesn't respond in any predictable way to their behavior. If he happens to be a "good boy" on occasion, it really has no connection to what the family has, or has not, done. The family, in fact, is accommodating themselves to the alcohol-

ic. Never sure why some times go better, they persist in trying. And trying some more. Meanwhile, the alcoholic stays his inconsistent, unpredictable self.

Eventually the family gives up and tries to live around the alcoholic. Alternately he is ignored or driving them crazy. Yet out of love and loyalty, all too long he is protected from the consequences of his drinking. In the marital relationship, if one spouse is alcoholic, the other gradually assumes the accustomed functions of the drinking partner. If the wife is alcoholic, the husband may develop contingency plans for supper in case it isn't ready that night. If the father is alcoholic, the wife may be the one who definitely plans to attend Little League games. If the father is up to it, fine; if not, a ready excuse is hauled out. This leads to resentments on both parts. The spouse carrying the load feels burdened; the alcoholic feels deprived and ashamed.

MARITAL RELATIONSHIPS

Wine makes a man better pleased with himself; I do not say that it makes him more pleasing to others.

SAMUEL JOHNSON

In the marital relationship, if one partner is alcoholic, you can count on sexual problems. In American society, concern over sexual performance seems to be the national pastime. Sexual functioning is not merely a physical activity. There are strong psychological components. How someone feels about oneself and one's partner is bound to show up in the bedroom. Any alcohol use can disturb physiological capacity for sex. Shakespeare said it most succinctly: alcohol provokes the desire but takes away the performance. In the male, alcohol interferes with erection, popularly referred to as "brewer's droop." The psychological realm has as strong an impact. Satisfying sexual relationships require a relationship, a bond of love and affection. In the alcoholic marriage, neither partner is able to trust that bond. There are doubts on both sides. Problems result in many ways. A slobbering drunk invites revulsion and rejection. By definition he is an unattractive, inconsiderate lover. Any qualities of love have, for the moment, been washed away by booze. Intercourse can also become a weapon. Wives or husbands can use the old Lysistrata tactic of emotional blackmail: refusing sex unless the partner changes behavior. Or both partners can approach intercourse as the magic panacea. If they can still make love, that can make up for everything else lacking in the relationship. Sexual fears and anxiety, which are rampant in the total population, are compounded in the alcoholic marriage.

AT WORK

Often, although the alcoholic is deeply mired in the symptoms of deterioration in the social, family, and physical areas of his life, he can still have his job. The job area seems to be the last part of the alcoholic's life to show the signs of his illness. The job is often the status symbol for both the alcoholic and the spouse. He might think or say: "There's nothing wrong with me. I'm still bringing in a good paycheck!" She is likely to make excuses to his boss for him to protect her livelihood.

Intervention

Intervention is, of course, possible at even the earliest signs. This is often *not* the case. That picture is gradually changing. Much effort is being made to alert employers to the early signs of alcoholism and to acquaint them with the rehabilitation possibilities. The employer is in a unique position to exert some pressure on the alcoholic at a relatively early stage. Recommending that he go for treatment may well be a precipitating factor in a recovery. The fact that the boss sees the problem and calls a spade a spade can go far in breaking down the denial system. Keeping his job may be important enough to get the alcoholic to begin to see his problem more realistically.

The alcoholic at an early stage often feels his cover-up, or diversionary, tactics are successful. Most people are unwilling to confront someone with a drinking problem until it is no longer possible to ignore it. (One study found that some person other than a family member had noticed a drinking problem on an average of seven years prior to an alcoholic's seeking help.) Often the alcoholic has no idea how obvious his difficulties are to his fellow employees. When an alcoholic is finally confronted, it can be a great shock to him to find out how much of his telltale behavior was in fact observed. His rationalization and denial systems actually convince him that *no one* on the job knows about his drinking problem.

Some contacts with local businesses can be most helpful to a counselor. Some rehabilitative programs employ spe-

Who hath woe? who hath sorrow? who hath contentions? who hath babbling? who hath wounds without cause? who hath redness of eyes? They that tarry long at the wine.

PROVERBS 28:31-32

cialists to consult with interested employers and aid them in setting up in-house referral programs. Check with the larger programs and state agencies in your area to become acquainted with these possibilities for referral.

RESOURCES AND FURTHER READING

Blane, Howard. *The personality of the alcoholic: guises of dependency.* New York: Harper & Row, Publishers, Inc., 1968.

Johnson, Vernon. *I'll quit tomorrow.* New York: Harper & Row, Publishers, Inc., 1973.

Weiner, Jack B. *Drinking.* New York: W. W. Norton & Co., Inc., 1976.

Whitney, Elizabeth. *The lonely sickness.* Boston: Beacon Press, 1965.

Or almost any biography, autobiography, or first-person account of an alcoholic.

CHAPTER SEVEN

Effects of alcoholism on the family

family portrait

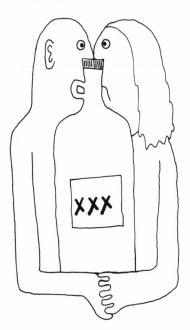

Alcoholism is often termed the *family illness,* referring to the tremendous impact an active alcoholic has on those around him. There is no way the family members can escape or ignore the alcoholic. The majority of the alcoholic's impairments are behavioral. So in the day-to-day interactions of family life, the family members are confronted with alcoholic behavior. The family is confused, bewildered, angry, and afraid. They act accordingly. Their responses characteristically are as impaired as the alcoholic's.

Certainly no family member ever caused alcoholism. Yet the family may, despite its best intentions, behave in a way that allows the alcoholic to continue drinking. They may protect the alcoholic, make excuses, buy into the alibis, cover up. They might call the employer, pretending the alcoholic has "the flu." Other facilitating behavior can include covering a bad check or retaining a good lawyer to beat a DWI charge. The alcoholic's actions are bound to increase the family's anxiety level. The alcoholic drinks more to relieve his own anxiety, which in turn ups the family's even higher. The higher the anxiety, the more the family members react by anxiously doing *more* of what they were already doing and then the alcoholic drinks more because of the higher anxiety, ad infinitum. The thing can become a spiraling squirrel cage or a collapse. The family is no better able to cope with the alcoholism than is the alcoholic.

JACKSON'S STAGES

Jackson describes the stages that occur as a family comes to grips with an alcoholic in its midst. Her stages were initially intended to describe the family in which the husband and father is the alcoholic. With modification, they probably describe any alcoholic family. These stages are sketched out here in order of appearance.

Denial. Early in the development of alcoholism, occasional episodes of excessive drinking are explained away by *both* marriage partners. Drinking because of tiredness, worry, nervousness, or a bad day is not unbelievable. The assumption is that the episode is an isolated instance and therefore no problem.

Attempts to eliminate the problem. Here the spouse recognizes that the drinking is not normal and tries to pressure the alcoholic to quit, be more careful, or cut down.

Simultaneously, the spouse tries to hide the problem from the outside and keep up a good front. Children in the family may well start having problems in response to the family stress.

Disorganization and chaos. The family equilibrium has now broken down. The spouse can no longer pretend everything is okay and spends most of the time going from crisis to crisis. Financial troubles are common. Under real stress, possibly questioning his or her own sanity, the spouse is likely to seek outside help.

Reorganization in spite of the problem. The spouse's coping abilities have strengthened. He or she gradually assumes the larger share of responsibility for the family unit. This may mean getting a job or taking over the finances. The major focus of energy is no longer directed toward getting the alcoholic partner to shape up. Instead, the spouse takes charge and fosters family life, despite the alcoholism.

Efforts to escape. Separation or divorce may be attempted. If the family unit remains intact, the family continues living around the alcoholic.

Family reorganization. In the case of separation, family reorganization occurs without the alcoholic member. If the alcoholic achieves sobriety, a reconciliation may take place. *Either* path will require both partners to realign roles and make new adjustments.

As mentioned, Jackson's formulations are focused on the family in which the husband is alcoholic. Families with an alcoholic wife and mother exist, too. An interesting difference is found in marriage outcomes, depending on which partner has the alcohol problem. The female alcoholic is much more likely to be divorced than is the male alcoholic. Several hypotheses are possible to account for the difference. In the past, various authors have speculated that women who marry alcoholics may have unconscious, neurotic needs to be married to weak, inadequate males. The implication is that because they have the need, they'll stay married to the drunk. The more accepted view now is that the difficulties seen in the alcoholic's wife come simply from the stress of living with him. Given the economic realities, it is not unlikely that the nonalcoholic wife stays in her marriage longer than the nonalcoholic husband because she feels the need of the husband's financial support to maintain the family.

Portrait of a woman who can't understand why her husbands were all alcoholics.

CHILDREN OF ALCOHOLICS

The children in an alcoholic family deserve some special attention. In an atmosphere of conflict, tension, and uncertainty, their needs for warmth, security, and even physical care may be inadequately met. In a family where adult roles are inconsistently and inadequately filled, children lack good models to form their own identities. It is likely that such children will have a hard time as they enter into relationships outside the home, at school, or with playmates. A troubled child may be the signal of an alcohol problem in a family. Although alcoholics comprise only 2% of the American population, their children account for approximately 20% of all referrals to child guidance clinics.

The family environment is not the only potential trouble spot for the child of an alcoholic. As discussed in Chapter 5, maternal alcohol use can influence fetal development. So the risk to a child can extend to earliest childhood, even before birth. In addition to the direct impact of the drug, behaviors associated with alcoholism may have direct effects on fetal development. Physical trauma, falls, malnutrition, or abnormalities of glucose metabolism are not uncommon in alcoholics. Any of these could have an impact on the developing baby.

The emotional state of the expectant mother probably influences fetal development. It certainly has an influence on the course of labor and delivery. The emotional state of the alcoholic expectant mother might differ dramatically from that of a normal, healthy, nonalcoholic expectant mother and be a source of problems. An alcoholic expectant father may exert some indirect prenatal influences. If he is abusive or provides little emotional and financial support, this could cause anxiety in the mother. Lack of support and consequent anxiety during pregnancy is associated with more difficult deliveries. In a similar vein, stress at certain times during pregnancy increases fetal activity. This, in turn, is linked to colicky babies. There are no specific data available on labor and delivery for either female alcoholics or wives of male alcoholics. It is known that increased maternal anxiety may precipitate problems of labor and delivery. Furthermore, it is known that these difficulties are related to developmental disorders in the children. One particular difficulty that children of alcoholics have more frequently than children of nonalcoholics is hyperactivity.

Another crucial time in any infant's life comes shortly after delivery. The very early interactions between mother and infant are important influences in the mother-child relationship. Medications that may be required for a difficult delivery may make the "bonding" more difficult. Both mother and infant, under the effects of the drug, are less able to respond to each other.

A new mother needs emotional and physical support to help her deal with the presence of the baby in her life. At a minimum, the baby requires food, warmth, physical comfort, and consistency of response from the mother. In the case of a family with an active alcoholic, one can't automatically assume everything is going smoothly. Any worker in contact with the family ought to question whether the infant is getting adequate care and should also check for any evidence of child abuse.

The teenager in the alcoholic family is not unlikely to have some difficulties with alcohol during adolescence. (These are discussed in the section on adolescents in Chapter 10.) Finally, another way in which the child of an alcoholic is vulnerable is in terms of genetic endowment. The issue of the causes of alcoholism is far from settled; yet a genetic component is suspected.

The effects of alcoholism are not limited to the alcoholic. We have barely scratched the surface of possible complications in the nuclear family. All the people directly involved with an alcoholic need more knowledge and more help to combat these effects.

RESOURCES AND FURTHER READING

Chafetz, M. et al. Children of alcoholics. *Quarterly Journal of Studies on Alcohol*, September, 1971, 32, 687-698.

Cork, R. Margaret. *The forgotten children*. Paperjacks, Addictions Research Foundation, Toronto, 1969.

Fox, Ruth. The effects of alcoholism on children. Proceedings of the International Congress of Psychotherapy. Basel, 1963. (Reprints available from the National Council on Alcoholism.)

Hindman, Margaret. Family therapy in alcoholism. *Alcohol Health and Research World*, 1976, 1(1), 2.

Hindman, Margaret. Child abuse and neglect: the alcohol connection. *Alcohol Health and Research World*, 1977, 1(3), 2.

Jackson, Joan. Alcoholism and the family. In D. J. Pittman and S. R. Snyder (Eds.), *Society, culture, and drinking patterns*. New York: John Wiley & Sons, Inc., 1962.

Treatment CHAPTER EIGHT

get the Alcoholic out of the Bottle

OVERVIEW

When one is acutely aware of the problems of alcoholism, the question arises: "How do you treat the alcoholic?" Or perhaps your question is more personal: "How can I help?" The first step is to consider how people get better and what treatment is about.

Treatment is nothing more (or less) than the interventions designed to short-circuit the alcoholic process and introduce the alcoholic to a sober, drug-free existence. Alcoholism is the third leading cause of death in the United States. It shouldn't be. In comparison to other chronic disease, it is significantly more treatable. *Any* alcoholic who seeks assistance and is willing to actively participate in rehabilitation efforts can realistically expect to lead a happy, productive life. Sadly, the same is not true for a victim of cancer, heart disease, or emphysema. The realization that alcoholism is treatable is becoming more widespread. Both professional treatment programs and AA are discovering that the alcoholic today is often younger and in the early or middle stages of alcoholism when he seeks help. It is imperative for the helping professions to keep firmly in mind the hopefulness that surrounds treatment.

Just as people initially become involved with alcohol for a variety of reasons, there is similar variety in what prompts treatment. For every person who wends his way into alcoholism, there is also an exit route. The role of the counselor or therapist is to serve as a guide, to share knowledge of the terrain, to be a support as the alcoholic regains his footing, and to provide encouragement. The counselor cannot make the trip *for* the alcoholic but can only point the way. The counselor's goal for treatment, the destination of the journey, is to assist the alcoholic in becoming comfortable and at ease in the world, able to handle his life situation. This will require the alcoholic to stop drinking. In our experience, a drinking alcoholic *cannot* be happy, at peace with himself, healthy, or alive in any way that makes sense, not to us, but to him. The question for the counselor is never "How can I make him stop?" The only productive focus for the counselor is "How can I create an atmosphere in which he is better able to choose sobriety for himself?"

Obstacles to treatment

If alcoholism is so highly treatable, what's been going wrong? Why aren't more people receiving help? The obsta-

It is a kindness to lead the sober; a duty to lead the drunk.

LANDOR

cles do need to be looked at. One big handicap is society's attitude toward alcohol and its use. Unfortunately, the alcoholic's chances of being treated for alcoholism are slim. Oh, he'll receive treatment: for depression, gastritis, cirrhosis . . . but less often for the alcoholism. Despite all the public education and information, there remains lurking the notion that talking about someone's drinking is in bad taste. It seems too private, somehow, none of anyone's business. Most of us have a good feel for the taboo topics—sexual behavior, people's way of handling their children. The way someone drinks is a large taboo. This is to be expected. An alcoholic has a stake in keeping *his* drinking and its associated problems off-limits. Should the drinking behavior be discussed, the alcoholic's rationalization combined with the tendency to "psychologize," analyze, and get to the why would spring another trap. The notion that someone drinks alcoholically *because* he's an alcoholic sounds circular and simpleminded. Thus, everyone scurries around to find the "real" cause. Alcoholism as a phenomenon, a fact of life, gets pushed aside and forgotten in the uproar. Unfortunately, even when alcoholism treatment is instituted, it often is seriously unbalanced, zeroing in on only a part of the symptomatology. When this happens, the alcoholism treatment can end up looking a lot like treatment for depression, or cirrhosis, or just a "rest cure." This is the other major source of recidivism and failure.

Factors in successful treatment

Having alluded to failure and some sense of what to avoid . . . on to success. Likelihood of success is greatly enhanced by simply keeping in mind the characteristics of the disease being treated. The following factors, always present in the alcoholic, need to guide the treatment process.

1. *Dysfunctional life-style*. The alcoholic's life-style has been centered on alcohol. If this is not immediately evident, it's because the particular alcoholic has done a better than average job of disguising the fact. Thus the counselor cannot expect a large repertoire of healthy behaviors that come automatically. Treatment will help build these, as well as dust off and rediscover behaviors from the past to replace the

warped "alcoholic" responses. This fact is what makes residential treatment desirable. Besides cutting down the number of easy drinking opportunities, it provides some room to make a new, fresh beginning.

2. *Few experiences of handling stress without alcohol.* Alcohol has been the alcoholic's constant companion. It's used to anticipate, get through, and then get over stressful times. The alcoholic, to his knowledge, is without any effective tools for handling problems. In planning treatment, be alert to what may be stressful for a particular client, and provide supports. In the process, the counselor can tap skills within the alcoholic to be turned to rather than the bottle.

3. *Psychological wounds.* Alcohol is the alcoholic's best friend and worst enemy. The prospect of a life without alcohol seems either impossible, or so unattractive as to be unworthwhile. The alcoholic feels lost, fragile, vulnerable, fearful. No matter how well put together the client can appear, or how much strength or potential the counselor can see, the client, by and large, is unable to get beyond his feelings of impotence, nakedness, nothingness. Even when being firm and directive, the counselor has to have a gentle awareness of this.

4. *Physical dysfunctions.* Chronic alcohol use takes its toll on the body. Even if spared the more obvious physical illnesses, there will be other subtle disturbances of physical functioning with which the alcoholic must contend. Sleep disturbance can last up to two years. Similarly, a thought impairment would not be unusual on cessation of drinking. The alcoholic in the initial stage of recovery will have trouble maintaining his attention. There will be diminution of adaptive abilities. During treatment, education about alcohol and its effects can help allay fears.

5. *Chronic nature of alcoholism.* A chronic disease requires continuing treatment and vigilance about the conditions that can prompt a relapse. This continued self-monitoring is essential to success in treatment.

That is a treacherous friend against whom you must always be on your guard. Such a friend is wine.

C. N. BOVEE

Recovery as process

Recall how the progression of alcoholism can be sketched out. Similarly, recovery is a process. It doesn't happen all at once. Gradually, in steps, the alcoholic becomes better able to manage his life. For the purpose of discussion, there are three distinguishable stages of recovery: the introductory phase, the active treatment phase, and the continuing maintenance of recovery. There is no clear-cut beginning or end point. Yet each phase has its observable hallmarks.

Preliminary or introductory phase. The preliminary or introductory phase begins when the problem of alcoholism comes to the foreground. This is happening when the alcoholic lets those nagging suspicions rise up that there is something wrong with his drinking, and he is unhappy. On his own initiative, he might make some initial inquiries. Or the first overture may be made by a perceptive physician or clergyman, or friends . . . someone who is sufficiently concerned to speak up and take the risk of being told he's meddling. At this point the alcoholic is a fish nibbling at the bait. He moves close and backs off. He wants to know, but he doesn't. Sure, his drinking causes him problems, but he doesn't want to (is scared to) stop. What he really wants to learn is how to drink well. He wants to drink without the accompanying problems. And, if he happens to be in touch with a counselor, the chances are pretty good he wants the counselor to teach him how. This represents an impossible request. (Hopefully, the counselor doesn't get sucked into trying.)

What *can* the counselor do? The first thing is to avoid getting into a defensive position. You need not defend why you can't be helpful in teaching the alcoholic how to drink successfully. That is guaranteed to push the alcoholic's seesaw and drive him away. There is, however, a mutual goal "to have things be okay." The counselor can buy into this without accepting the client's means of achieving it. The task of the therapy will be to assist the alcoholic to see his behavior and its consequences accurately. As this occurs, the client will be confronted with the impossible nature of his request. The counselor will be most successful by being open, honest, patient. The counseling is doomed if you are seduced into playing the "patsy" or try to seduce the client by being the "good guy, rescuer." Having a co-worker with whom to discuss cases and their frustrations can help keep sight of the objectives.

Alcoholism is a disease that requires the client to make a self-diagnosis for successful treatment to occur. Treatment, full steam ahead, cannot begin until the alcoholic, inside himself, attaches that label to cover all that is going on with him. A head, or intellectual, understanding doesn't suffice. It must come from the heart. In fact, the whole thing can be confusing. He certainly doesn't have to be happy. He simply needs to know it's true. Then without hope of his own, he borrows the counselor's belief that things can change.

If it is a small sacrifice to discontinue the use of wine, do it for the sake of others; if it is a great sacrifice, do it for your own sake.

S. J. MAY

Active treatment phase. At this point of acknowledgement, seeing alcohol as the culprit, and with a desire to change, the alcoholic by himself is at a dead-end. If he knew what to do, he'd have done it. Thus he, in essence, turns the steering of his life over to the counselor or therapist. The counselor, in turn, needs to respond by providing clear, concrete, simple stage directions. The alcoholic requires a rehabilitative regimen set forth for him. He needs his environment simplified. The number of decisions he is confronted with must be pared down. He is able to deal with little more than "How am I going to get through this day (or hour) without a drink?" Effort needs to be centered on doing whatever is necessary to buy sober time. To quote the old maxim: "Nothing succeeds like success." A day sober turns on the light a little. It has become something that is possible. For the alcoholic, this is an achievement. It doesn't guarantee continued sobriety, but it demonstrates the possibility. In the sober time, the alcoholic is gaining skills. He is discovering behavior that can be of assistance in handling those events which before would have prompted drinking.

Although we are not attempting to discuss specific techniques of treatment here, a mention of AA is nonetheless in order. Anyone in the alcoholism treatment field will acknowledge that clients who take up AA have a much better chance of recovery. This is not accidental. AA has combined the key ingredients essential for recovery. It provides support, it embodies hopes. It provides concrete suggestions without cajoling. Its slogans are the simple guideposts needed to reorder a life. And its purpose is never lost.

The necessity for a direct and uncluttered approach to

the alcoholic cannot be overstressed. He isn't capable of handling anything else. This is one of several reasons for the belief that alcoholism has to be the priority item on any treatment agenda. The only exceptions are life-threatening or serious medical problems. For the alcoholic to work actively and successfully on a list of difficulties is overwhelming. Interestingly enough, when alcoholism treatment is undertaken, the other problems often fade. Furthermore, waiting to treat the alcoholism until some other matter is settled invites the alcoholic's ambivalence to surface. This waiting feeds the part of him that says, "Well, maybe it isn't so bad after all," or "I'll wait and see how it goes." Generally the matters are unsolvable because an active drinking alcoholic has no inner resources to tackle anything. He's drugged.

Focusing on alcoholism as a priority, the alcoholic's acceptance of this, and providing him room and skills to experience sobriety is the meat of therapy. As this takes place, the alcoholic is able to assume responsibility for managing his life, using the tools he's acquired. With this, the working relationship between the counselor and client shifts. They collaborate in a different way. The counselor may be alert to potential problematic situations. But the client increasingly takes responsibility for identifying them and selecting ways he can deal with them. Rather than being a guide, the counselor is a resource, someone for the client to check things out with. At this point, the alcoholic's continuing treatment has begun.

Continuing treatment phase. The alcoholic, as do other persons with chronic disease, learns the importance of being able to identify situations, and his responses to them, that may signal a flare-up. For the alcoholic, this entails maintaining a continuing awareness of his alcoholic status, if sobriety is to continue. The alcoholic certainly will not continue to see the counselor for a lifetime as a reminder of his need to be vigilant. But he will need to develop other alternatives, if he is to succeed in staying sober.

"Why do I drink?" This is the recurrent theme of many active alcoholics and those beginning active treatment. In our experience, focusing on this question even when it seems most pressing to the client is of little value. It takes the client off the hot seat. It looks to the past and causes "out there." The more important question is the nitty-gritty of the present moment: "What can be done now?" If there is a time to deal with the "whys," it comes during the continuing treatment phase. Don't misunderstand. Long hours spent on studying what went wrong, way back, is *never* helpful. Rather, the why can be discerned from the present, daily life events, on those occasions when taking a drink is most tempting. Dealing with these can provide the alcoholic with a wealth of practical information about himself, for his immediate use. Dealing with the *now* is of vital importance. The alcoholic, who has spent his recent life in a drugged state, has had less experience than most of us (which isn't much) in attending to the present. His automatic tendency is to analyze the past and/or worry about the future. The only part of his life that he can hope to handle effectively is the present.

A client's hope for change often must be sparked from the counselor's belief in that possibility. Your attitudes about your clients and their potential for health exerts a powerful influence. This doesn't mean you cannot and will not become frustrated, impatient, or angry at times. Whether therapy can proceed depends on what you do with these feelings. You can only carry them so long before the discomfort becomes unbearable. Then you will either pretend they aren't there or unload them on the client. Either way your thinking can become "he can never change," "this guy is hopeless," or "he's just not ready." When that happens, counseling is not possible, even if the people continue meeting. A better approach is to have a co-worker with whom you can discuss these feelings of impotence and frustration. Doing this makes it easier to say "I know he can change, even if *I* can't imagine how it will happen. Certainly stranger things have happened in the history of the world." And therapy can proceed. But if an impasse in working with a particular client isn't broken through, the client should be referred to a co-worker.

Treatment is a process involving people. People have their ups and downs, good days, bad days. Some you think will make it, won't. Some you are sure don't have a chance will surprise you. There will be days when you'll wonder why you ever got into this. On others it will seem a pretty good thing to be doing. Remembering that it is an unpredictable process may help you keep your balance.

DRINKING HISTORY

In our opinion, a drinking history should become an integral part of an interview with any troubled person, whether the person has come to a physician or hospital with a physical problem or to a social worker, psychiatrist, psychologist, or clergymember concerning a mental or emotional problem. The reasons for this should now be clear. As we have previously noted, this is a drinking society; most people drink at least some alcohol. We have also noted that alcohol is a chemical and not as benign a one as previously thought. It simply cannot be ignored as a possible factor in whatever brings a person to a caregiver of any kind. This does not mean that you need suspect, or even be looking for, alcoholism alone. The purpose of a drinking history is simply to get as clear a picture of alcohol use as you would of other medical aspects, family situation, job difficulties, feelings, or whatever. It is part of the information-gathering process, which is later added up to give you an idea of what is going on in the person's life and how best to proceed.

There are many sample drinking history forms floating around—for doctors, for nurses, etc. Our bias is that the attitude of the questioner is as important, if not more important, than the actual list of questions. If asking about drinking strikes you as an invasion of privacy, a waste of time, or of little use because the presenting problem is clearly *not* alcohol related, then you are going to be uncomfortable asking and will probably get unreliable answers from a now uncomfortable client. If your bias is the opposite, and you see alcohol lurking in the corner of every problem, again discomfort and unreliable answers will probably be your lot. Somehow you need to begin with a more objective stance. Alcohol might or might not be a factor, just as any other aspect of the client's life might or might not be of concern.

When to ask. It takes practice to do a good drinking history. It also takes recognition of timing and a good look at what is in front of you. It may seem redundant to say, but an intoxicated or withdrawing client cannot give you good information. You wouldn't expect accurate information from someone going under anesthetic or coming out of it. Unfortunately, some of the forms we have seen are supposed to be given on admission or intake with no recognition of this factor. In other words, use your common sense. Try to ask the questions you need to at a time when the person is at least relatively comfortable both emotionally and physically. Ask them matter-of-factly and nonjudgmentally, remembering that *your own drinking pattern is no yardstick for others*. For example, when someone responds to the question "How much do you usually drink?" with "About four or five drinks or so," don't stare openmouthed.

What to ask. Basically, the information needed is what does the client drink, how much, how often, when, where, and is it or has it been a problem in any area of his life, including physical problems. These questions get stated in different ways, depending on the form referred to or the information required by your agency. In general, however, we lean to a more informal approach than sitting there filling out a form as you ask the questions in order. Another issue we think as important as the above information, but not included on most forms, is the question of what the drinking does *for* the client. Questions such as "How do you feel when you drink?" "What does alcohol do for you?" and "When do you most often want a drink?" can supply a lot of information.

How to ask. If the questions are asked conversationally along with other questions regarding general health, social aspects, and other use of drugs or medications, most people will answer them. The less threatened you are by the process, the more comfortable the questionee will be.

Special considerations

The remarks above have been directed primarily at asking anybody about drinking. A word or two must be said for the benefit of those working in a designated alcohol treatment program. Here, the person may be referred or come in with a good idea that alcohol is a problem or wanting to prove that it isn't. Either attitude is going to color the responses. Because of alcohol treatment designation, the questions can be much more forthright and in depth; however, the responses are quite likely to be more guarded. Particularly responses to how much and how often. They can range all the way from a defensive "a few and just socially" to a bragging "a whole case of beer whenever I feel like it." The grain of salt theory can be applied here and so noted in your record keeping. It is not, however, an occasion for an "Aw, come on!" response from you. Simply record the answer and reserve your comment for the appropriate place in the records. A clearer picture will emerge as therapy continues (if it does). Remember, the client will usually need to feel somewhat comfortable with you before total honesty can occur. And there's always the real possibility that he doesn't *know* exactly how much or how often. The key thing for the counselor is to get as much reasonably reliable information as possible in order to proceed with appropriate treatment or referral.

Another point to consider is that you don't always have to get all the history at one sitting. If a client comes to a treatment facility smelling of alcohol, clearly uncomfortable, and somewhat shaky, you need to know immediately how much alcohol he has been drinking, for how long, and when the last drink was taken. You also need to know about other physical problems and what happened on other occasions when drinking was stopped. These questions are necessary to determine whether the client needs immediate attention from a physician.

One method of gathering information when a client is not in immediate physical difficulty is used regularly at a treatment facility in our area. Clients are asked to review their drinking beginning with the first drinking experience they remember. This chronological review gives the counselor a complete picture of the drinking pattern and also serves to give clients the opportunity of looking at the developing drinking habits for the first time. It often helps them to see the shifts and changes that signaled/led to an emerging problem and can thus be used as a therapeutic lever.

Sample questions

Let us stress again that the kind of information needed and the kinds of questions used to obtain the information vary from place to place. For example, a physician will need very different information than a clergymember. Some sample questions that could be used in almost any setting follow:

How old were you when you started using alcohol regularly?

How often do you drink alcoholic beverages?

What kinds of alcoholic beverages do you drink?

How much of each kind do you usually drink on any one occasion?

Has drinking created problems for you with your family, friends, or job?

Have you ever been injured because of drinking? Be specific.

Have you ever been arrested because of drinking?

Have you ever had treatment for alcohol problems or alcohol-related illness?

Have you ever been unable to complete a task or function because of alcohol?

Have you noticed a change in the amount of alcohol it takes to get the effect you desire? If yes, describe the change.

What reactions occur when you stop drinking?

Have you ever experienced a period of time you don't remember when drinking?

These are only a few possible areas to explore, but the answers to such questions can provide you with clues as to whether to ask more or drop the subject.

In closing, we must add that a questionnaire can never be a substitute for good clinical evaluation. It may be of some help in bringing the alcohol issue to the fore in treatment planning. But most of the questionnaires we have seen would not be able to clearly identify a person in the early stages of a developing problem, and the later stages are usually clear enough that a questionnaire is unnecessary. Accurate diagnosis still remains in the realm of clinical judgment, and in the very early stages it's in the realm of prediction. Still, one *very* good reason for always taking an alcohol history is to get people used to examining their drinking. It can also help people begin to understand that alcoholism can develop in anyone at any time and that our drinking habits are certainly as vital to our health as diet, exercise, and sleep. We have too long avoided the issue and have made our drinking patterns seem far less important than whether we smoke, drink coffee, or eat junk foods. Simply asking about drinking whenever someone seeks help of any kind can also help remove the "finger pointing" aspect. It is so rare to be asked about drinking that the askee often feels threatened by the mere mention. When it becomes a routine part of interviews, this threatening feeling can begin to disappear.

INDIVIDUAL COUNSELING

Earlier we defined treatment as all the interventions intended to short-circuit the alcoholism process and to introduce the alcoholic to effective sobriety. This could be put in equation form as follows: Treatment = individual counseling + client education + family therapy + family education + group therapy + medical care + AA + Ala-non + Antabuse + vocational counseling + activities therapy + spiritual counseling + ... As you can see, individual counseling is only a small part of the many things that can comprise treatment. So what is it? A very simple way to think of individual counseling is simply the time, and place, and space in which the rest of the treatment gets organized and planned. One-to-one counseling is a series of interviews. During the interviews the counselor and client work together to define problems, explore possible solutions, and identify resources, with the counselor providing support, encouragement, and feedback to the client as he takes action. Before proceeding to a discussion of how the counselor does this, first a digression.

One of the difficulties in thinking about, discussing, or writing about counseling is knowing where to begin. It all seems more than a little overwhelming. One of the problems is that most of us have never seen a real counselor at work. We've all seen police officers, telephone linemen, carpenters, or teachers busily at work. So we have some sense of what is involved and can imagine what it would be like. The counselor's job is different. It's private and not readily observable. Unfortunately, most of our ideas about counselors come from books or television. Now, it doesn't take too much television viewing to get some notion that a good counselor is almost a magician, relying on uncanny instincts to divine the darkest, deepest recesses of the client's mind. You can't help thinking the counselor must have a T-shirt with a big letter S underneath the button-down collar. TV does an excellent job of teaching us that things are not always as they seem. Yet, remember, in real life they often—indeed usually—are. Everyone is quite adept at figuring out what is going on.

Observation

Each day we process vast amounts of information without much thought. Our behavior is almost automatic.

Without benefit of a clock, we can make a reasonable estimate of the time. Or when going into a store, without too
much trouble, we can distinguish the clerk from fellow
customers. Sometimes, though, we can't find a person who
seems to be a clerk. Take a couple of minutes to think about
the clues you do use in separating the clerk from the customers. One of the clues might be dress. Clerks might wear
some special outfit, such as a smock or apron. Or in colder
weather, customers off the street will be wearing or carrying their coats. Another clue might be behavioral. The
clerks stand behind counters, the customers in front. Customers stroll about casually looking at merchandise, while
clerks systematically arrange displays. Another clue could
be the person's companions. Clerks are usually alone, not
hauling children or browsing with a friend. Although we've
all had some experience of guessing incorrectly, it happens
rather rarely. In essence, this is *the good guys wear white
hats principle*. A person's appearance provides us with
useful, reliable information about him. Before a word of
conversation is spoken, our observations provide us with
some basic data to guide our interactions.

Hopefully, you are convinced everyone indeed has
keen observational powers. Usually, people simply do not
reflect on these skills. The only difference between a counselor and others is that a counselor will cultivate these observational capacities, will listen carefully, and will attend
to *how* something is said and not merely the content. The
counselor will ask: "What is the client's mood?" Is the mood
appropriate to what's being said? What kinds of shifts take
place during the interview? What nonverbal clues, or signs,
does the client give to portray how he feels?

So, in a counseling session, from time to time,
momentarily tune out the words and take a good look.
What do you *see*? Reverse that. Turn off the picture and
focus on the sound. One important thing: the questions you
ask yourself (or the client) are *not why* questions. They are
what and *how* questions that attempt to determine what is
going on. (Strangely enough, in alcohol counseling, successful treatment can occur without *ever* tackling a why
kind of question. But ignoring what or how issues may
mean you'll never even get into the right ball park.)

So what is the importance of observation? It provides
data for making hypotheses. A question continually before

An alcohol counselor's first task is to observe the client.

the counselor is "What's going on with this person?" What you see provides clues. You do not pretend to be a mind reader. Despite occasional lapses, you do not equate observations, or hunches, with ultimate truth. Your observations, coupled with your knowledge of alcohol, suggest where you might focus attention. An example: a client whose coloring is awful, who has a distended abdomen and a number of bruises, will alert the counselor to the strong possibility of serious medical problems. The client may try to explain this all away by "just having tripped over the phone cord," but the counselor will urge the client to see a physician.

You do your work by observing, by listening, and by asking the client (and yourself) questions to gain a picture of the client's situation. The image of a picture being sketched and painted is quite apt to capture the counseling process. The space below is the canvas. The total area includes everything that is going on in the client's life.

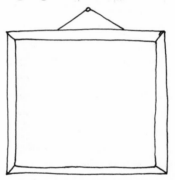

As the client speaks with the counselor, this space gets filled in. Now the counselor is getting a picture of the client's situation. Not only do you have the "facts" as the client sees them, you can see the client, his mood and feelings, and also get a sense of what the world and picture *feels* like. As this happens, the empty space gets filled in and begins to look like this:

You have a notion of the various areas that make up the person's life: family, physical health, work, economic situation, community life, how the person feels about himself, etc. You are also aware of how alcohol may affect these areas. As necessary, you will guide the conversation to ensure that you have a total picture of the client's life. You are also aware that if the client is experiencing difficulty, having a problem, it means the pieces are not fitting together in a way that feels comfortable. Maybe some parts have very rough edges. Maybe one part is exerting undue influence on the others. So you also attempt to see the relationship and interaction between the parts.

Initial interview

The initial interview is intended to get a sense of the general picture. As a result of the initial interview, the alcohol counselor will want to be able to answer the following questions:

1. What is the problem the client sees?
2. What does he want?
3. What brings him for help *now*?
4. What is going on in his life (the "facts" of the family situation, social problems, medical problems, alcohol use—how much, how long)?
5. Is there a medical or psychiatric emergency?
6. What are the recommendations?

Certainly there is much other information that could be elicited. But the answers to the above form the essential core for making decisions about how to proceed.

What next?

Counseling is an art, not a science. There isn't a series of rules that can be mechanically followed. However, one guideline is in order for an initial interview. It is especially apt in situations in which someone is first reaching out for help. *Don't let the interview end without adopting a definite plan for the next step.* Why? People with alcohol problems are ambivalent. They run hot and cold. They approach and back off from treatment. The person who comes in saying, "I'm an alcoholic and want help," is very, very rare. You are more likely to meet the following: "I think I may have a problem with alcohol, sort of, but it's really my _____ that's bugging me." The concrete plan adopted at the close of the interview may be very

Counseling is an art NOT A SCIENCE

simple. The plan may be nothing more than agreeing to meet a couple of times more, so that you, the counselor, can get a better idea of what's going on. Set a definite time. Leaving future meetings up in the air is like waving good-bye. It's not uncommon for the alcoholic to try to get off the hook by flattering the counselor. "Gee . . . you've really helped me. Why don't I call you if things don't improve? Why, I feel better already, just talking to you."

Despite the title Alcohol Counselor, a client first coming to treatment is not coming to you to have you "do your treatment routine" on him. It's not unlikely that he wants a clean bill of health. He wants to figure out why his drinking isn't "working" any more. The only thing that may be clear is the presence of drinking. The client is often unaware of the relationship of his drinking to the problems in his life. As he paints a picture of what's going on in his life space, the counselor will certainly see things the client is missing or ignoring.

Client's view of his world   *Counselor's view of client's world*

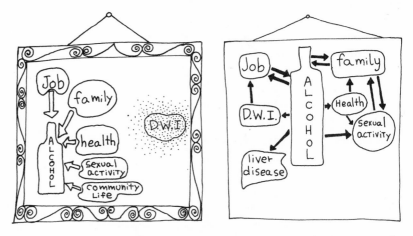

You can see the client is alcoholic. In your opinion, the client may need a rehabilitation facility. However, at the moment, the client is unable to use the treatment. First, it's necessary for him to make some connections, that is, get his arrows pointed in the right direction.

Confrontation

Confrontation is a technique used by the counselor to help the client make the essential connections. Confrontation does *not* equal attack. According to *Webster's*, to confront means "to cause to meet: bring face to face." Several examples of what the counselor may do to bring the client face to face with the consequences of his behavior are have a family meeting, so that the family's concerns can be presented; make a referral to a physician for treatment and consultation on the "stomach problems"; or refer the client to an alcohol discussion group. The counselor endeavors to structure situations in which the client is brought face to face with facts.

Feedback

In assisting the alcoholic to "see" what is going on, the counselor's observation skills pay off. The alcoholic has a notoriously warped perception of reality. The ability of the counselor to "merely" provide accurate feedback to the client, giving specific descriptions of behavior, of what the client is doing, is very valuable. The alcoholic has lost his ability for self-assessment. It's quite likely that any feedback from family members has also been warped and laced with threats, so that it's useless to the alcoholic. In the counseling situation, it may go like this: "Well, you say things are going fine. Yet, as I look at you, I see you fidgeting in your chair, your voice is quivering, and your eyes are cast down toward the floor. For me, that doesn't go along with someone who's feeling fine." *Period.* The counselor simply reports his observations. There isn't any deep interpretation. There's no attempt to ferret out hidden unconscious dynamics. The client isn't labeled a liar. Your willingness and ability to simply describe what you see is a potent therapeutic weapon. The alcoholic can begin to learn how he does come across, how others see him. Thus, use of observation serves to educate the client about himself.

Education

In addition to self-awareness, the client also needs education about alcohol, the drug, and the disease of alcoholism. Provide facts and data. There are a host of pamphlets available from state alcohol agencies, insurance companies, and AA. Everyone likes to understand what is going on with them. This is becoming increasingly apparent in all areas of medicine. Some institutions have hired patient educators. Patient education sessions on diabetes, heart disease, cancer, and care of newborns are becoming commonplace. The importance of education has two thrusts in alcoholism. The first is to help instill new attitudes toward alcoholism: that it is a disease, has recognizable signs, and is treatable. The hope is to elicit the alcoholic's support in helping to manage and treat his problem. The other reason for educating alcoholics is to handle feelings of guilt and low self-esteem. The chances are pretty good that the alcoholic's behavior has been downright crazy. Not just to others, it's also been inexplicable to the alcoholic. The fact that he has been denying a problem confirms this. There's no need to deny something unless it's so painful, so out of step with values, that it can't be tolerated. Learning facts about alcohol and alcoholism can be a big relief to the alcoholic. Suddenly, things make sense. All the crazy behavior becomes normal, at least for an active alcoholic. That's a significant difference. Successful recovery appears to be related to a client's acceptance of the disease concept. Energy can be applied to figuring out how one can live around the disease, live successfully, *now*. The client is relieved of the need to hash around back there, in his past, to uncover causes, to figure out what went wrong. He needn't dwell on his craziness; it becomes merely a symptom. And it is a symptom he isn't doomed to re-experience if he works on maintaining sobriety.

Client responsibility

The counselor expects the client to assume responsibility for his actions. You do not buy into the client's view of himself as either a pawn of fate or helpless victim. An ironic twist is present. You make it clear that you see the client as an adult who is accountable for his choices. Simultaneously, you are aware that an alcoholic, when he consumes alcohol, is abdicating control of his life to a drug. By definition, an alcoholic cannot be responsible for what transpires after even one or two drinks. Therefore, being responsible ultimately means that the attempt to manage alcohol must be abandoned. Here again, facts about the drug, alcohol, and the disease, alcoholism, are important. A large chunk of the client's work will be to examine the facts of his own life in light of this information. People's ability to alibi, to rationalize, and to otherwise explain away the obvious varies. But the counselor consistently holds up the mirror of reality. You play back to the client the client's story. You share your observations. In this way the client is enabled to move toward the first step of recovery, admitting his inability to control alcohol.

Word of caution

One word of caution to the newcomers to the field: alcoholics are notorious con artists. They've had to be. Anyone who has managed to continue drinking alcoholically in spite of the consequences has learned many sneaky little tricks. These do not disappear with the first prod, push, or pull toward treatment. Habits die hard. The habit of protecting his right to drink (even to death) is a long-standing one for most alcoholics. When he finds that you are probably not going to hand out a simple "three-step way to drink socially," all the considerable cunning at his command will rise up in defense.

Gee, you've really helped me to see exactly what I have to do. I'll _____, _____, _____, and _____, and everything will be just fine. Thanks so much. You've made my life for me.

Well, you know, both my parents were alcoholics. I even had a grandfather who was. But you know, I really don't drink like that at all! It really only started when Johnny had that awful operation, and I spent hours at the hospital, and then my husband was called away to South America, and I needed *something* to just boost me over those awful times. But my husband's due home next week, and I'm just sure now that I know all the facts you've given me, that I'll just stop by myself, and everything will be just fine! Thank you so much. You've changed my life.

I can't imagine why my wife says what she does about my drinking. She must really be down on me, or jealous, or something. . . . After all, I only have a couple of beers with the guys after work . . .

Speaking of _____, did you hear about that new research they've been doing? You know, the stuff that talks about having a dog helps. I bet if I just get a dog and take something for my nerves (after all, my nerves are the *real* problem), I'll be just fine! Etc., etc., etc.

Most alcoholics are far more inventive than these examples show. Add tears, or a charming smile, or bruises from a beating, and you've been exposed to quite a smoke screen. If they're not at the moment falling down, slobbering, throwing up, or slurring their words, it's hard *not* to believe them. There they sit—full of confidence, hopeful, and *very* friendly. Experience has shown that at some point, you'll

I've heard him renounce wine a hundred times a day, but then it has been between as many glasses.

DOUGLAS JERROLD

either see, hear from, or hear about these people, and their situations will have gone downhill. They don't know how familiar their stories are—to them, they're unique. They are not lying. They are simply trying to hang on to the only help they *feel* they have—the bottle. You may be able to help them loosen their grip by *not* allowing these pat replies to go unchallenged, by giving them something else to grasp.

Problem identification and problem solving

In counseling, problem identification and problem solving is a recurring process. No matter what the problem, there are always two kinds of forces in action. Some factors help maintain the problem. Other forces are pushing toward change. These can be sketched out in a diagram, as shown below. Suppose the problem being presented is "I don't like my job." The line going across represents the current situation. The arrows pointing upward stand for the factors that ease or lighten the problem. The arrows pointing downward represent the factors aggravating the problem.

If the goal of the client is to be more content at work, this might happen in several ways. The positive forces can be strengthened or others added. Or attempts can be made to diminish the negative ones. A similar sketch might be made for alcoholic drinking.

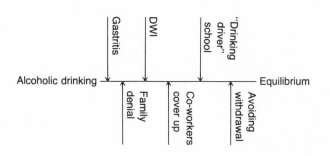

This kind of chart can help the counselor decide what factors might be tackled to disturb the present equilibrium.

Left to his own devices, the alcoholic would piddle along for years. Since he's sitting in front of you, something has happened to jiggle the equilibrium. This can be a force for change. Take advantage of it. Jiggle his equilibrium further. In the example just given, to take away the family denial or co-worker cover-up would blow his whole act. It is becoming widely acknowledged that for the counselor to precipitate such a crisis is the most helpful thing to do.

COMMON THEMES IN TREATMENT

Early in the recovery process, many alcoholics have a tendency to become quite upset over very small matters. They look well, feel well, and sound well. But they really aren't quite there yet. This can be very trying for both counselor and client. Remembering and reminding them of how sick they have recently been makes this less threatening. The steps after any major illness seem slow and tedious. There are occasional setbacks. Yet, eventually, all is well. It works that way with alcoholism, too. It is simply harder to accept, since there aren't any bandages to remove, scars to point to, or clear signs of healing to check on. It can't be emphasized enough that it *takes time*.

During this early phase of treatment, one point often overlooked is the alcoholic's plain inability to function on a simple daily basis. It is almost inconceivable to therapists (or anyone else for that matter) that a person who seems reasonably intelligent, looks fairly healthy after detoxification, and is over 21 can have problems with when to get up in the morning or what to do when he *is* up! Along with family, work, and social deterioration caused by the alcoholic life-style, the simple things have gotten messed up too. Alcoholics may have gargled, brushed their teeth, and chewed mints continually while drinking in an effort to cover up. They may, on the other hand, have skipped most mealtimes and eaten only sporadically with no eye to their nutritional needs. They may have thrown up with some regularity. But as we have seen in Chapter 5, their sleep is not likely to be normal. Getting dressed without trying to choke down some booze to quell the shakes may be a novel experience. It may have been years since the person has performed the standard daily tasks in a totally drug-free state.

SAC-1975

Alcoholics are rather like Rip Van Winkles during the early weeks of their recovery. Everything they do is likely to feel strange. The face looking back at them from the mirror may even seem like a stranger's. They became used to the blurred perceptions they had experienced while drinking. It's terribly disconcerting to find virtually every task one faces a whole new thing. While it used to take two very careful days to prepare Thanksgiving dinner, it now requires only a few hours. The accompanying wine for the cook, trips back to the store for forgotten items (and by the way, a little more booze), the self-pity over *having* to do it, the naps necessary to combat the fatigue of the ordeal, the incredible energy devoted to control the drinking enough to get everything done . . . all these steps are eliminated.

The newly sober alcoholic is continually being faced with the novelty of time. It's either time left over, or the experience of not enough time, or near panic over "what to do next." Many clients will need help in setting up schedules. After years of getting by on the bottle, they have to regain a sense of the "real" time it takes to accomplish some tasks. He may plan to paint the entire house in two days or, conversely, decide that he can't possibly fit a dentist appointment, a luncheon engagement, and a sales call into one. She may feel it's all she can manage to make the beds, do the dishes, and dust today. Tomorrow she intends to make new living room drapes in time for that evening's dinner party! The perception of time is as distorted as other areas of perception. Reassurance that this is a common state of affairs, along with assistance in setting realistic daily goals, is greatly needed. This is one reason newcomers to AA find the slogans "Keep it simple" and "First things first" so helpful.

The alcoholic may not mention the dilemmas over time and schedules to you. There may be a sense of shame over such helplessness in the face of simple things. But a gentle question from you may open the flood gates. This provides the opportunity to help bring order out of chaos. You can offer the alcoholic some much needed guidance in remastering the details of daily living. It's all too often that the wail is heard, "I don't know! The house was a mess . . . I was a mess . . . I just couldn't handle it, so I drank!"

Another area in which the counselor has to reorient the alcoholic to reality involves the misperception of events.

The faulty memories caused by the drugged state will need to be reexamined. One cannot always wait for some sudden insight to clear things up. For example, he is talking to you about difficulties he has had with his wife. He remembers her as a nagging bitch on his back about a "few little drinks." You might remind him that on the occasion in question, he was picked up for driving while intoxicated with a blood alcohol content of 0.20—clearly not a few. Then go on to point out that since he has misperceived the amount he was drinking to such an extent, he may have misperceived his wife's behavior. The opportunity is there, if indicated, to educate the client briefly on the distortions produced by the drug, alcohol, and to suggest that sober observations of his wife's behavior are more valid. Or possibly suggest a couple's meeting; but keep clearly in front the issue of the alcohol use.

Portrait of a man who has had 4 drinks and thinks someone has insulted him

Different strokes for different folks

Another easy trap to fall into is to expect the same course of recovery to occur for most clients. *Alcoholics don't get sick at the same rate, and they don't get well at the same rate.* One will be up and at 'em and lookin' good in very short order; another will seem to be stuck, barely hanging on, forever. And there are all the degrees in between. What's a hang-up for one is a breeze for another. Don't assume you *know* what is going to be a problem for any one particular alcoholic. We've tried to point out some of the most common, but there are lots of surprises around still. There are just no formulas or easy prescriptions that will work every time. There is no substitute for knowing *this* alcoholic and dealing with who sits before you.

Still later

At a point, after about three months, when the sober alcoholic reaches some level of comfort with his new state, the focus can shift slightly again. This doesn't mean all the problems previously discussed are totally overcome or that work is not proceeding along some of the above paths. It simply means that other problems may now be surfacing. Some are fairly common, and counselors must be alert to them. It is also at this point that some assessment should be made about whether to refer the client on to other professionals if the present caregiver is not equipped to handle this next phase. The problems are tricky ones, usually in finding a balance point between two extremes of behavior that are equally dangerous for the client. A recent article by John Wallace, a psychologist who has had long experience working with alcoholics, deserves close attention. He compares these extremes to rocks and whirlpools that must be avoided in the recovery "voyage." Another analogy could be the extremes of a pendulum before it settles into a steady rhythm. Steady rhythms have certainly been missing from the alcoholic pattern. The issue for the helping person is to clearly recognize the dangers inherent in the extremes and be prepared to guide the alcoholic strategically to the more realistic, and safer, middle ground.

Denial

One of the first difficulties is the denial problem. The tendency, when faced with the alcoholic's massive rejection of reality, is to want to force him to face all the facts *right now*. The trouble with this approach is that self-knowledge is often bought at the price of anxiety, and anxiety is a drinking trigger. What to do? Provide lots of support to counteract the initial anxiety caused by the acceptance of the reality of the drinking itself. Then, gradually, keep supporting the small increments in awareness that occur in the sober experience. It is difficult, but necessary, to remember that the denial of some particular issue is serving a useful purpose at the time, keeping overwhelming anxiety at bay until more strength is available. The counselor must decide how much anxiety the client can tolerate. The question facing the counselor is whether the denial is still necessary to ward off anxiety or whether it has become counterproductive, blocking further progress.

Guilt

Other problems occur over the issues of guilt and its fraternal twin, self-blame. It is clearly desirable to mitigate the degree of both. It is also necessary to avoid the pitfalls of their opposites, rejection of social values and blaming others. Although excessive guilt leads to the guilt/drinking spiral, some degree of conscience and sense of responsibility is necessary to function in society. The helper needs to be clear on this issue. A counselor must be able to point out unnecessary burdensome guilt on the one hand and yet allow honest guilt its expression. Dealing with both kinds, appropriately, is essential. On the blame issue, the alcoholic needs help in accepting personal responsibility where necessary. However, it can be helpful to point out that the disease itself, rather than self/others may be the true cause of some of the difficulties.

Compliance/rebellion

Two other unhealthy extremes are often seen, particularly early in treatment: compliance or rebellion. In either case, strong confrontation is not a good strategy to choose. It seems simply to produce more of either behavior. The compliant client becomes a more "model" client; the rebellious one says: "Aha! I was right. You *are* all against me," and drinks. Moderation is again the key. The aim is to help the client to acknowledge the alcoholism and accept the facts of his situation.

Feelings. Feelings, and what to do with them, provide another dual obstacle to be faced. The dry alcoholic is likely to repress feelings entirely. He does this to counteract their all too uncontrolled expression during the drinking experiences. Respect for this need to repress the emotions should prevail in the initial stages of recovery. But the eventual goal of the helper is to teach the alcoholic to recognize emotions and deal with them appropriately. Alcoholics need to learn, or relearn, that feelings need not be repressed altogether or, conversely, wildly acted out. Instead, a recognition and acceptance of them can lead to better solutions.

These are by no means the only examples of extremes that alcoholics fall victim to. The therapist needs to be wary when dealing with *any* extreme behavior or reaction to avoid having the client plunge into the opposite danger. It should be noted that some of these problems are continuing ones and may require different tactics at different stages in the recovery process.

Dependency issues

One of the most provocative points in Wallace's article concerns dependency issues. Many articles, and indeed whole books, have been written about dependency and alcoholism. Sometimes, the alcoholic is depicted as a particularly dependent type who has resolved his conflict inappropriately by the use of alcohol. It is doubtful that this point of view needs to be taken as a theoretical framework for the development of alcohol treatment programs. However, it must be noted that many alcoholics do tend toward stubborn independence versus indiscriminate dependence in their relationships. They seem to have an evil genius for attracting the very people they don't need—ones who, in fact, are harmful to them. The need for loving relationships, the development of unsatisfactory ones, and the consequent pain and misery are responsible in an unusually large number of instances for relapses. The alcoholic needs, maybe more than most, to realize that people are all interdependent to some degree. The trick is to recognize the dependent need and ask, as Wallace so aptly states: "1. Upon *whom* should I be dependent? 2. For *what?* 3. At what *cost* to me?" These questions should be asked in regard to all the relationships, not simply the primary love one. It may well turn out that dependency is being channeled into one relationship instead of spread out more effectively. Once these questions are squarely faced, selectivity and judgment stand a better chance; the extremes, with their threat to sobriety, can be more successfully avoided.

Getting stuck

Speaking of dependency, anyone working with alcohol-troubled people is bound to hear this one some time: "Sending someone to AA just creates another dependency." The implication of this is that you're simply moving the dependency from the bottle to AA, and ducking the real issue. That the dependency shifts from alcohol to AA or a counselor for the newcomer is probably true. We think that's a plus. We also think no one should get stuck there. By "there," we mean in a life-style just as alcohol-centered as before. The only difference is that the center is "not drinking" instead of "how to keep drinking." Granted, physical health is less threatened, traumatic events less frequent, and maybe even job and family stability have been established. Nonetheless, it's a recovery rut (maybe even a trench!). That some do get stuck is, unfortunately, true. But that is no reason to condemn the whole process. After all, weaning takes time, and no one implies it is easy or without the possibility of some setbacks. The infant doesn't usually go from the breast to the coffee mug in one easy jump.

There are probably many factors that account for the "stuckness." One might be an "I never had it so good, so I won't rock the boat" feeling, a real fear of letting go of the life preserver even when safely ashore. Another could be that some counselors (and some AA members) are better equipped to deal with the crisis period of getting sober and not with the later issues of growth and true freedom. Time constraints are too often the cause of the counselor's inability to encourage the letting go/stretching phase. They are quite often overwhelmed with numbers of clients truly in crisis. They simply have no time or energy to put out for the clients who are "getting along O.K." Counselors who are not content with their clients' just getting by could aid the process by referring them to extra types of therapy and groups that promote personal exploration and growth. This is a delicate situation; the adjunctive treatments are not to be seen as substituting for whatever has worked so far. Rather, they are an addition to it, whether it is AA, individual counseling, or whatever.

The counselor who does have time and does work with clients on a long-term basis should beware of getting stuck in back-patting behavior. The phrase, "Well, I didn't do much today, but at least I stayed sober," is OK once in awhile. When it becomes a client's standard refrain, over a long period of time, it should be questioned as a satisfactory life-style. Those who work around treatment facilities are all too aware of groups of alcoholics who hang around endlessly, drinking coffee, talking to other alcoholics exclusively, and clearly going nowhere. For some, who, for instance, may have suffered brain damage or some other disability, this may be the best that can be hoped for. However, we suspect that many are there simply because they are not being helped and encouraged to proceed any further. These are the alcoholics most clearly visible to the health care professionals and may be one reason for the low expectations they have for recovering alcoholics. They don't see the ones who are busy, involved, highly functioning individuals. It's our contention that counselors and caregivers can increase the number of the latter and unstick more and more, if they are sensitive to this issue.

The reason for the emphasis on lots of treatment over a fairly long period throughout this treatment section is simple. The people most successful in treating alcoholism are those who recognize that anywhere from eighteen to thirty-six months are necessary for the alcoholic to be well launched in a healthy life-style. It might be said that recovery requires an alcoholic to become "weller than well." To maintain sobriety and avoid developing alternate harmful dependencies, the alcoholic must learn a range of healthy alternative behaviors to deal with tensions arising from living problems. Nonaddicted members of society may quite safely alleviate such tensions with a drink or two. Since living, problems, and tensions go hand in hand, being truly helpful implies helping the alcoholic grow to a higher level of health than might be necessary for the general population.

GROUP WORK

Group therapy has become an increasingly popular form of treatment for a range of problems, including alcohol abuse. (Of course, with AA dating back to 1935, alcoholics have been working toward recovery in groups for forty years, long before group therapy became popular or alcohol treatment was even known.) Why the popularity of group treatment methods? The first response often is, "It's cheaper," or "It's more efficient; more people can be seen." These statements may be true, but a more fundamental reason exists. Group therapy works. It works very well with alcoholics. Some of the reasons for this can be found in the characteristics of alcoholism, plus normal human nature.

For better or worse, people find themselves part of a group. And whatever being a human being means, it does involve other people. We think in terms of our family, our neighborhood, our school, our club, our town, our church. On the job, at home, on the playground, wherever, it's in group experiences where we feel left out or, conversely, find a sense of belonging. Through our contacts with others, we feel OK or not OK. As we interact, we find ourselves sharing our successes or hiding our supposed failures. It's through groups we get strokes on the head or a kick in the pants. There's no avoiding the reality that other people play a big part in our lives. Just as politicians take opinion polls to see how they're doing with the populace, so do each of us run our surveys. The kinds of questions we ask ourselves about our relationships are "Do I belong?" "Do I matter to others?" "Can I trust them?" "Am I liked?" "Do I like them?" To be at ease and comfortable in the world, the answers need to come up more ayes than nays. The practicing alcoholic doesn't fare so well when he takes this poll. For the myriad reasons discussed before, his relationships with other people are poor. He's isolated and isolating, rejects and is rejected, feels helpless and refuses aid. With his warped view of the world, he's oblivious to the fact that it's been the drinking getting him into trouble. While he's wed to the bottle, other bonds can't be formed. Attempts to make it in the world sober will require his reestablishing real human contacts. Thus groups, the setting in which life must be lived, become an ideal setting for treatment.

Group as therapy

Being a part of a group can do some powerful therapeutic things. The active alcoholic is afraid of people "out there." The phrase "tiger land" has been used by alcoholics to describe the world. That's a fairly telling phrase! Through group treatment, hopefully the alcoholic will *re-experience* the world, his world, differently. The whole thing need not be a jungle—other people can be a source of safety and strength. Another big bonus from a group experience is derived from the alcoholic's opportunity to become *reacquainted* with himself. A group provides a chance to learn who he is, his capabilities, his impact on and his importance to others. Interacting honestly and openly provides opportunity to adjust and correct the mental picture of himself. He gets feedback. Group treatment of persons in a similar situation reduces the sense of *isolation*. Alcoholics tend to view themselves *very* negatively and house an overwhelming sense of shame for their behavior. Coming together with others proves one is not uniquely awful. Yet mere confession is not therapeutic. Something else must happen for healing to occur. Just as absolution occurs in the context of a church, in a group that functions therapeutically, the members act as priests to one another. Members hear one another's confession and say, in essence, "You are forgiven, go and sin no more." (A short lesson in linguistics: "sin" is derived from the Greek word meaning "to miss the target." It doesn't imply evil, or bad,

Drinking makes such fools of people, and people are such fools to begin with that it's compounding a felony.

ROBERT BENCHLEY

as is so often assumed.) That is to say, group members can see one another apart from the alcoholic behavior. They can also often see a potential that is unknown to the person himself. This is readily verified in our own lives. Solutions to other people's problems are *so* obvious, but not so solutions to our own. Members of the group can see that people need not be destined to continue their old behaviors. Old "sins" need not be repeated. Thus they *instill hope* in one another. Interestingly enough, one often finds that people are more gentle with others than with themselves. In this regard, the group experience has a neat boomerang effect. In the process of being kind and understanding of others, the members are in turn forced to accord themselves similar treatment.

What has been discussed is the potential benefit that can be gleaned from a group exposure. How this group experience takes place can vary widely. Group therapy comes in many styles and can occur in many contexts. Being a resident in a halfway house puts the client in a group, just as the person who participates in outpatient group therapy. Group therapy means the use of any group experience to promote change in the members. Under the direction of a skilled leader, the power of the group processes is harnessed for therapeutic purposes. Being an effective group leader is a real skill that comes only with practice. Anyone who hopes to do group counseling or group therapy will find it helpful to enroll in seminars or courses on group work. And then, try it, working as a co-leader with an old hand or under supervision. The comments in this section can never substitute for such training.

Group work with alcoholics

In contemplating group work with alcoholics, the leader will need to consider several basic issues. What is the purpose of the group? What are the goals for the individual members? Where will the group meet? How often? What will the rules be? The first question is the keystone. The purpose of the group needs to be clear in the leader's mind. There are many possible legitimate purposes. Experience shows that *not* all can be met simultaneously. It is far better to have different types of groups available, with members participating in several, than to lump everything into one group and accomplish nothing.

Some of the major group focuses include education, self-awareness of alcohol use, support for treatment, problem solving, and activity/resocialization.

Educational groups attempt to impart factual information about alcohol, its effects, and alcoholism. There is a complex relationship between knowledge, feelings, and behavior. Correct facts and information don't stop alcoholic drinking. But they can be important in breaking down denial, which protects the alcoholic drinking. Besides battering denial, educational efforts assist the already motivated client. Information provides an invaluable framework for understanding what has happened and what treatment is about. The client acquires some cognitive tools to better participate in his own treatment. Educational groups generally include a lecture, film, or presentation by a specialist in the alcohol field, followed by a group discussion.

Wine is a mocker, strong drink is raging.
PROVERBS 28:29-30

Another kind of educational activity, developed by Leona M. Kent in California, is the AA Training Group. In a series of ten sessions, the clients are introduced to the structure, philosophy, and jargon of AA. The intent is to help the referral process to AA of persons in treatment programs. Many of these clients are resistive, or confused, and apprehensive about AA. Normally, in AA, this kind of information is shared informally between a sponsor and a newcomer. Without an introduction, some clients wouldn't ever get close enough to understand how the AA program works.

Self-awareness and support groups are intended to assist the members to honestly grapple with the role of alcohol in their lives. The group function is to support sobriety, to identify the characteristic ways in which people sabotage themselves. In these groups, the emphasis is on the here and now. The participants are expected to deal with feelings as well as facts. The goal is not intellectual understanding of why things have, or are, occurring. Rather, the hope is to have members discover how they feel and learn how feelings are translated into behavior. They then *choose* how they would prefer to behave, and try it on for size.

A *problem-solving* group is directed at tackling specific problem or stress areas in the group members' lives. Either discussion, role play, or a combination may be used. For example, how to say no to an offer to have a beer or how to handle an upcoming job interview could be appropriate topics. The goal is to develop an awareness of potential stress situations, to identify the old response pattern and how it created problems, and then to try new behaviors. These sessions thus provide practice for more effective coping behaviors.

Activity groups are least likely to resemble the stereotype of group therapy. In these groups an activity or project is undertaken, such as a ward or client government meeting or a planning session for a picnic. The emphasis is on more than the apparent task. The task is also a sample of real life; thus it provides a practice arena for the clients to identify areas of strength and weakness in interpersonal relationships. Here, too, the clients have a safe place to practice new behaviors.

Group functions

No matter what the kind of group, a number of functions will need to be performed. For any group to work effectively, there are some essential tasks, regardless of the goal. Initially the leader may need to be primarily responsible for filling these roles:

- initiating—suggesting ideas for the group to consider, getting the ball rolling
- elaborating or clarifying—clearing up confusions, giving examples, expanding on other person's contribution
- summarizing—pulling together loose ends, restating ideas
- facilitating—encouraging others' participation by asking questions, showing interest
- expressing group feelings—recognizing moods and relationships within the group
- giving feedback—sharing your response to what is happening
- seeking feedback—asking for others' responses to what you are doing

But as time goes on the leader needs to teach the group members to share the responsibility for these functions. Giving a lecture or showing a film on how to be a group member won't do it. Instead, through your own behavior, you serve as a model. You set the example, not only of how to act in group, but demonstrate more generally what healthy behavior looks like.

Different types of group therapy can be useful at different times during recovery. During the course of an inpatient stay, a client might well attend an educational group, an AA Training Group, a problem-solving group, and a self-awareness group. In addition, he could attend outside AA meetings. In this example, the client would be participating in five different types of groups. On discharge from the residence, the client would return for weekly group sessions as part of follow-up, and with his spouse might join a couples group. None of these group experiences would be intended to substitute for AA. The most effective treatment plans will prescribe AA *plus* alcohol-related group therapy. They are no more mutually exclusive than is AA or group therapy, along with medical treatment of cirrhosis.

Groups as a fad

A word of caution. Group experiences have become something of a fad. There is a bandwagon phenomenon. Marathon, encounter, TA, gestalt, sensitivity, what have you are seemingly offered everywhere: school, church, job, women's clubs. The emphasis placed on groups here does not imply the alcoholic should ride the group therapy circuit! On the contrary, the alcoholic seeking *alcohol* treatment in a group *not* restricted to alcoholics is likely to waste his and other people's time. As was stated earlier, until he's taken some step to combat the alcohol problem, there's little likelihood of working on other problems successfully. Inevitably, the alcoholic will raise havoc in a mixed group. The prediction we'd make is that the alcoholic will have others running in circles figuring out the whys, get gobs of sympathy for his predicament, and remain unchanged. Eventually the other group members will wear out, end up treating him just as his family does, and experience all the same frustrations as the family. But in a group with other alcoholics and a leader used to the dynamics of alcoholism, it's a different story. The opportunity to maintain the charade is diminished to virtually zero because everyone knows the game thoroughly. The agenda, in this latter instance, is clearly how to break out of the game.

He says if everyone would get off his back, he could let go of the bottle.

FAMILY TREATMENT

Members of an alcoholic's family often need treatment as much as the alcoholic. Often they will be the ones asking for assistance first. They are entitled to as much compassion, aid, and assistance as the drinker. In contacts with a family, energy should be directed toward handling *their* problems, *not* treating the alcoholic in absentia. What does the family need? Education about alcoholism, the disease, will be one thing. Another is some aid in sorting out their behavior to see how it fits into, or even perpetuates, the drinking problem. Most importantly, family members require support to live their own lives *despite the alcoholic*. Paradoxically, by doing this, the actual chances of short-circuiting alcoholism are enhanced.

Counseling techniques in working with families are the same as working with the alcoholic. Both individual counseling and group work can be useful. Family therapy is another possibility. Here the family is seen as a total group and counseled as a unit. The basic notions behind this approach are that the family behaves as a unit, has characteristic ways of interacting. No matter how sick it looks, these interactions and behaviors are the family's attempt to minimize pain and disruption. The family is trying to maintain a balance. When one person is identified as "sick" or "the one with a problem," other family members may allow the illness to continue. Working with the family as a group allows the therapist to see the family together. Ineffective behaviors can be identified as they occur, and support provided for desired change. Family therapy is a special skill similar to, yet different from, group work. You, the alcohol counselor, might refer families to a skilled family therapist or work with one as a means of also enhancing your own skills.

Once the alcoholic does seek help, it is equally important to include the family. Unfortunately, what is more probable is that the family will be called in to give background information and then ignored. Attention will be paid again only if problems arise and counselor or treatment staff feel the spouse or family isn't being supportive or sympathetic. No one seems too interested in the problems the spouse or family has had or is having. The alcoholic's entering treatment, especially residential treatment, may itself impose immediate problems. The spouse may be concerned about more unpaid bills, fears of yet more broken promises, etc. When there are immediate concerns, long-range benefits may offer little consolation. Counseling the family may help them weather the immediate storm and look forward to the future with hope. Many treatment programs run separate groups for family members as a part of the alcoholic's treatment program.

Suggestions for working with families

Here are some concrete suggestions for dealing with alcoholic families no matter what the stage of treatment. You are the most objective person present. It's up to you to evaluate and guide the process.

Concentrate on the interaction, not on the content. Don't become the referee in a family digression.

Teach them how to check things out. People tend to guess at other peoples' meanings and motivations. They then respond as though the guesses were accurate. This causes all kinds of confusion and misunderstandings and can lead to mutual recriminations. The counselor needs to put a stop to these mind reading games, and point out what's going on.

The counselor must *be alert to "scapegoating."* A common human tendency is to lay it all on George. This is true whatever the problem. The alcoholic family tends to blame the drinker for all the family's troubles, thereby neatly avoiding any responsibility for their own action. Help them see this as a no-no.

Any good therapy stresses *acceptance of each person's right to his own feelings.* One reason for this is that good feelings get blocked by unexpressed bad feelings. One of the tasks of a therapist is to bring out the family's strengths. The focus has been on the problems for so long that they have lost sight of the good points.

Be alert to avoidance transactions. This includes such things as digressing to Christmas three years ago in the midst of a heated discussion of Daddy's drinking. It's up to you to point this out to them and get them back on the track. In a similar vein, it may fall to you to "speak the unspeakable," to bring out in the open the obvious, but unmentioned, facts.

In making these patterns clear to the family, you can *guide them into problem-solving techniques as options.* You can help them begin to use these in therapy, with an eye to teaching them to use them on their own.

After a time of success, when things seem to be going

better, there may be some resistance to continuing therapy. The family fears a setback and wants to stop while they're ahead. Simply point this out to them. They can try for something better or terminate. If they terminate, leave the door open for a return later.

Pregnancy in the alcoholic family

You may recall some of the particular family problems that relate to pregnancy and the presence of young children in the family. A few specific words should be said about these potential problematic areas. The first is contraceptive counseling. Pregnancy is not a cure for alcoholism in either partner. In a couple in which one or both partners are actively drinking, they'd be advised to make provision for the prevention of pregnancy until the drinking is well controlled. It's important to remember that birth control methods that are adequate for an ordinary couple may not be adequate when alcoholism is present. Methods that require planning or delay of gratification are likely to fail. Rhythm, foam, diaphragms, or prophylactics are not wise choices if one partner is actively drinking. A woman who is actively drinking is not advised to use the pill. So the alternatives are few: the pill or IUD for the partner of an active male alcoholic, an IUD for the sexually active female alcoholic. In the event of an unwanted pregnancy, the possibilities of placement or therapeutic abortion should be considered. If the woman is alcoholic, a therapeutic abortion certainly should be considered. At the moment, no amniotic fluid assay test exists that can establish the presence of fetal alcohol syndrome, but the possibility is there when the mother is actively drinking.

Should pregnancy occur and a decision be made to have the baby, intensive intervention is required. If the expectant mother is the alcoholic, every effort should be made to get her to stop drinking. Regular prenatal care is also important. Counseling and support of both parents if alcohol is present is essential to handle the stresses that accompany any pregnancy. If the prospective father is the alcoholic, it is important to provide additional supports for the mother.

Portrait of a young child whose father is nice to him when sober, but beats him when drunk.

Children in the alcoholic family

A few words are in order on behalf of older children in an alcoholic family. In many cases, children's problems are

related to stress in the parents. Children may easily become weapons in parental battles. With alcoholism, children may think their behavior is the cause of the drinking.
A child needs to be told that this is *not* the case. In instances where the counselor knows that physical or severe
emotional abuse has occurred, child welfare authorities
must be notified. In working with the family, additional
parenting persons may be brought into the picture. Going
to a nursery school or day care center may help the child
from a chaotic home.

Recovery and the family

It might be expected, if one considers the family as a
unit, that there are stages or patterns of a family's recovery
from alcoholism. This has not yet been adequately studied.
No one has developed a "valley chart" that plots family
disintegration and recovery. Counselors who have had considerable involvement with families of recovering alcoholics
have noticed and are now beginning to discuss some common themes of the family's recovery.

One observation suggests that the family unit may experience growth pains which parallel those facing the alcoholic. It has long been a part of the folk wisdom that the
alcoholic's psychological and emotional growth ceases when
the heavy drinking begins. So when sobriety comes, the
alcoholic is going to have to face some growing-up issues
that the drinking prevented him from attending to. In the
family system, what may be the equivalent of this Rip Van
Winkle experience? Consider an example of a family in
which the father is an alcoholic, whose heavy drinking occurred during his children's adolescence, and who begins
recovery just as the children are entering adulthood. If he
was basically "out of it" during their teenage years, they
grew up as best they could, without very much fathering
from him. When he "comes to," they are no longer children
but adults. In effect, he was deprived of an important
chunk of family life. There may be regrets. There may be
unrealistic expectations on the father's part about his
present relationship with his children. There may be inappropriate attempts by him to "make it up," regain the missing part. Depending on the situation, the counselor may
need to help him grieve. Or there may be the need to help
him recognize that his expectations are not in keeping with
his children's adult status. Hopefully, he may be able to

find other outlets to experience a parenting role or reestablish and enjoy appropriate contacts with his children.

Divorced or separated alcoholics

Issues of family relationships are not important just for the alcoholic whose family is intact. For the alcoholic who is divorced and/or estranged from the family, the task during the early, active treatment phase will be to help him make it without family supports. Other family members may well have come to the conclusion long ago that cutting off contacts with the alcoholic was necessary for their welfare. Even if contacted when the alcoholic enters treatment, they may refuse to have anything to do with him or his treatment. However, with many months or years of sobriety, the issue of broken family ties may emerge. The recovered alcoholic may desire a restoration of family contacts and have the emotional and personal stability to attempt it, be it with parents, siblings, or the alcoholic's own children.

If the alcoholic remains in follow-up treatment with a counselor, the counselor ought to be alert to this. If the alcoholic is successful, it will still involve stress; very likely many old wounds will be opened. If the attempt is unsuccessful, the counselor will be able to provide support and help the person find a new adjustment in the face of his unfulfilled hopes. As family treatment becomes an integral part of treatment for alcoholism, the hope is that fewer families will experience a total disruption of communications in the face of alcoholism. A more widespread knowledge of the symptoms of alcoholism may hopefully facilitate reconciliation of previously estranged families.

Al-Anon

Finally Al-Anon, a support group for the families of alcoholics, has been found helpful. It provides a place in which the family is free to discuss the problems of living with an alcoholic. It focuses on their own behaviors and helps them to get out of an "alcoholic-centered" existence. The program is designed to help them learn better coping behavior, the theory being that one can only change oneself. We don't wish to belie the importance of Al-Anon by our brevity. This program is significantly similar to that of AA, and a lengthy description of both would be redundant.

ALCOHOLICS ANONYMOUS

Volumes have been written about the phenomenon of AA. It has been investigated, explained, and defended by laypeople, newspapers, writers, magazines, psychologists, psychiatrists, doctors, sociologists, anthropologists, and clergy. Each has brought a set of underlying assumptions and a particular vocabulary and professional or lay framework to the task. The variety of material on the subject reminds one of trying to force mercury into a certain-sized, perfectly round ball.

In this brief discussion, we certainly have a few underlying assumptions. One is that "experience is the best teacher." This text will be relatively unhelpful compared to attending AA meetings over a period of time, watching and talking with people in the process of recovery actively using the program of AA. Another assumption is that AA works for a wide variety of people caught up in the disease and for this reason deserves a counselor's attention. AA has been described as "the single most effective treatment for alcoholism." The exact whys and hows of its workings are not of paramount importance, but some understanding of it is necessary to genuinely recommend it. Presenting AA with such statements as "AA worked for me; it's the only way," or, conversely, "I've done all I can for you, you might as well try AA," might not be the most helpful approach.

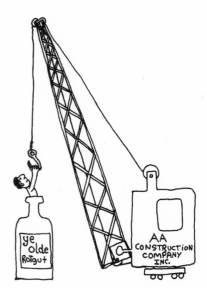

History

AA had its beginnings in 1935 in Akron, Ohio, with the meeting of two alcoholics. One, Bill W., had had a spiritual experience that had been the major precipitating event in beginning his abstinence. On a trip to Akron after about a year of sobriety, he was overtaken by a strong desire to drink. He hit upon the idea of seeking out another suffering alcoholic as an alternative. He made contact with some people who led him to Dr. Bob, and the whole thing began with their first meeting. The fascinating story of this history is told in *A. A. Comes of Age.* The idea of alcoholics helping each other spread slowly in geometric fashion until 1939. At that point, a group of about a hundred sober members realized they had something to offer the thus far "hopeless alcoholics." They wrote and published the book *Alcoholics Anonymous,* generally known as the Big Book. It was based on a retrospective view of what they had done

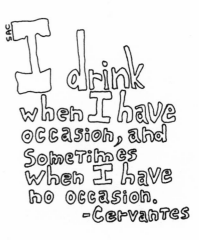

I drink when I have occasion, and sometimes when I have no occasion.
—Cervantes

that had kept them sober. The past tense is used almost entirely in the Big Book. It was compiled by a group of people who, over time, working together, had found something that worked. Their task was to present this in a useful framework to others who might try it for themselves. This story is also covered in *A. A. Comes of Age.* In 1941, AA became widely known after the publication of an article in a national magazine. The geometric growth rapidly advanced until 1972, when figures estimated an active membership of 750,000 alcoholics attempting to loosen their grip on the bottle.

Organization

AA has very little form as an organization. It functions around the Twelve Steps and the Twelve Traditions. The traditions cover the organization as a whole, with stress laid on the autonomy of individual groups. The groups are based on the principles outlined in the preamble and the traditions. The focus is on sobriety, anonymity, and individual application of The Program, which includes meetings, attempting to work the Twelve Steps, and service to other alcoholics. "The Twelve Steps and the Twelve Traditions," an AA publication, is another recommended reading.

There are open meetings (open to any spouses, interested parties, etc.) and closed meetings (only professed alcoholics attend the latter). Both types divide into speaker or discussion meetings. The former format has one to three speakers who tell what it was like drinking (for the purpose of allowing newcomers to identify), what happened to change this, and what the sober life is now like. A discussion meeting is usually smaller. The chairman may or may not tell his story briefly as above, or "qualify" in AA jargon. The focus of the meeting is a discussion of a particular Step, topic, or problem with alcohol, with the chairman taking the role of facilitator.

Meetings plus . . .

Attendance at meetings is not all there is to AA. An analogy to medical care may help. The AA meeting might be like a patient's visit to a doctor's office. The office visit doesn't constitute the whole of therapy. It's a good start; but how closely the patient follows the physician's advice and recommendations and acts on what is prescribed makes the difference. Sitting in the doctor's office doesn't do it. So too with AA. The person who is seriously trying to use AA as a means of achieving sobriety will be doing a lot more than attending meetings. Persons successful in AA will spend time talking to and being with other more experienced members. Part of this time will be spent getting practical tips on how to maintain sobriety. Time and effort goes into learning and substituting other behaviors for the all-pervasive drinking behavior. AA contacts will also be a valuable resource for relaxation. It's a place a newly recovering alcoholic will feel accepted. It's also a space in which the drinking possibilities are greatly minimized. In his early days with AA, a member may spend a couple of hours a day phoning, having coffee with, or in the company of, other AA members. Although it is strongly recommended that a new member seek a sponsor, he will be in touch with a larger circle of people. Frequent contact with AA members is encouraged, not only to pass on useful information. Another key reason is to make it easier for the new members to reach out at times of stress, when picking up a drink would be so easy and instinctively natural. The new member's contacting a fellow AA member when a crunch time comes makes the difference in many cases between recovery and relapse.

Slogans

Slowly the new member's life is being restructured around *not* drinking, and usually the slogans are the basis for this: "One day at a time," "easy does it," "keep it simple," "live and let live," "let go and let God," etc. Although they sound trite and somewhat corny, remember the description of the confused, guilt-ridden, anxious product of alcoholism. Anyone in such a condition can greatly benefit from a simple, organized, easily understood schedule of priorities. A kind of behavior modification is taking place in order that a growth process may begin. Some new members feel so overwhelmed by the idea of a day without a drink that their sponsor and/or others will help them literally plan every step of the first few weeks. They keep in almost hourly touch with older members. Phone calls at any hour of the day or night are encouraged as a way to relieve anxiety.

Goals

AA stresses abstinence and contends that nothing can really happen for a drinker until "the cork is in the bottle." Many other helping professionals tend to agree. A drugged person—and an alcoholic *is* drugged—simply cannot comprehend, or use successfully, many other forms of treatment. First the drug has to go.

The goals of each individual within AA vary widely; simple abstinence to a whole new way of life are the ends of the continuum. Individuals' personal goals may also change over time. That any one organization can accommodate such diversity is in itself something of a miracle.

In AA, the words "sober" and "dry" denote quite different states. A "dry" person is simply not drinking at the moment. "Sobriety" means a more basic, all-pervasive change in the person. Sobriety does not come as quickly as dryness and requires a desire for, and work toward, a contented, productive life without reliance on mood-altering drugs. The Twelve Steps provide a framework for achieving this latter state.

The Twelve Steps

The initial undrugged view of the devastation can, and often does, drive the dry alcoholic back to the bottle. But the Twelve Steps of AA, as experienced by the sober members, offer the possibility of another solution: hope for another road out of the maze.

Step 1, "We admitted we were powerless over alcohol —that our lives had become unmanageable," acknowledges the true culprit, alcohol, and the scope of the problem, the whole life. Step 2, "Came to believe that a Power greater than ourselves could restore us to sanity," recognizes the craziness of the drinking behavior, and allows for the gradual reliance on some agent outside (God, the AA group, the therapist, or a combination) to aid an about-face. Step 3, "Made a decision to turn our will and our lives over to the care of God as we understood Him," enables the alcoholic to let go of the previous life preserver, the bottle, and accept an outside influence to provide direction. It has now become clear that as a life preserver, the bottle was a dud, but free floating can't go on forever either. The search outside the self for direction has now begun.

Step 4, "Made a searching and fearless moral inventory

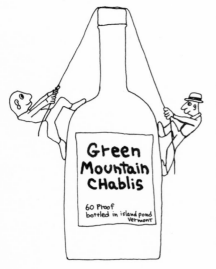

Green
Mountain
CHablis

60 Proof
bottled in island pond
Vermont

of ourselves," allows a close look at the basic errors of thinking and acting that were part of the drinking debacle. It also
gives space for the positive attributes that can be enhanced
in the sober state. An inventory is, after all, a balance
sheet. Number 5, "Admitted to God, to ourselves, and to
another human being the exact nature of our wrongs,"
provides a method of cleaning the slate, admitting just how
awful it all was, and getting the guilt-provoking behavior
out in the open instead of destructively "bottled up."

Steps 6 and 7, "Were entirely ready to have God remove all these defects of character," and "Humbly asked
Him to remove our shortcomings," continue the mopping-
up process. Step 6 makes the alcoholic aware of the tendency to cling to old behaviors, even unhealthy ones.
Step 7 takes care of the fear of repeated errors, again instill-
ing hope that personality change is possible. (Remember,
at this stage in the process, the alcoholic is likely to be
very short on self-esteem.)

Steps 8 and 9 are a clear guide to sorting out actual
injury done to others and deciding how best to deal with
such situations. Step 8 is "Made a list of all persons we had
harmed and became willing to make amends to them all."
Step 9 is "Made direct amends to such people wherever
possible, except when to do so would injure them or
others." They serve other purposes, too. First they get the
alcoholic out of his bag of blaming others for life's difficulties. They also provide a mechanism for dealing with
presently strained relationships and for alleviating some of
the overwhelming guilt the now sober alcoholic feels.

Steps 10 to 12 are considered the continuing maintenance steps. Step 10, "Continued to take personal inventory and when we were wrong promptly admitted it,"
ensures that the alcoholic need not slip back from his
hard-won gains. Diligence in focusing on his own behavior
and not excusing it keeps the record straight. Step 11,
"Sought through prayer and meditation to improve our
conscious contact with God as we understood Him, praying
only for knowledge of His will for us and the power to carry
that out," fosters continued spiritual development. Finally,
Step 12, "Having had a spiritual awakening as a result of
these steps, we tried to carry this message to alcoholics and
to practice these principles in all our affairs," points the way
to sharing the process with others. This is one of the vital

keys Bill W. discovered to maintain sobriety. It also implies that a continued practice of the new principles is vital to the sober life.

A word can be said here about "Two Steppers." This phrase is used to describe a few individuals in AA who come in, admit they are alcoholics, dry out, and set out to rescue other alcoholics. However, it is often said in AA that "you can't give what you don't have." This refers to a quality of sobriety that comes after some long and serious effort applying the entire Twelve Steps. It is interesting to note that "carrying the message" isn't mentioned until Step 12.

No AA member serious about the program and sober for some time would ever imply that the Steps are a one-shot deal. They are an ongoing process that evolves over time (a great deal of it) into ever-widening applications. When approached with serious intent, the Steps enable a great change in the individual. That they are effective is testified to not only by great numbers of recovering alcoholics, but also by their adoption as a basis for such organizations as Overeaters' Anonymous, Gamblers' Anonymous, and Emotions Anonymous. These other organizations simply substitute their own addiction for the word alcohol in Step 1.

A therapist/counselor/friend should be alert to the balance required in this process. The newly dry alcoholic who wants to tackle all 12 Steps the first week should be counseled "Easy does it." The longer dry member hopelessly anguished by Step 4, for instance, could be advised that perfection is not the goal and a stab at it the first time through is quite sufficient. The agnostic having difficulty with "the God bit" can be told about using the group or anything else he chooses for the time being. After all, the spiritual awakening doesn't turn up until Step 12 either.

Resistances

Water taken in moderation cannot hurt anybody.

MARK TWAIN

An objective opinion of AA is hard to find. Quite honestly, some workers do show resistances to AA. At times one gets the sense that AA isn't considered to be "real" treatment. Why these feelings? Often, we don't have the foggiest notion. Nonetheless, our suspicion is that a number of factors may feed into this attitude. One reason is that any worker in the field of alcoholism will periodically lose touch with what the disease of alcoholism is really like. The literal hell that is the life of the active alcoholic is forgotten.

That is who AA is for. Yet at times, we forget that the primary purpose of AA is to help people escape their hell. Then we begin to act as if AA were supposed to do other things, for example, be a growth group or handle marital problems. Another point of possible professional resistance is that we sometimes take our resistive client's objections too seriously. We buy their criticisms of AA. We accept their not "liking" AA as a valid reason for their not going. But we don't expect (or care!) if they "like" to see their doctors, or "like" to use other forms of treatment! Similarly, treatment people don't usually see the people who try AA and succeed the first time around, who don't need other kinds of help. There's a natural human tendency when we see someone operating differently to think one of us must be wrong. If I don't want it to be me, that means it must be you . . . or AA. Another point of friction seems to be connected to the fact that AA does not build termination into the program. More will be said about this below. What professional workers forget is that any chronic disease is only terminated by death. Even when under control, regular checkups are routine practice. Finally, professionals sometimes have mistakenly gotten the impression that AA, as an organization, holds AA and other therapies to be incompatible. This is not the case. Nothing in the AA program would support this. Certainly, an occasional client member will give this impression, in which case, as a counselor, you can help clear up this misconception. So much for the friction points and back to AA.

View of recovery

One thing assumed in AA is that recovery is a serious, lifelong venture. Safety does not exist, and some kind of long-term support is necessary. This seems to be the case, and a lot of experience supports the assumption. Alcoholics, like all of us, have selective memories and are inclined, after varying periods of dryness, to remember only the relief of drinking and not the consequent problems. Some kind of reminder of reality seems to be necessary. Any alcoholic of long-term sobriety will be able to tell about the sudden desire to drink popping up out of nowhere. Those who don't succumb are largely grateful to some aspect of their AA life as the key to their returning stability. No one knows exactly why these moments occur, but one thing is

Against diseases the strongest fence is the defensive virtue, abstinence.

ROBERT HERRICK

certain: they are personally frightening and upsetting. They can reduce the reasonably well-adjusted recovering alcoholic to a state very like his first panic-ridden dryness. The feelings could be compared to the feelings after a particularly vivid nightmare. Whatever the reason for the phenomenon, these unexpected urges to drink do spring up. This is one reason why continued participation in AA is suggested. Another is the emphasis (somewhat underplayed from time to time) on a continued growth in sobriety. Certainly, groups will rally round newcomers with a beginner's focus and help them learn the basics. But in discussion meetings with a group of veterans, the focus will be on personal growth within the context of the Twelve Steps. AA may advertise itself as a "simple program for complicated people," but an understanding of it is far from a simple matter. It involves people, and people are multifaceted. It's simplicity is deceptive and on the order of "Love thy neighbor as thyself." Simple, and yet the working out of it could easily take a lifetime.

In closing, we again strongly urge you to attend a variety of AA meetings and speak at some length with veteran members. So much has been written about AA, plus in some respects it's so understandable an approach, that people assume they know what it's about without firsthand knowledge. Just as you would visit treatment programs, or community agencies to see personally what they're about, so too, go to AA.

Referral

A few words about making an effective referral to AA. Simply telling someone to go probably won't work in most cases. The worker needs to play a more active role in the referral. AA is a self-help group. What AA can do and offer is by far best explained *and* demonstrated by its members. The counselor can assist by making arrangements for the client to speak to a member of AA or can arrange for a client to be taken to a meeting. Helping professionals, whether alcoholic or not, often have a list of AA members who have agreed to do this. Even if the counselor is an AA member, a separate AA contact is advisable. It is less confusing to the client if AA is seen as distinct from, although compatible with, his other therapy. The counselor need not defend, proselytize for, or try to sell AA. AA speaks for itself eloquently. You do your part well when you get the client to attend, to listen with an open mind, and to stay long enough to make his own assessment.

SPIRITUAL COUNSELING

There is increasing effort to educate and inform clergy about alcohol abuse and alcoholism. The focus of the effort is to equip pastors, priests, rabbis, ministers, and chaplains who come into contact with alcoholics or their families to assist in early identification and help get the alcoholic into treatment. Presumably the merits of this effort are self-evident. There is plenty of room in the alcohol field for many different kinds of care-providers. This section on spiritual counseling is not about this educational outreach to clergy. Instead, we wish to discuss the contribution that clergy members, priests, or rabbis may make to the recovery process in their pastoral roles.

Alcoholics may have a need for pastoring, "shepherding," or spiritual counseling as do other members of the population. In fact, their needs in this area may be especially acute. Attention to these needs may play a critical part in the recovery process.

It is not easy to discuss spiritual matters. Medical, social work, psychology, or rehabilitation textbooks do not include chapters on spiritual issues as they affect prospective clients or patients. The split between spirituality and the "rest of life" has been total. In our society, that means for many it has become an either/or choice. Since defining crisply what we mean by spiritual issues is not easy, let's begin by stating what it is not. By spiritual we do not mean the organized religions and churches. Religions can be thought of as organized groups and institutions that have arisen to meet spiritual needs. But the spiritual concern is more basic than religion. In our view, the fact that civilizations have developed religions throughout history is evidence of a spiritual side to human beings.

There are also experiences, difficult to describe, which hint at another dimension different from but as real as our physical nature. They might be called "intimations of immortality" and occur among sufficient numbers of people to give more evidence for the spiritual nature of humankind.

In a variety of ways we can see an awakened interest in

It is hard to believe in God, but it is far harder to disbelieve in Him.

EMERSON

spiritual concerns in contemporary America. This is especially true among younger persons. Whether it's transcendental meditation, Zen Buddhism, Indian gurus, Jesus "freaks," the "Moonies," mysticism, or the more traditional Judeo-Christian Western religions, people are flocking in. They are attempting to follow these teachings and precepts, with the hope that they will fill a void in their lives. It's taken almost as an article of faith that "making it," in terms of status, education, career, or material wealth, can still leave someone feeling there's something missing. This "something" is thought by many to be of a spiritual nature. This missing piece has even been described as a "God-shaped hole."

Alcoholism as spiritual search

How does this fit in with alcohol and alcoholism? First, it is worth reflecting on the fact that the very word most commonly used for alcohol is "spirits." This is surely no accident. And look how alcohol is used. It is often used in the hope it will provide that missing something or at least turn off the gnawing ache. From bottled spirits, a drinker may seek a solution to life's problems, a release from pain, an escape from circumstances. For awhile it may do the job. But eventually it fails. To use spiritual language, you can even think of alcoholism as a pilgrimage that dead ends. Alcohol is a false god. To use the words of the New Testament, it is not "living water."

If this is the case, and alcohol use has been in part prompted by spiritual thirst, the thirst remains when the alcoholic sobers up. Part of the recovery process must be aimed at quenching the thirst. AA has recognized this fact. It speaks of alcoholism as a threefold disease, with physical, mental, and spiritual components. Part of the AA program is intended to help members by focusing on their spiritual needs. It is also worth nothing that AA makes a clear distinction between spiritual growth and religion.

Clergy assistance

How can the clergy possibly be of assistance? Ideally, the clergy are people within society who are the "experts" on spiritual matters. (Notice we say *ideally*.) In real life, clergy are human beings, too. The realities of religious institutions may have forced some to be fund raisers, social directors, community consciences, almost everything but spiritual mentors. But there are those out there who are and maybe many more who long to act as spiritual counselors and advisors.

One of the ways the clergy may be of potential assistance is to help the alcoholic deal with "sin" and feelings of guilt, worthlessness, and hopelessness. Many alcoholics, along with the public at large, are walking around as adults with virtually the same notions of God they had as a 5-year-old. He has a white beard, sits on a throne on a cloud, checks up on everything you do, and is out to get you if you aren't "good." This is certainly a caricature but also probably very close to the way most people really feel if they think about it. The alcoholic getting sober feels remorseful, guilt-ridden, worthless, endowed with a host of negative qualities, and devoid of good. In his mind, he certainly does not fit the picture of someone God would like to befriend or hang around with. On the contrary, he probably feels that if God isn't punishing him, he ought to be! So the alcoholic may need some real assistance in updating his concept of God. There's a good chance some of his ideas will have to be revised. There's the idea he has that the church, and therefore (to him) God, is only for the "good" people. A glance at the New Testament and Christian traditions doesn't support this view, even if some parishes or congregations act that way. Jesus of Nazareth didn't exactly travel with the smart social set. He was found in the company of fishermen, prostitutes, lepers, and tax collectors! Whether a new perspective on God or a Higher Power leads to reinvolvement with a church, assists in affiliation with AA, or helps lessen the burden of guilt doesn't matter. Whichever it does, it's potentially a key factor in recovery.

Again to use spiritual language, recovery from alcoholism involves a "conversion experience." The meaning of conversion is very simple: "to turn around" or "to transform." Contrasting the sober life to the alcoholic's drinking days certainly testifies to such a transformation. A conversion experience doesn't necessarily imply blinding lights, visions, or a dramatic turning point, although it might. And if it does involve a startling experience of some nature, the sober alcoholic will need some substantial aid in dealing with or understanding this experience.

Carl Jung

It is interesting to note that an eminent psychiatrist recognized this spiritual dimension of alcoholism and recovery over forty years ago, in the days when alcoholism was considered hopeless by the medical profession. The physician was Carl Jung. Roland H., who had been through the treatment route for alcoholism prior to this, sought out Jung in 1931. He saw Jung as the court of last resort, admired him greatly, and remained in therapy with him for about a year. Shortly after terminating therapy, Roland lapsed back into drinking. Because of this unfortunate development, he returned to Jung. On his return, Jung told Roland his condition was hopeless as far as psychiatry and medicine of that day were concerned. Very desperate and grabbing at straws, Roland asked if there was any hope at all. Jung replied that there might be, provided Roland could have a spiritual or religious experience—a genuine conversion experience. Although comparatively rare, this had been known to lead to recovery for alcoholics. So Jung advised Roland to place himself in a religious atmosphere and hope (pray) for the best. The "best" in fact occurred. The details of the story can be found in an exchange of letters between Bill W. and Jung, published in the AA magazine, *The Grapevine*.

In recounting this story many years later, Jung observed that unrecognized spiritual needs can lead people into great difficulty and distress. Either "real religious insight or the protective wall of human community is essential to protect man from this." In talking specifically of Roland H., Jung wrote: "His craving for alcohol was the equivalent on a low level, of the spiritual thirst of our being for wholeness, expressed in medieval language; the union with God."

You would be hard pressed to find a drinker who would equate his use of alcohol with a search for God! Heaven only knows they are too sophisticated, too contemporary, too scientific for that. Yet an objective examination of their use of alcohol may reveal otherwise. Alcohol is viewed as a magical potion, with the drinker expecting it to do the miraculous.

Counselor's role

If convinced that there is a spiritual dimension that may be touched by both alcoholism and recovery, what do you as a counselor do? First, we recommend cultivating some clergy in your area. It seems many communities have at least one member of the clergy who has stumbled into the alcohol field. And we do mean stumbled. It wasn't a deliberate, intellectual decision. It may have occurred through a troubled parishioner who's gotten well, or one whom the clergyman couldn't tolerate watching drink himself to death any longer and so blundered his way through an intervention, or he has gotten involved with alcoholics and finds more and more showing up on his doorstep for help. This is the one you want. If you can't find him, find one you are comfortable talking with about spiritual or religious issues. That means one with whom you don't feel silly or awkward and, equally important, who doesn't squirm in his seat either at talk of spiritual issues. (Mention of God and religion can get people, including some clergy, as uncomfortable as talk of drinking can!)

Once you find a resource person, it's an easy matter to provide your client with an opportunity to talk with him. One way to make the contact is to simply suggest the client sit down and talk with Joe Smith, who happens to be a Catholic priest, or whatever. It may also be worth pointing out to the client that the topic of concern is important and the individual mentioned may be helpful in sorting it out. Set up the appointment and let the clergyman take it from there. Some residential programs include a clergyman as a resource person. He may simply be available to counsel with clients, or he may take part in the formal program, for example, by providing a lecture in the educational series. But his presence and availability gives the message to clients that matters of the spirit are important and not silly.

How do you recognize the person for whom spiritual counseling may be useful? First off, let's assume you've found a clergyman who doesn't wag a finger, deliver hellfire and brimstone lectures, or pass out religious tracts at the drop of a hat. He's a warm, caring, accepting, and supportive individual. A chat with someone like that isn't going to hurt anyone. So don't worry about inappropriate referrals. Nonetheless, there are some persons for whom the contact may be particularly meaningful. Among these are persons who have a spiritual or religious background but are not experiencing it as a source of support, but rather as a condemnation. Others may, in their course of

Temperate temperance is best. Intemperate temperance injures the cause of temperance.

MARK TWAIN

sobriety, be conscientiously attempting to work the AA program, but have some problem that is hanging them up. Another group who may experience difficulty are Jewish alcoholics. "Everyone knows Jews don't become alcoholics." This presents a problem for those who do. It's been said there is double the amount of denial and consequent guilt for them. Since the Jewish religion is practiced within the context of a community, there may also be a doubled sense of estrangement. A contact with a rabbi may be very important. It is worth pointing out that someone can be culturally or ethnically Jewish, but not have been religiously Jewish. The intrusion of an alcohol problem may well provide the push to the Jewish alcoholic to explore his spiritual heritage. The alcohol counselor is advised to be sensitive to this and supportive.

The counselor, as an individual, may or may not consider spiritual issues important personally. What the caregiver needs is an awareness of the possibility (even probability) of this dimension's importance to a client and a willingness to provide the client with a referral to an appropriate individual.

RELAXATION THERAPY/MEDITATION

A recovering alcoholic is likely to face a multitude of problems. One of these is a high level of anxiety. It can be of a temporary nature, the initial discomfort with his nondrinking life, or more chronic if he's the "nervous" type. Whether temporary or chronic, it is a darned uncomfortable state, and the alcoholic has a *very* low tolerance for it. Many alcoholics have used alcohol for the temporary and quick relief of anxiety. What is now remembered (and longed for!) is the almost instant relief of a large swig of booze. When alcohol or drugs are no longer an option, the alcoholic has quite a problem: how to deal with anxiety. Many simply "sweat it out"; some relapse over it.

Relaxation

There are some positive things that can be done to alleviate their anxiety, or anyone's, for that matter. One is relaxation therapy. It is based on the fact that if the body and breathing are relaxed, it is impossible to *feel* anxious. The mind rejects the paradox of a relaxed body and a "tense" mind. Working with this fact, some techniques evolved to counter anxiety with relaxation. Generally, the therapist vocally guides a person through a progressive tensing and relaxing of the various body parts. The relaxing can start with the toes and work up, or with the scalp and work down. The process involves first tensing the muscles, then relaxing them at the direction of the therapist. These directions are generally given in a modulated, soft voice. When the client is quite relaxed, a soothing picture is suggested for him to hold in his mind. The client is then given a tape of the process to take home, with instructions on its use, as an aid in learning the relaxation. With practice, the relaxed state is achieved more easily and quickly. In some cases, he may finally learn to totally relax with just the thought of the "picture." Once thoroughly learned, the relaxation response can be substituted for anxiety at will. Relaxation therapy is a very useful type of behavior modification. It is often used to aid people to overcome an abnormal fear, such as a fear of crowds. It would be helpful to find someone experienced in this kind of therapy to recommend to your clients who are particularly anxious or nervous.

Meditation

Although meditation has different goals, depending on the type practiced, the process of reaching a meditative state is somewhat similar to relaxation. A fairly relaxed state is necessary before meditation can begin. Some schools of meditation use techniques quite similar to relaxation methods as a lead-in to the meditation period. In yoga, there are physical exercises coupled with mental suggestions as a precursor. Studies have shown that altered physiological states accompany meditation or deep relaxation. Altered breathing patterns and different brain wave patterns are examples. These changes are independent of the type of meditation practiced. The real physical response in part accounts for the feelings of well-being after meditation periods. Those who practice meditation find it, on the whole, a rewarding experience. Many also find in the experience some form of inspiration or spiritual help. There are several highly advertised schools of meditation receiving attention these days. You might investigate those which are available for clients who express an interest in meditation.

A word of caution. Alcoholics tend to go overboard. Meditation should never be a substitute for their other prescribed treatment. Also, there are extremists in every area of life, and meditation is no exception to exploitation. That is why some personal knowledge of what is available, who's using it, and how it affects those who do use it is necessary before advising your alcoholic client to try it. Meditation is only helpful if it alleviates the alcoholic's anxiety and allows him to continue learning how to function better *in* the world, not out of it.

What is a meditation?

Perhaps a meditation is a daydream, a daydream of the soul as the beloved and God, the lover, their meeting in the tryst of prayer, their yearning for one another after parting; a daydream of their being united again.

Or perhaps a meditation is the becoming aware of the human soul of its loneliness and the anticipation of its being united with the One who transcends the All and is able to come past one's own defenses.

Or perhaps, again, it is a standing back with the whole of the cosmos before one's mind's eye as one's heart is being filled with the sheer joy of seeing the balance of the All and one's own self as part of it.

Or perhaps a searching into one's own motives, values, and wishes, with the light of the Torah against the background of the past.

Or perhaps . . .*

BEHAVIORAL THERAPY

The terms *behavioral therapy* and *behavior modification* have been bandied about by many folks, some of whom are poorly informed about them. Here we would like to give you a brief rundown of the pertinent factors, plus point out some of the things that have muddied the waters. Unfortunately, in too many facilities the terms have been used so casually and imprecisely that what is being discussed is not correctly termed behavior modification at all.

Obviously, any therapy has as its goal the modification of behavior. However, behavioral therapy is the clinical application of the principles psychologists have discovered about how people learn. The basic idea is that if a behavior can be learned, it can also be changed. This can be done in

*From Siegel, R., Strassfeld, M., and Strassfeld, S. *The Jewish Catalogue.* Philadelphia: The Jewish Publication Society of America, 1973.

several ways. To put it very simply, one way is to introduce new and competing behavior in place of the old or unwanted behavior. By using the principles by which people learn, the new behavior is reinforced (the person experiences positive results), and the old behavior is in effect "squeezed out." Another technique is to negatively reinforce (punish) the unwanted behavior; therefore it becomes less frequent. Recall the discussion of Johnson's model for the development of drinking behavior in Chapter 6. That explanation was based on learning principles. People *learn* what alcohol can do; alcohol can be counted on in anyone's early drinking career to have dependable consequences.

Behavioral therapy is a field of psychology that has been developing rapidly over the past fifteen years. In the course of this development, several techniques have been devised that have been used in the treatment of alcoholism.

Historically, one of the first behavioral methods to be used in alcohol treatment was *aversion therapy.* In this case, a form of punishment was used to modify behavior. The behavior was drinking and the goal was abstinence. Electric shock and chemicals were the things primarily used. The alcoholic would be given something to drink and as he swallowed the alcohol, the shock would be applied. Or a drug similar to disulfiram would induce sickness. The procedure was repeated periodically until it was felt that the drinking was so thoroughly associated with unpleasantness in the subject's mind that he would be unlikely to continue drinking alcohol. Although short-term success was assured, the results over the long haul have been questioned. As Miller writes in "A Comprehensive Behavioral Approach to the Treatment of Alcoholism": "Historically there have been many fads in the treatment of alcoholism. . . . Behavioral therapists have also been guilty of this faddism in the form of aversion therapy. There is a recent awareness on the part of behavior therapists that this rather naive approach to a complex clinical problem such as alcoholism is unwarranted."

Aversion therapy of this form is now used very rarely. More effective behavioral approaches have been developed. Also it has become well accepted that an effective behavioral treatment program cannot be based on a single behavioral technique. Nor can one expect all patients to be

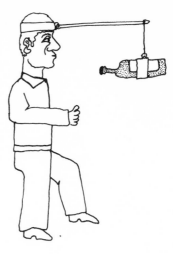

Eat not to fullness; drink not to elevation.

BENJAMIN FRANKLIN

successfully treated by the routine application of the same procedure. Just as not all patients are given the same kind and dose of a medication, neither can they be given the same behavioral treatment; a careful individual assessment is required for both.

Complex behavior needs complex treatment

Alcoholism is now being seen not as a single behavior, but as a complex set of behaviors. Therefore, a variety of techniques would be expected to be used in its treatment. Thus, behavioral therapists believe that a very detailed assessment is required to develop a treatment program that will meet the needs of the individual.

Two of the most widely used groups of techniques today are those based on *systematic desensitization* and behavior modification through *positive reinforcement*. Systematic desensitization is a technique earlier discovered to be effective in the treatment of phobias and anxieties. In a set of exercises the client approaches a situation in his imagination that leads to anxiety. As the anxiety builds up, he is directed to use relaxation techniques he has been taught. Gradually, going step by step, he uses the relaxation to turn off the anxiety, and eventually the situation itself becomes much less anxiety provoking. In alcohol treatment, this approach has been used for persons whose drinking has been partially prompted by stressful, anxiety-producing situations. The theory is that by providing the alcoholic with another coping behavior besides drinking, he will have other alternatives open to him.

Behavior modification by positive reinforcement is based on the assumption that a reward system to reinforce nondrinking behavior would thereby reduce the chances of drinking. It also recognizes that some rewards are involved with alcoholic drinking and something else positive needs to be substituted. Within residential treatment settings, these techniques might include making privileges contingent on the client's behavior in other areas, such as participating in treatment activities or going to AA. For outpatient work, this approach may be used to foster better family functioning. For example, positive rewards such as going to a movie, going out to dinner, or fishing on a Saturday afternoon can be agreed on as payoffs for the family as they try to develop new behaviors.

Behavioral techniques are becoming more widely used in reestablishing or developing social skills. One example of this is assertiveness training, which can be used to help alcoholics learn how to refuse drinks under social pressure. The relaxation techniques described earlier are also based on behavioral techniques.

Behavioral therapy is a skill just as are other kinds of therapy. Reading one or two articles on behavioral approaches doesn't make one a skilled behavioral therapist, any more than reading a medical journal turns someone into a physician! The techniques can be very helpful in focusing effectively on a particular circumscribed area of difficulty that an alcoholic is having, such as with anxiety. Although not every alcohol treatment facility will have a behavioral therapist on the staff to make an assessment and prescribe a program to intervene, they are available in many mental health clinics or other social service agencies. A referral may be helpful. With this consultation and direction by the therapist, you may well find that the client is better able to use the other forms of treatment.

DISULFIRAM (ANTABUSE)

In the late 1940s, by a series of accidents, a group of Danish scientists discovered that a drug they were testing for other purposes, disulfiram, led to a marked reaction when alcohol was ingested by a person who had taken it. Disulfiram chemically alters the metabolism of alcohol by blocking out an enzyme necessary for the breakdown of acetaldehyde, an intermediate product of alcohol metabolism. Acetaldehyde is normally present in the body in small amounts, in somewhat larger ones when alcohol is ingested, and in toxic amounts when alcohol is taken into the body after disulfiram medication.

This adverse physical reaction is characterized by throbbing in the head and neck, flushing, breathing difficulty, nausea, vomiting, sweating, tachycardia (rapid heartbeat), weakness, and vertigo. The intensity of the reaction can vary from person to person and varies with the amount of disulfiram present and the amount of alcohol taken in. Disulfiram is excreted slowly from the body, so the possibility of a reaction is present for four to five days after the last dose and in some cases longer. Because of this reaction, Antabuse, the trade name for disulfiram, has been widely used in the treatment of alcoholism.

Prescription, administration, and use

Over the years since disulfiram's discovery, trial and error and research have led to some suggestions for its prescription, administration, and use in alcohol treatment. Disulfiram is not a *cure* for alcoholism. At best, it can only postpone the drink for the alcoholic. If he chooses to use disulfiram as an adjunct to AA, psychotherapy, group therapy, etc., it can be most useful in helping him *not* take an impulsive drink. Since it stays in the system for such a long time, whatever caused the impulsive desire for a drink can be looked at. It possibly could be worked through during the five-day grace period to forestall the need for the drink entirely.

Anyone who wishes to use it should be allowed to do so, provided he is physically and mentally able. The client should first be thoroughly examined by a physician to determine his physical state. Some conditions contraindicate disulfiram usage. There is still some debate as to the need for such caution on the newer prescribed lower dosages, but only the client's doctor can decide this point. In many cases physicians consider the risks of a disulfiram reaction not as dire as continued drinking certainly would be. Its administration should usually be supervised for at least a time. Preferably the spouse should *not* be the one expected to do this. Ideally, a visit to an outpatient clinic for the doses is desirable. Also, ideally, it should be used in combination with other support therapies.

The client taking disulfiram should be thoroughly informed of the dangers of a possible reaction. He should be provided with a list of substances (such as cough syrup, wine sauces, paint fumes, etc.) that contain some alcohol and can cause a reaction. The person should carry a card or wear a med-alert disk stating he is taking disulfiram. Some medications given to accident victims or in emergency situations could cause a disulfiram reaction compounding whatever else is wrong. There is no way to be able to tell if an unconscious person has been taking disulfiram without such a warning.

A client who wishes to use disulfiram often begins taking the drug in a hospital setting after primary detoxification. Generally, one tablet (0.5 Gm) daily for five days is given, then half a tablet daily thereafter. During the initial five days the patient is carefully monitored for side effects.

Once the client is receiving the maintenance dose, he can continue for as long as he and his therapist feel it to be beneficial.

Disulfiram seems also to free the alcoholic's mind from the constant battle against the bottle. When someone decides to take the pill on a given day, he has made one choice which will postpone that drink for at least four or five days. If he continues to take it daily, that fourth or fifth day is always well out ahead. He can then begin to acquire or relearn behaviors other than drinking behaviors, and the habits of sobriety can take hold.

Disulfiram has been described as a crutch (which is not really out of place when one's legs are impaired!). Instead, one might think of it as a way of buying sober time until the alcoholic's "legs" are steadier and other healthy supports are found. The supports may be available already, but the alcoholic has to be able to use them successfully. Until then, these supports would fit him no better than a basketball player's crutch would fit a 10-year-old boy!

RESOURCES AND FURTHER READING

Albrect, Gary. The alcoholism process: a social learning viewpoint. In P. G. Bourne and R. Fox (Eds.), *Alcoholism progress in research and treatment.* New York: Academic Press, Inc., 1973.

Alcoholics Anonymous. New York: Alcoholics Anonymous Publishing, 1955.

Blum, Eva, and Blum, Richard. *Alcoholism: modern psychological approaches to treatment.* San Francisco, Calif.: Jossey-Bass, Inc., Publishers, 1972.

P. G. Bourne and R. Fox (Eds.). *Alcoholism progress in research and treatment.* New York: Academic Press, Inc., 1973.

Clinebell, Howard. *Understanding and counseling the alcoholic.* New York: Abingdon Press, 1968.

Coudert, Jo. *The alcoholic in your life.* New York: Warner Paperbacks, 1974.

Fox, Ruth. Disulfiram (Antabuse) as an adjunct in the treatment of alcoholism. In R. Fox (Ed.), *Alcoholism: behavioral research and therapeutic approaches.* New York: Springer Publishing Co., Inc., 1967.

Johnson, Vernon. *I'll quit tomorrow.* New York: Harper & Row, Publishers, Inc., 1973.

Leach, Barry. Does Alcoholics Anonymous really work? In P. G. Bourne and R. Fox (Eds.), *Alcoholism progress in research and treatment.* New York: Academic Press, Inc., 1973.

Miller, Peter. A comprehensive behavioral approach to the treatment of alcoholism. In Ralph Tarter and A. Arthur Sugerman (Eds.), *Alcoholism: interdisciplinary approaches to an enduring problem.* Reading, Mass.: Addison-Wesley Publishing Co., Inc., 1976.

Norris, John. Alcoholics Anonymous and other self-help groups. In Ralph Tarter and A. Arthur Sugerman (Eds.), *Alcoholism: interdisciplinary ap-*

proaches to an enduring problem. Reading, Mass.: Addison-Wesley Publishing Co., Inc., 1976.

Scarf, Maggie. Tuning down with T.M. *New York Times Magazine,* Feb. 9, 1975.

The drinking game and how to beat it. New York: Benco, 1970. (Distributed by the National Council on Alcoholism.)

Thiebout, Harry. Surrender vs. compliance in therapy. *Quarterly Journal of Studies on Alcohol,* 1953, *14,* 58-68.

Wallace, John. Between Scylla and Charybdis: issues in alcoholism therapy. *Alcohol Health and Research World,* 1977, *4*(1), 15-22.

Wineberg, Jon. Counseling recovering alcoholics. (Reprints available from Hennepin County Alcoholism Program, Minneapolis.)

CHAPTER NINE Alcohol, plus

SUICIDE EVALUATION AND PREVENTION

The suicide rate in alcoholics is fifty-five times that of the general population. Before we all commit suicide ourselves over these statistics, we should look at why suicide and alcohol are related, and what we can do about it.

Types of suicide: succeeders, attempters, and threateners

For practical purposes, there are several different groups to be considered when examining suicide. *First* are the *succeeders*, those who succeed *and intended to.* Classically, these are lonely white men over 50 years of age or lonely teenagers. They use violent means such as a gun or hanging, and their methods are calculated and secretive. Second are those who succeed but *did not* intend to. These are the *attempters*. Classically they are white women, ages 20 to 40, often with interpersonal conflicts, whose "method" is pills, and whose action is an impulsive response. Attempters die by mistake or miscalculation. For example, they lose track of dosage, or something goes wrong with their plans for rescue. The attempter's intent is not so much to die, as to elicit response from the environment. Emergency room psychology, which dismisses this patient with a firm kick in the pants, is inappropriate. Someone who is trying to gain attention this way is in reality quite sick and deserves care. Third are the *threateners*, who use suicide as a lethal weapon: "If you leave me, I'll kill myself." They are often involved in a pathological relationship. These people usually do not follow through, but are frightened and guilt-ridden. It is a good idea for the therapist to challenge the threat and quickly remove the deadlock it has created.

Statistics and high-risk factors

The real statistic to keep in mind is that suicide is the second leading recorded cause of death in people under 18 or over 65. Sixty percent give some prior indication of their intent, thereby making it preventable. Typical indications might be "I have a friend . . .," "What would you think if . . .," stockpiling drugs, or giving away possessions. Take note of new behaviors as cues. For example, people doing things they have never done before may often indicate they have suddenly decided to commit suicide and are now at peace. Examples might be *suddenly* playing cards, dancing, or taking out the garbage when they have never made a practice of this before.

Certain high-risk factors should be identified if present: recent loss of a "loved" person; single, widowed, and/or childless people; people living in urban areas; being unemployed, nonreligious, or "oppressed." High-risk emotional factors include anger plus hopelessness, broken or pathological family/friend communications, and marital isolation. Verbal high-risk cues take the form of both direct statements: "I'm going to kill myself," or indirect indications: "I won't be around to give you any more trouble." People entering and *leaving* a depression are especially vulnerable, as are those with chronic illnesses like arthritis, high blood pressure, ulcers, and malignancies.

Fifty percent of all suicides are alcohol related. Several reasons explain this correlation. First, the chemical nature of alcohol tends to release certain brain areas from control. The guarding mechanisms are let down. Hidden thoughts and impulses are released. (You have all witnessed the intoxicated guy calling the boss an SOB.) Second, because of the chemical action of alcohol, a state is created wherein the integrative capacity of the brain is diminished. It is a condition of loss of aspects of memory, priorities, and concentration. Third, when alcohol is used as a medicine, it is unfortunately a good one to initially produce a mood of relaxation and pseudostability. In this state, people may think things are just the way they should be. They feel cool, calm, and collected. Suicide at this point may seem relevant and a good idea: "I'll just jump. It's the rational solution." More alcohol acts as a true depressant with obvious potential consequences. Finally, alcohol may also bring out psychological weakness. It may place people on the edge of reality, tip the scales, lead to loose associations, bring out psychosis, loosen normal fears, produce voices saying things like: "The thing to do is rid the world of you," or "The world is better off without you." In all these cases, alcohol acts as a catalyst, both physically and psychologically.

The most fertile ground for suicide is in cases of clinical depression. Most people who have the "blues" are not suicidal. They might think, "Gee, I wish I were dead, things are going so badly," or "I don't know how I'll make it. I might just drive off the road if things don't get better."

But things usually do get better. On the other hand, a clinical depression is characterized by a consistently low mood over a period of weeks, plus weight changes, sleep problems, and other physical symptoms. Pessimism is a part of the illness, just as fever is a part of the flu. Feelings of how bad things are are part of the depression. Depression, therefore, is bad enough alone, but combined with alcohol, it is a potent mix. "There is no way out." "I'm a bad person—the only way out is to kill myself."

How to ask

The therapist should *always* ask about suicide with any person who is depressed. The thing to remember is that we have never killed anybody *by* asking. We have certainly missed helping people we could have helped by *not* asking. There is no way to instigate a suicidal attempt by common sense asking. It will come as a relief to your clients if you do ask them. Use your own emotional barometer to find out whether they are depressed or whether they're sad. Check yourself in an interview every so often. Block out the client for a moment and ask, "How am I feeling right now? Am I sad, angry, scared? What am I feeling?" It is probably a pretty good barometer of how the client is feeling. The client often says he feels great; check your own gut reactions and trust them.

Ask every client about suicide, but let rapport develop first. Do not just have the client come in and immediately ask him intimate questions like "I'm Dr. G., how's your sex life?" or "Been hallucinating lately?" or "Hi—Wanna kill yourself?" He will probably want to kill *you*. Let rapport develop, and later say, "Now, we've talked about a lot of things these last twenty minutes. Have any of them ever gotten you to the point of feeling you couldn't go on any longer?" Don't leave it there; explain that when you say that, you mean suicide. Always say the word "suicide." Do not just ask clients if they ever thought of "throwing in the towel" or some other euphemism. They can take you pretty literally and might say, "Well, no. I dried myself pretty well this morning." You have to get yourself to say "suicide." Practice. It is not so easy to come right out and say it. The first few times it bombs something like this. "Gee, we've talked about a lot of things. Have any of them ever gotten you to the point of thinking about committing s--s--ah---s-th--." It's almost the kind of thing you need to practice in front of a mirror. "Su-i-cide. Suicide."

Clients may say, "Boy, you're kidding!" but it's not a hostile response. If anybody does say "Yes"—and he probably will tell you if he has been thinking about it—get as much information as you can. Then go on to say, "Well, when was the time you thought of it last?" "How about today?" Whenever the client was thinking of it last, find out what he was doing, how he thought about it, when he thought of it, and get his plans for it as specifically as possible. In cases of most serious intent, the client will probably say, "Well, not only have I been thinking of it today, but I've been cleaning my gun, it's in my car, my car's outside." In other words, get *all* the data.

What to do

Try to diffuse the situation psychologically and in a practical way. For instance, offer alternatives. Say something like, "On the other hand, what specific reasons do you have for living?" Try to get to a positive thing. Start initiating reasons to live. The more seriously depressed the client, the fewer reasons he will see to live. Remember, that's part of the illness. He will say, "Nothing," and cry. At that point, try to reiterate things he told you earlier about himself that are reasons to live—a child, a spouse, a business, or whatever. Give him the reason to live: "That child really needs you." If he doesn't come up with anything, give him sixty seconds to think of something—one reason—then support that enthusiastically; "You're right. Tremendous!" Back the client up! Fill in the picture, and lead him into ways he can do this practically. If it is a child, for example, ask where the child is now. How can the parent be of help?

Another important thing is to make a referral, whenever possible, to a mental health clinic or mental health specialist. As a counselor, you have a key role in identifying potential suicides. You cannot expect yourself to single-handedly treat and manage the situation. Request a consultation for further evaluation. Possibly the person is in a real depression and needs the supervision of an inpatient facility and/or medications. So, call up and make an appointment *before* the client leaves the office. In conjunction with the mental health clinic, a decision can be made about how quickly the person should be seen—immediately, later to-

day, or tomorrow. If the client is already being seen by a therapist, contact the therapist. A therapist who is unaware of the situation will want to know and will also be able to provide guidance for you, so that you are working together. Don't be afraid you are stepping on anyone's toes. Anybody contemplating suicide cannot have too many people in his corner.

In passing, maybe here we can lay to rest any discomfort that arises from the philosophical debates on whether someone has a right to commit suicide. Looking at it from the practical side of the issue, anyone who thinks he does will just up and do it. He wouldn't be in your office. Anyone who "happens" into a counselor's office, or phones, and acknowledges suicidal thoughts, directly or indirectly, is not there by chance. They are seeking help in settling their internal debate over life vs. death. The counselor, as do other helping people, must come down clearly on the side of living. Similarly, when depressed, a client cannot *rationally* make this decision. Once the depression clears, most clients are very pleased you prevented their action on suicide plans.

If a client has a weapon, ask him to check it at the reception desk (or elsewhere on the premises). If it's at home, ask him to have someone else take possession of it and notify you when that is done. *Never* let a client who is suicidal (he usually improves during the interview) leave your office without your double-checking all the great plans he has for the rest of the day. Be specific. Call home to make sure someone will be there if that's the expectation. Give the client chores and support. Get something for him to do. Have somebody there to watch him around the clock and to give him the attention he needs. Set up another appointment to see him within 48 hours. Have him call you to check in later that day, or you call him. Be specific. Say, "I'd like to call you between 4 and 5," or at least "this afternoon." It is better not to give an exact time because that's often hard to meet. This kind of paternalism is needed at this time. The weaning and fostering of independence comes later. Give reinforcements. "What do you like to do?" "What do you have to do?" "Do it and let me know how it goes."

The only times in talking with a client that you may precipitate something going wrong are the following three times. It's simple logic, but it's also a trap.

1. If the client's theme is rejection and loss, for example, he feels his mother's death shows she did not love him, be careful *you* do not reject him or put him off.

2. If you agree with the client about how bad things are, for example, the client says, "I am a worthless person. I beat my child," you may easily get into your own negative feelings about this. You might communicate "Well, you are right, that was a horrible thing to do." Do not crucify clients. Do not support their punitive guilt response.

3. The client says how bad he feels. You are tempted to say "I understand how badly you feel. I often feel that way myself." You're trying to sympathize and share his misery, but the client interprets this as permission to feel the way he does. You are getting away from the reasons the client has to live and are underscoring his pessimism. It is better to reinforce his reasons to live.

Other thoughts about evaluation and prevention come to mind. Get histories of previous suicide attempts. Anyone who has tried it once has a poor track record. A family history of suicide plus a broken home in childhood also increases the risk. With someone who has either attempted suicide or is thinking about it, reduce his isolation from family and friends. Consider hospitalization under close supervision if supports are lacking. Remove guns, ropes, pills, etc. Have him give you the weapon personally. Shake hands with the client as he leaves the office, and give him "something of yourself" to take with him to put in wallet or purse, such as a piece of paper with your name and phone number. Try to make sure the client has only a one- to two-day supply of medication and *no* barbiturates such as glutethimide (Doriden), ethchlorvynol (Placidyl), methyprylon (Noludar), methaqualone (Quāalude), meprobamate (Equanil, Meprospan, Miltown), or chloral hydrate. A seven-day supply, of tricyclic antidepressants (1,000 mg) or a five-day supply of meprobamate (Miltown) (8,000 mg) can be lethal.

Now a special situation. If you happen to get involved in an emergency where someone is about to shoot, jump, etc., try to be calm. Keep your voice down. Do not ask philosophical questions, but ask practical questions. "What's your name?" "Where are you from?" Try to have a nonthreatening conversation. This is a grueling situation and can last for hours. Wear the person down. *Do not ever be a hero.* Do not rush a person with a gun. Stay alive to help the people who can be helped.

Trust your gut reactions. Don't feel that if you are unsuccessful, it's your fault. Don't ever forget that your job with suicidal clients is not to be God. Being his helper is enough.

PSYCHIATRIC DIAGNOSES

Working with alcoholics brings you into contact with psychiatrists and other mental health professionals. Some of the terminology they use could be confusing. Words used in connection with diagnosis may be particularly so. The intent of this section is to review some of the major diagnoses, so that you will recognize them and have a general sense of what is implied by their usage.

Diagnosis begins with observation. In describing what you observe about a person, you are confronted with obvious limitations both in time and space. Clearly it is necessary to abbreviate or signify what you observe in a single word or phrase, so that communication with someone else is possible. Pulling together all your observations into a single idea or concept is the process of diagnosis. The diagnosis is the name you apply to what you see.

It is useful to think of observation as a process of hearing and seeing. We hear what someone tells us about what it is like for him. This is a report about his inner state, not an observation of the inner state itself. Although a person can tell us what he looks like, we can usually see for ourselves; hence, his appearance is not a report, but a direct observation. We are constantly comparing, especially in the process of diagnosis, what we see and what we hear. For example, when someone reports he is nervous and panicky inside, we often see increased color, sweating, and movement. What is heard and seen might be said to be consistent. On the other hand, if someone reports that he is depressed, but does so with a broad smile, this might seem inconsistent. This consistency (or lack of it) between what you see and what you hear is often important in judging the nature and severity of the situation.

In considering the many psychiatric diagnoses, it is possible to fit them into six main categories: retardation, dementia, psychoses, neuroses, character disorder, and situational reaction.

Retardation and dementia. These terms refer to a limitation of the ability to think about and respond to the environment meaningfully. These terms imply that the limitation is permanent, although special care can reduce this limitation. Retardation refers to this limitation as it appears in infants and children. Dementia refers to a limitation appearing in later life. In both cases, the limitation is based on diffuse damage to the brain. These diagnoses are relatively straightforward, usually based on the results of psychological testing. The lack of normal mental endowment has consequences for behavior. Generally, someone who is retarded or demented is less skilled in all areas. He is not as skilled in presenting his thoughts, in handling feelings, and in dealing with complex emotional situations. Although retardation and dementia are psychiatric diagnoses, they can also become a label, attached to someone as closely as his name. This certainly has an impact. It can alter how someone is treated, and alter his perceptions of himself. While words such as retardation or dementia can convey information and thus facilitate communication, they can also be an excuse for segregation and mistreatment.

Psychoses. *Psychosis* is a second major category. It refers to any disorder in which there is an observable disturbance of perception and function. Persons with a psychosis may be in significant disagreement with others as to what is reality. The psychotic individual has his own idiosyncratic notions of reality. Sitting in a room full of people, he might claim to be alone. Possibly, if we think of the statement in philosophical or poetic terms, it could make sense. However, as a statement of "fact" on which to base further interaction, it breaks down. Attempts to communicate are very difficult because the psychotic perceives reality very differently. This altered perception can be very subtle or very marked. The preference here is to think of it as a very gross disturbance. For example, suppose you were to see someone undressing in the parking lot outside your office, and then jumping on a car roof. Were you to ask why, a logical explanation might be given. But it wouldn't be an adequate explanation to get you to do it too. If the person is psychotic, the lingering question after the explanation would be, "But why are you doing *that?*" If

Dear, Are you sure this is Just A Scotch and Soda?

only the perception of reality were disturbed, then such persons would rarely come to our attention. However, there is also a disturbance of function. It's because we observe strange behavior that we inquire about someone's perceptions and belief about the world. Ordinarily, we simply don't challenge one another. For someone to qualify as psychotic, you should expect there would be fairly uniform agreement among others that he's not on the same wavelength, but instead is "nuts" or "really bouncing off the walls" to use some popular expressions.

What are the causes of psychoses? They can be divided into three major headings. The first is *organic brain syndrome*. An organic brain syndrome can result from any traumatic or toxic insult to the central nervous system. Acute alcohol intoxication, as an example, can lead to bizarre behavior. Other drugs, including prescription drugs, can also have an impact. Anything that impairs the function of the brain—too little oxygen, too much carbon dioxide, or a blow to the head—can cause organic brain syndrome. Treatment attempts to correct the underlying causes: if it's a tumor, surgery; if it's drugs, withdrawal.

Schizophrenia is another cause of a psychotic state. In contrast to organic brain syndrome, the schizophrenic tends not to be disoriented. That is, he knows who he is, where he is, the time, etc. Among psychiatrists, there is not 100% agreement as to the basic essentials that make up a diagnosis of schizophrenia. The usual requirements are the presence of faulty sensory perceptions that have no basis in reality, such as hearing voices no one else can hear. The schizophrenic would have to be *convinced* these sensory perceptions are true. As a response to these false perceptions, or hallucinations, false ideas may appear. The false ideas about reality are delusions. Since schizophrenia is a potent label, it is a diagnosis that should be made with care. A ten-minute interview wouldn't do, or possibly even an hour. Several observations over time would be necessary.

Affective illnesses are another basis for psychoses. Affect refers to mood and emotion; what you feel and how you show it. Here there are two extremes: people who are depressed, and those who are manic. People can fluctuate between these two extremes; this is called *bipolar illness*. People who are manic show characteristic behavior. Often they've grand schemes, which to others seem quite out-landish. Their conversation is very rapid, quick, pressured. Often they jump from topic to topic. If there were a conversation about the State of the Union, a manic person might say, "and, yes, New Hampshire is a very pretty state. Governor Thompson is the governor of the state, and the governor of my car is out of kilter. The left tire is flat, out of air like a balloon Suzy got at the circus. . . ." Although there is a logical connection between these thoughts, there's an inability to concentrate on one. Each thought is immediately crowded out by the next. Someone who is manic is often aggressive and irritable. They may feel themselves very attractive and sexually irresistable. Persons who are manic are perpetually in high gear and have difficulty sleeping. Simply being in their company might well make you feel exhausted.

Depression, which is the other side of the coin, has all the opposite characteristics. Rather than being hyped up, these people grind to a halt. Depressed people feel *very* down. Speech is slow, movements are slow. Rather than a flood of things, they say nothing. Biological changes can accompany depression: disturbances of the normal sleep pattern, constipation, retarded motor activity, loss of appetite. In severe depression, thoughts of suicide are not uncommon. The person feels worthless and can think of no reason to live. Whether extremely high as in mania, or very low as in depression, either way there's a distortion of reality.

The appropriate treatment of psychosis involves use of medications, either the antipsychotic agents, also called major tranquilizers, or the antidepressant agents. (A separate discussion on medications appears later in the chapter.) Psychoses simply do not lend themselves to psychotherapy. Talking therapies are of little use when someone's perception of reality and thought processes are so seriously altered.

Neuroses. A third major category of psychiatric disorders is the *neuroses.* Neurosis differs from all the other disorders. It's quite possible that a person with a neurosis would not be detected simply by his behavior, unless someone were a very sharp observer. There may be no observable signs. The key to neurosis is that something is *felt* to be wrong. The diagnosis is based on a self-report of distress, usually anxiety. Rather than other people saying, "Hey, you *act* strange," the neurotic says, "I *feel* strange." Why the strange feelings? To explain neuroses, the assumption must be made that there is an unconscious, which can express itself through feelings of something out of kilter. It is further assumed that if these hidden things are uncovered, the neurotic will feel better. Everyone has had the experience of forgetting, but with the proper stimulus, the light goes on. Freud felt that there was more to it than that. Painful things, things that are hard to deal with and cause inner conflict, are repressed—put into the unconscious—especially things from early childhood. These painful events continue to lurk about and can break through into consciousness in disguised form. The type of neurosis comes from the form the conflict takes as it breaks out.

In *anxiety neurosis*, the person is overwhelmed by indefinable fears and concerns. He finds himself apprehensive even though he is aware there is no particularly good reason for it. A person with an *obsessive-compulsive neurosis* finds himself continuing to do things he doesn't want to do. Yet he cannot *not* do them. *Hysterical neurosis* has a different meaning than our everyday use of the word hysterical. It does not mean to be highly excited or to have temper tantrums. Rather, in this context it refers to a physical problem that develops because of the unconscious conflict. Although there is no physical reason, someone may become blind or have a limb paralyzed. *Phobias* are another form of neurosis. Here all the unconscious conflict comes out in the fear of something such as open spaces, tall buildings, snakes, etc. How incapacitating this can be is a function of the type of fear and the person's surroundings. A fear of tall buildings could be crippling in New York City, but be minimally disturbing if home is rural New England. The most prevalent treatment for neurosis is some variety of psychotherapy.

Before moving on to the next category of psychiatric disorder, a word of caution. Neurosis is probably a label that could be properly ascribed to any of us. Each of us has some quirks of personality that may occasionally annoy us, but are not incapacitating. If I check the car at night to be sure the headlights are off, even though I am *sure* they are, that's neurotic behavior. But most likely I only need to check *once*. I might be annoyed at myself for doing this from time to time, but not sufficiently upset to enter therapy and have my neurotic trait treated.

Character disorder. *Character disorder* is a fourth classification of psychiatric illness. Here, the "symptom" is likely to be a nuisance and bother to others, but not to oneself. Unlike neurosis, there are observable behaviors and objective disturbance of function. This behavior is likely to get the person into trouble with others. The behavior is not psychotic or necessarily bizarre. It's more likely to be termed illegal, obnoxious, inconsiderate, or antisocial. Alcoholism, as well as drug addiction, is classified here. Excessive drinking and drug use are the behaviors that bring difficulties. Even if the alcoholic or drug addict is perfectly content, his behavior would still cause those about him to complain. *Sociopathy* is another variety of character or behavior disorder. At times it seems sociopath is a label used by people to show their anger. But there *are* people always out to con the rest of the world, disrespect laws, and whose motto is "every man for himself." Another variety of character disorder goes by the awful phrase *borderline character*. This, too, is an angry phrase, probably in response to feelings generated in the therapist by such clients. The borderline is characterized by impulsiveness, unreliability, vacillation, and ambivalence toward help. One day he comes in tearful, seeking assistance and support in getting his life in order. Two days later, he is off to California with a new lover. Four months later, again he returns to your doorstep.

The most effective single treatment of character or behavioral disorders is an intensive peer experience. The thought is that character disorder represents a life-style that is maladaptive. The best correction is an experience with others in the same boat, to learn together more effective ways of coping with the world. This includes things like AA, halfway houses, and drug rehabilitation houses.

Situational reaction. *Situational reaction* is the final category. This is not so much a diagnosis of illness as it is a statement of normal response to an abnormal situation. In a sense, there are an irreducible number of tragedies in life: deaths, illnesses, accidents. People at such times may well feel the need of outside assistance as they cope with the problematic situation. If the crisis response continues too long, such as someone actively grieving the death of a spouse a year later, then it might be suspected there are other things going on with the person. Treatment of situational adjustment reaction usually is some kind of psychotherapy.

In conclusion, psychiatric diagnosis is not an exact science. From time to time there may be differences of opinion. Yet diagnosis is based on behaviors that are usually observable. This section is meant to provide some guidelines as to what is meant by various diagnoses and what behaviors are associated with them.

MENTAL STATUS EXAMINATION

The mental status examination is one of the techniques used by psychiatrists and other mental health workers. The purpose is to guide observation and assist the interviewer in gathering essential data about mental functioning. It consists of standard items, which are routinely covered, ensuring nothing important is overlooked. The format also helps mental health workers record their findings in a fashion that is easily understood by their colleagues.

Three aspects of mental functioning are always included: mood and affect, thought processes, and cognitive functioning. Mood and affect refer to the dominant feeling state. They are deduced from general appearance, what the client reports, posture, body movement, and attitude toward the interviewer. Thought processes zero in on how the client presents his ideas. Are his thoughts ordered and organized, or does he jump all over the place? Are his sentences logical? Is the content (what he talks about) sensible, or does it include delusions and bizarre ideas? Finally, cognitive functioning refers to intellectual functioning, memory, ability to concentrate, comprehensions, and ability to abstract. This latter portion of the mental status examination involves asking specific questions, for example, about current events, definitions of words, or meanings of proverbs. The interviewer considers the individual's education, life-style, and occupation in making a judgment about the responses.

If the alcohol counselor can get some training in how to do a simple mental status examination, it can be helpful in spotting clients with particular problems. It can also greatly facilitate your communication with mental health workers. Just telling a psychiatrist the fellow you are referring to him is "crazier than a bedbug" isn't very useful.

MEDICATIONS

Alcoholism does not exist in a vacuum. Alcoholics, as do other people, have a variety of other problems: some physical, some mental. They may be receiving treatment

or treating themselves. The treatment probably involves drugs, prescribed or over the counter. The more one knows about drugs in general, the more helpful one can be to a client. Alcoholics in particular tend to seek instant relief from the slightest mental or physical discomfort. Taking a good drug history (even though it might be done conversationally) is a definite must in dealing with alcohol problems. Following are some of the questions you would want to have in mind: "What? Is it prescribed and when was it prescribed? Is the client following the prescription? Is he afraid of the drug? Is the drug having the desired effect or are the side effects canceling out the benefits? Should the physician be notified if the client is misusing the drug or mixing it with alcohol and possibly many other medications from several other doctors?" This is only a sample of the kind of information to be elicited.

There may be tremendous confusion surrounding drugs. Often this arises from a communication gap. The doctor prescribes a certain medication intended to have a particular effect on a particular patient. The patient is unclear (and usually doesn't question) what the purpose is. He takes the drug without letting the physician know, in fact, what is occurring. Every drug has multiple simultaneous actions. Only a few of these effects are being sought when any drug is prescribed. These intended effects are called *therapeutic effects*. All other effects would be the side effects in that instance. In selecting a medication for a patient, the doctor seeks a drug with the maximum therapeutic impact and minimal side effects. Only feedback from the patient enables the doctor to make adjustments, if necessary. The regimen for taking a drug is as important as what is taken. There's a good reason for specifying before or after meals, for example. Often, as the patient begins to feel better, he stops or cuts the dosage of prescribed drugs. One danger in this is that he's taken enough of a drug for relief of symptoms, but not enough to remove the underlying cause. Any client should be encouraged to consult with his physician *before* altering the way he takes his medications. Since treatment requires good communication, he should be helped to ask any questions about his treatment and the drugs involved.

Psychotropic drugs

The group of medications with which the alcohol counselor may have frequent contact are the *psychotropic drugs*.

Any drug that acts on the mind, thereby influencing behavior or mood, falls into this category. These drugs are likely to be of the greatest concern to the counselor. At the same time, they may be the most widely misunderstood. There is no denying that psychotropic drugs are widely prescribed. During 1974, 24% of the population took some form of psychotropic medication. Two years prior to that, 144 million prescriptions were written for minor tranquilizers alone, just one subgroup of the psychotropic drugs. Few persons would deny that such drugs are not only widely prescribed, but *over*prescribed. Because of their mood-altering properties, such medications may be candidates for abuse. "Down with drugs" is not apt to be an effective banner for a counselor, however. All psychotropic medications are not alike. Each has its appropriate use. Not all are uniformly potential problems for clients. Consequently, a counselor is well advised to become familiar with the major types of psychotropic drugs and their appropriate uses.

A discussion of the three major categories of psychotropic drugs follows. Each has a different combination of actions and is properly prescribed for different reasons. These are the antipsychotic agents, antidepressant agents, and antianxiety agents.

The *antipsychotic* drugs are also called the *major tranquilizers.* This second name isn't really a very good way to describe their action. It's probably introduced confusion for 'the layman, but the phrase sticks. Antipsychotic agents, as the name implies, are drugs that relieve the symptoms of psychoses. In addition to the antipsychotic effect, these drugs also have a tranquilizing and a sedative action. They calm behavior and induce drowsiness. Different drugs in this group have differing balances of the three actions. The drug prescribed would be selected on the basis of the patient's constellation of symptoms. Thus a drug with greater sedative effects might well be selected for a person exhibiting psychotic and agitated behavior.

The antipsychotic medications most frequently encountered are listed below.

I don't care if he's a colonel. He still needs a major tranquilizer.

Brand name	Generic name	Daily dosage range (mg)
Thorazine	Chlorpromazine	100-1,000
Mellaril	Thioridazine	30-800
Stelazine	Trifluoperazine	2-30
Trilafon	Perphenazine	2-64
Navane	Thiothixene	6-60
Haldol	Haloperidol	3-50

These drugs interact with alcohol. Some possible effects include raising the seizure threshold and slowing the metabolism of alcohol.

On occasion, an antipsychotic agent will be prescribed, not to relieve psychotic symptoms, but for its sedative or tranquilizing properties. This is because these preparations are less likely to be abused than the usual sedatives or antianxiety agents. Generally it is safe to assume persons whom these drugs have been prescribed for are thought to have, or to have had, a serious disorder. Medication may be prescribed not only during an acute phase, but afterward, to maintain an adequate level of functioning.

In working with alcoholics, a justified concern centers on the possible abuse of additional drugs. The abstinent alcoholic is less likely to abuse these medications than some other types of psychotropic drugs. These compounds are not chemically similar to alcohol and are therefore not subject to cross-tolerance or addiction.

The *antidepressants*, another major class of psychotropic drugs, do just what the name implies. They are used to treat the biological component of depression. They are not intended to help someone who is simply having a blue day. It takes a period of time of regular use for these medications to have their full action. Therefore, not an uncommon initial complaint of patients is that the medicine isn't helping. Commonly experienced side effects are sedation and tranquilization. These are most pronounced when the person first begins taking the drug. The physician may choose to have the patient take the drug at bedtime, so the sedation effect will not interfere with daytime function.

The most common antidepressants follow.

Brand name	Generic name	Daily dosage range (mg)
Tofranil	Imipramine	75-150
Elavil	Amitriptyline	75-150
Aventyl	Nortriptyline	75-200

There is no clear evidence that antidepressant agents are addicting. Again, in combination with alcohol, problems can rise with additive effects.

Lithium carbonate is worth special mention. Dissimilar to the antidepressants in chemical composition, it is nonetheless the mainstay of treatment in manic-depressive illness. Lithium has been invaluable in the control and leveling of wide mood swings associated with this illness. The dosage is geared to body weight, and the level of lithium is monitored periodically through blood samples. Any patient taking lithium should be seeing his physician regularly. An insufficient level of lithium will not help in control of symptoms. With too high a level, the patient may have a toxic reaction. Although it is unclear how lithium works, not only does it help during an acute episode, but just as importantly it reduces or prevents the intensity of subsequent episodes. Any patient taking lithium should be strongly advised to consult his physician if he is considering stopping this medication. Lithium is not a psychoactive drug that is at all likely to be abused by the patient.

The final group of psychotropic drugs are the *antianxiety agents*. Drugs in this class, along with barbiturates, are the ones most likely to be trouble for alcoholics. The major action of these drugs is to promote tranquilization and sedation. Quite properly, alcohol can be included in any list of drugs in this class. The *antianxiety* agents are also called the *minor tranquilizers*. They have no antipsychotic or significant antidepressant properties. Two of the top three most widely prescribed drugs in the United States are antianxiety agents: Librium and Valium. Most of these prescriptions are *not* written by psychiatrists but by general practitioners, surgeons, internists, and orthopedists.

Alcohol and the minor tranquilizers in combination potentiate one another. Because of their similar pharmacology, they are also virtually interchangeable. It's simply a matter of getting the correct dosage. This phenomenon is the basis of cross-addiction. Thus, Librium becomes an excellent drug to manage withdrawal from alcohol and for detoxification. Essentially, the Librium is substituted for the alcohol, and then the patient tapered off the Librium. This interchangeability with alcohol is what makes Librium a very poor drug for alcoholics except for detoxification purposes. There is always the danger of creating an additional dependency.

The most common antianxiety agents follow.*

Brand name	Generic name	Daily dosage range (mg)
Librium	Chlordiazepoxide	10-100
Valium	Diazepam	6-40
Equanil, Miltown	Meprobamate	600-1,200
Atarax, Vistaril	Hydroxyzine	30-100

*We have lumped the antianxiety agents together for the purpose of this discussion. However, there are differences among them based on their chemical composition that have significance if abuse occurs. These will be elaborated on in the following section.

In the main, Americans are very casual about drugs. Too often, prescribed drugs are not taken as directed, are saved up for the "next" illness, or are shared with family and friends. If the attitude toward prescription drugs is so casual, over-the-counter preparations are treated as candy. Because a prescription is not required does not render these preparations harmless. Some possible ingredients of over-the-counter drugs are antihistamines, codeine, scopolamine, and of course alcohol. These can cause difficulty if taken in combination with alcohol. Or they may themselves be targets of abuse.

In working with clients, a good drug history is imperative. You probably can't attack the national problem of casual drug use. But you can aid your client by helping him sort out his medications and discuss his drug use with his physician.

POLYDRUG USE

There is increasing concern about polydrug use and abuse. This refers to simultaneous use of different mood-altering drugs, either one with another, or another drug in combination with that all-time favorite, alcohol. Different patterns of multiple drug use might be identified. One is most common among teenagers (or was several years ago). Naive drug users, they often took whatever was available, without particular regard for, or knowledge of, the specific effects. There were reports of teenage parties with "fruit salad." "Fruit salad" was a bowl of pills, with each guest contributing whatever he could glean from the family medicine cabinet. In what, to us, sounds like chemical roulette, the kids would take a handful of pills and supposedly "turn on" for the evening. From time to time, emergency rooms would be confronted with sick kids who had ingested unknown drugs in unknown quantities. This is polydrug abuse, although admittedly not the variety you are most likely to encounter.

Another form of polydrug abuse does not involve simultaneous use, but sequential use or abuse. Generally, people have their drug of choice, whether it is licit or a street drug. However, if what they want is unavailable, they will use something else that is—just like the cigarette smoker who is forced to settle for another brand when the vending machine is out of "his brand." It's only a temporary switch.

Then there are the folks who use multiple drugs in an attempt to achieve different particular moods or feeling states. You name the mood, and they have a formula of drugs in combination to achieve it. This may mean uppers in the morning, downers to unwind later in the day, drugs to counteract fatigue, drugs to promote sleep, drugs to feel "better." Those most likely to get into this drug use pattern are persons with relatively easy access to drugs: nurses, physicians, pharmacists, and their spouses. This does not imply the medications are being stolen. Easy access can mean asking someone to write you a prescription as a favor. Anyone who works near the health care system or knows a physician is likely to make an informal request at some point. It may be for the birth control pills you didn't realize had run out, or poison ivy lotion, or just a few Librium because you are under a lot of stress now. Although the dynamics of this type of drug use have not been adequately described, in all probability it starts out innocently. The aim is not to get high, but to cope. Accustomed to the use of medications, often working at a pace beyond reasonable expectations for mere mortals, people may try a little chemical assistance to get by. Despite all their book knowledge of pharmacology, before they know it, they are in trouble. The drugs are no longer something to be used in special situations; they are essential for simply existing. Alcohol may well become a part of this picture.

It should be added that persons who work in the alcohol field are no more immune than anyone else. The intake worker who relieves the incoming client of his booze and pills may very quickly acquire an impressive stash in the desk drawer. Or there are the workers who dispense medication. One for the client every four hours, and occasionally one for me?

It is our impression that the most frequent polydrug use does not involve illicit drugs or fit the patterns just described. Although alcohol workers all know of some horror story in which other drug use developed from injudicious use of medication prescribed as a part of identified alcohol treatment, this appears to be becoming increasingly less common. Yet polydrug use is reportedly on the rise. It is our suspicion that much polydrug use involving alcohol begins when people in the early stages of alcoholism start to ride the doctor circuit, in search of a physical answer to their problems. The complaint may be "nerves," "headaches," or "sensitive stomach," coupled with other vague complaints. These people do not go to their physicians deliberately trying to con them into a prescription. They truly want to be fixed up. Their drinking may not even look that different. Quite possibly the budding alcoholic may openly tout alcohol as a Godsend, given how he feels.

> PHYSICIAN (dutifully taking the drinking history): How much do you drink?
>
> PATIENT: Oh, not too much, mostly when I go out socially.
>
> PHYSICIAN: How much is that, and how often?
>
> PATIENT: Oh, not much, one or two drinks at a party, on occasion a cocktail before dinner. But I tell you, these headaches have been murder. And I've sometimes said, "I may not be a drinker, but I will be if they continue."
>
> PHYSICIAN: They're that bad . . .

It all sounds straightforward. Our friend has tests done; nothing emerges to pin the headaches on. He is reporting stress at work, and eventually he walks out of the doctor's office with a prescription for a minor tranquilizer. This fellow may be headed for trouble.

Or there may be the patients who have always been high-strung "nervous types", who are likely to get flapped easily. Somewhere along the line, they got some pills for their nerves. These pills just work wonders. They like to have a supply handy, "just in case." These patients often become quite skilled in reporting symptoms to ensure the pill bottle in the medicine cabinet is always full. In this day of medical specialists, they might be seeing more than one doctor. And they may have each one writing the same prescription. As time goes on, the occasions warranting a pill become more numerous. Alcohol can come in here also. They simply may not be told of the dangers of mixing the medications with alcohol. Or they may dismiss the information if they are told. They are rarely informed of the time required to metabolize the drug from the system (or alcohol, for that matter) and simply think, "Oh, I took that two hours ago. A drink wouldn't hurt now!" This is a frequently seen phenomenon. After all, how many people do you know who believe alcohol is a terrific way to calm the nerves?

Withdrawal

Just as tolerance develops for alcohol, so too can tolerance develop for some other psychotropic medications, especially barbiturates, sedatives, and the minor tranquilizers. More are required to keep doing the same job. Add to this the all-American viewpoint that discomfort is pointless when chemical comfort is only a swallow away. With the development of tolerance, withdrawal syndromes may accompany abstinence. Several of these will be briefly described.

Barbiturates have been around since the beginning of this century. Central nervous system depressants, like alcohol, they have an abstinence syndrome very similar to alcohol's. At lower doses, withdrawal symptoms will most likely be limited to anxiety and tremulousness. At high levels, more serious withdrawal symptoms may develop. These can include convulsions and a "DT-like" syndrome of delirium, disorientation, hallucinations, and severe agitation. Barbiturate withdrawal presents a medical situation as serious, and potentially as life threatening, as that accompanying alcohol withdrawal.

Drugs included within the category of minor tranquilizers can be subdivided into different groups depending on their chemical compositions. These differences are important when it comes to withdrawal and potential problems of abuse. Librium and Valium both belong to the subgroup known as the benzodiazepines. When drugs of this subgroup are abused, withdrawal symptoms may be present if use is abruptly stopped. Withdrawal symptoms can include tremulousness, sweating, and possibly convulsions. A full-blown "DT-like" picture is *not* associated with the benzodiazepines. For other subgroups of drugs in the minor tranquilizers category, withdrawal can be much more serious. Be particularly alert to abuse of Miltown or Equanil, the brand names of meprobamate, Doriden (a glutethimide), and Quāālude (methaqualone); withdrawal syndromes for these can be as dangerous as those associated with alcohol or barbiturates. (Doriden and Quāālude have hypnotic, sleep-inducing properties and may have been prescribed for sleep. Don't overlook "just a few sleeping pills" in pursuing a drug history.)

Combine physical dependence on alcohol along with dependence on another drug, and the problems of detoxification are increased. Actually the task confronting the physician is to manage detoxifications. That is what is done, sequential detoxification, withdrawal of one drug at a time.

Medical management can be a very delicate process in these situations. It is critical for multiple dependencies to be identified when someone first enters treatment. If alcohol detoxification is not going smoothly, the first question to be asked is: "Are there other drugs involved?"

Active alcoholics—other drug use

Multidrug use does not have importance only in terms of detoxification. It clearly has an impact on the drinking career. One observation is that the alcoholism process is accelerated when other drug use is present. This would not be unexpected, since the liver is the organ involved in the metabolism of many drugs. But more rapid physical deterioration is not the only problem. Depending on the drugs involved, there can be difficulties of a more acute nature on any drinking occasion. The effects may be additive, so there will be increased central nervous system depression. This can be a life-threatening situation.

In addition to physical problems that can occur with alcohol and other drug use, there are other difficulties for the active alcoholic. There are any number of ways the alcoholic can use other drugs. One way is to use other drugs to maintain and control the drinking. (Alcohol is the drug of choice.) Along the line, the alcoholic may have learned the warning signs of alcoholism. So by using pills, alcohol consumption may be maintained within what the drinker has decided are safe limits. What would *really* hit the spot would be a nice, stiff drink before a meeting. But instead the drinker settles for a capsule. He doesn't drink during the day, so he doesn't consider himself an alcoholic. So drug use can help the alcoholic keep alcohol use within "acceptable" limits. The drinking career can thereby, in his mind, be managed and extended.

Another pitfall is that other drug use can prevent the reality of the alcohol problem from sinking in. The minor tranquilizers are also known as the antianxiety agents. It might be said that anxiety is what will eventually move the alcoholic near treatment. This happens when his problems are such that he cannot explain them away or successfully drink them away, when the pain is no longer alcohol soluble. A little digression on anxiety. Anxiety, it seems to us, has been getting an unduly harsh press. Some anxiety is essential for normal, healthy functioning. It's an internal signal

of potential danger and at times is essential for the preservation of life. The antianxiety agents, by turning off anxiety, may create a false sense of well-being. The individual using antianxiety agents will still intellectually know what is happening, but the emotional impact is blunted. The active alcoholic has plenty to be anxious about. Although pills may help turn it off, they will be unable to alter the source of the anxiety, which is the drinking and its consequences. Even if the alcoholic is at a point where the drinking is very troubling, when under the influence of pills, the drinking may not seem all that bad. So some anxiety seems necessary to produce change. We have a friend who says, "No one ever changes until it's too painful not to." This observation comes from long experience in a professional helping role. Removal of the alcoholic's pain can be a block to recovery. In the mildly mulled state of minor tranquilization, it may seem much easier to the alcoholic simply to continue the life pattern as before, including the drinking.

Polydrug use and abuse can take many forms, and there are great individual variations on these themes. It is not a subject that can be dismissed with any pat answers. It should be looked for when any drug, including alcohol, is being used, and particularly when abuse is present. Suitable treatment will have to be determined on an individual basis. Finally, there *are* some, few sober alcoholics who may need some tranquilizing agent to keep them comfortable enough to remain sober. Great care will need to be exercised by the physician prescribing for this type of problem. But a blanket statement that no drugs are allowed to any abuser can prove a very harmful attitude.

RESOURCES AND FURTHER READING

Cole, Jonathon, and Ryback, Ralph. Pharmacological therapy. In Ralph Tarter and A. Arthur Sugerman (Eds.), *Alcoholism: interdisciplinary approaches to an enduring problem.* Reading, Mass.: Addison-Wesley Publishing Co., 1976.

Ray, Oakley. *Drugs, society, and human behavior* (ed. 2). St. Louis: The C. V. Mosby Co., 1978.

CHAPTER TEN **Special populations**

217

WOMEN

The alcohol problems of women is not a topic you will find much discussed until very recently. If you judged the presence of alcohol problems in women by the number of articles published on the subject, in either the scientific or popular press, you'd be forced to conclude there weren't any until the mid-1970s, when suddenly an epidemic struck! Alcoholism, heavy drinking, and problem drinking were long thought to be the concern principally of men. The reasons for this view are complex. Women's roles are changing as will be discussed later. But, for centuries, women carried the burden of idealization. Women were "purer," objects to be loved and set on pedestals. There was (and still is to some extent) a virgin-prostitute dichotomy. Women fell clearly on one side or the other. Thus "ladies" didn't smoke, drink (never mind the Lydia Pinkham's), or swear. Although the picture has changed somewhat—women do smoke, drink, and swear now in varying degrees—vestiges of the pedestal still remain. "A woman drunk is worse than a drunk man." Therefore, not very many women drink too much. Therefore, if you encounter a woman alcoholic, pretend she isn't there. She is depressed, or suicidal, or mentally ill, or it will go away, or she is grieving the loss of her husband, etc. The alcoholic woman was, and to an extent still is, ignored by all. Her family, if she had one, hid her from view as much as possible. And she died, early and often. Even in the beginning years of AA (1935-1945) she was a rarity, a real minority.

For many years the estimates were that only one out of every seven alcoholics was a female. Only recently have some authorities come to the conclusion that there are almost as many female alcoholics as males. That the view of women and alcohol has changed little is evidenced by the title of a recent article in the September, 1977, issue of *Good Housekeeping* magazine: "The *Shocking* Facts about Women and Alcohol." (The emphasis is ours.) To whom it was to be a shock wasn't clear—presumably, the readers. One of the shocks was that nearly half the estimated 10 million alcoholics are female. Another was "that the husbands of 9 out of 10 of these women will leave them." (Only one out of every ten women married to alcoholic men leave their husbands.) Also, housewives make up the largest

single category of women alcoholics. The article also mentioned the risk factor of alcohol during pregnancy, which has been discussed earlier. These facts were certainly not news to anyone working in the alcohol field. That a major women's magazine calls these facts shocking says much about the avoidance of this issue by our society. If 5 million women were at risk because of some other illness, the hue and cry would be much greater.

Paucity of previous research

What is really known about alcohol problems as they affect women is appallingly little. Schuckit, in a review of the literature, found that between 1928 and 1970 there were only twenty-eight studies of women alcoholics published in the English language! Since then, several people have been industriously trying to fill the void. Previously, it was assumed that reported findings from studies of male alcoholics could just be extrapolated to females. There is a great deal of work currently under way to describe fully the characteristic manifestations of the disease in women, to pinpoint both the differences and similarities, to do studies on alcohol's physiological effects on women, to study the societal factors that influence the course of the disease and the treatment, and much more. The results to date are important, but tend mainly to point to areas of investigation that should be pursued. The most thoughtful writing on current research efforts generally ends with a statement that more information is required before firm statements can be made. We are at a stage where we are realizing how much we do not know. All that was thought to be known is rightfully being questioned and reexamined.

Women's roles and alcohol use

Women do not become alcoholics in a vacuum, any more than do other populations. Society plays a part as an influence. Women's roles in society now are less clearly defined than they once were. There are some hints and many questions as to how the changes taking place may affect the rates of alcoholism. As was seen in Chapter 4, cultural influences are only one of the three interwoven "causes" of alcoholism. One would suspect that the genetic factor, to date studied only in men, will likewise play a part in the development of alcoholism in women as well. Any

MONUMENT TO AN
ALCOHOLIC HOUSEWIFE

differences in women's psychological makeup distinguishing them from men have yet to be explored adequately. But research is going forth in this area, also. Culturally, several typical life-styles of today's women can be described and compared to those of the past. From this one can consider how these roles might influence women's use of alcohol.

There is first the now much denigrated role of housewife. These women now comprise a little under 50% of the female population. This role is subject to great variations on a theme, depending on social status, financial status, age, and area of the country in which one lives. Housewives range from those who enjoy the country club, fully electric kitchen, outside paid help, and volunteer work life-style to those women less financially advantaged who must do all their own work with little, if any, timesaving devices. One common thread for both, however, is that their schedules are built primarily around those of their families. They do whatever they have to do around and because of the husband's job and hours and children's school and extracurricular activities. Their activities may have a fractured quality. Interruptions, minor crises, and unfinished business seem to be constant. There is also a sameness to their routine, which varies only with the seasons—school, vacation, holidays. Boredom, too much to do, and too little reward are fairly common complaints. Today's housewife may have some advantages, such as wash and wear clothing, convenience foods, and electric appliances, but there were some things about the "good old days" that really were! One of these positive things was support—extended families nearby. People tended to be less mobile. They grew up, married, and remained living in the same area. Grandparents, aunts, sisters, and cousins were around for help with children, during illnesses, or when canning time came around. Certainly an "all for one and one for all" feeling wasn't always present, but there were usually at least some family members close by to call on for aid. For many women today, their families are far away, with visits only once or twice a year. Supports are either friends or, when there aren't many of these, agencies of one kind or another. When daily life got to be too much in the past, women had the option of a grandmother or two or other women in the family to help out. Today women have to pay sitters or housekeepers.

We suspect that one outlet no longer available was "the vapors." Women in the old stereotypic view were "weaker," more "emotional," and "delicate." It was accepted practice to take to their beds under stress. This was possible because there was usually someone to take over for a brief period, to allow for the temporary collapse. It could well be that this acted as a safety valve and actually was beneficial. In order to justify the expense of temporary household help today, the woman *really* has to be sick in a big way. Who knows how many tranquilizers and drinks are used to ward off what was previously taken care of by a day or two in bed!

Today's increased pace also enhances the use of alcohol. Children don't just go to school, come home, study, and help with chores. There are Boy Scouts, play rehearsals, dancing and music classes, riding lessons, Little League, babysitting jobs, and most of these trips require a chauffeur. And they are often in conflict with the things the other children have scheduled. Add to this the vicissitudes of life, minor accidents, pets, and so on. After a fractured, harried day, a drink may be a very welcome way to unwind enough to get dinner on the table and relax or do the laundry, or entertain business associates of the husband. . . . There is also the psychological impact created by the self-questioning most housewives now are subject to, with the implication often that such a role is unrewarding, unnecessary, and behind the times. Whether this be true or not, the question is being raised.

Some figures now show that over half of adult women work outside the home. Many do so out of financial necessity. Most of this group are not trained professionally and must take the jobs available to them. The magazine articles of late have focused primarily on women who like their work and have some skills and/or training that allow them a choice. This has glamorized the working woman and distorted the picture. Many women are still forced by need to support themselves and their children or add to the family income to survive. And many of these women are in low-paying, highly unsatisfying jobs. Some are not working outside the home because they want to. Often these women are also stuck with the more traditional view of a woman's role. Therefore, they still carry the greater burden at home and in essence hold two full-time jobs.

Others work out of a need to have more in life than unmade beds, dishes, and cleaning something all the time. With more options open, women are no longer forced to stay at home if they find that unrewarding. For these women, work outside the home is something they are glad to be able to do. More younger women are choosing careers they plan to pursue whether they marry or not. They are more aware of the financial realities and the probability that they will be spending at least a portion of their adult life working outside the home. They are more aware of the possibilities of divorce and having to be more self-reliant. As a consequence, they are more realistic in preparing themselves to do something that will be financially and personally rewarding.

There have always been some, and will be more and more, women who wish to pursue a professional career. Whether it is the law, medicine, the arts, education, or the business world, these women are pursuing something they really wish to do. Their careers are very important to them; they don't wish to put them in second place. The times may be changing sufficiently to make this easier for women to do. If changes are coming in the professional world, it seems they come at the rate of the proverbial snail. It still is harder for a woman to advance professionally or at a rate financially equal to that of her male counterpart. A recent survey of colleges and universities showed women still not holding positions of real power and being paid less than men in comparable positions. It is doubtful the picture is much different in other segments of society.

What happens to working women back in the home? A recent survey of working women with families showed that they had reduced the amount of housework they did by only about 35% when they began full-time employment. Thus, they will then have many of the same pressures of women who work at home plus whatever other pressures are incurred on their jobs. Alcohol has always been an accepted way to "relax" after a hard day at work for men. It is rather natural to assume that women would find the same to be true for them. They can also add all the other reasons men give for drinking: entertaining clients, to be one of the "girls" or "boys." Since equal opportunities for women have not totally arrived and society still holds the view generally that most household chores "belong" to women, the situation for most working women is far from ideal. They

I'd like another whiskey sour please.

are faced with many compromises that are unsatifsactory to them. And dissatisfaction and alcohol have long been companions.

Some suggestions

With this background on the changing roles of women and how they might prompt the use of alcohol, and in light of what was first discussed on how little is definitively known about women and alcohol, what suggestions might be given to caregivers? Some few things do come out as valid points to remember when working with women with alcohol problems. Often mentioned in research recently is the fact that many women can point to a specific trigger for the onset of their drinking. This might be a divorce, an operation, death of a spouse, children leaving home, a depression, or some other significant event. This response occurs much more frequently on women's questionnaires than on men's. If a woman comes to you at such a stressful time in her life, check out her drinking habits and proceed accordingly. If she doesn't have a problem, you can do a little education about the dangers of trying to cope with her difficulties with alcohol. Alert her to the higher risk she runs at this time. If she already has a problem, the general remarks about treatment apply. Do not let yourself, the client, or the family brush it aside as something that will pass when the crisis is resolved.

It has been tentatively shown that women's alcoholism progresses somewhat differently from men's. For one, the

Drink because you are happy, but never because you are miserable.

G. K. CHESTERTON

whole disease process appears telescoped; it starts later and gets worse faster. For another, the Jellinek phases are not as clear-cut in women. They show many of the same characteristic developments that men do, but the order in which they appear is different. Thus, you can't automatically assume a woman is or isn't in a particular phase because she does or does not manifest the symptoms described there. (It should be recalled that the Jellinek chart was based on the average progression seen in male alcoholics. One cannot ever expect the symptoms to show up in order: one, two, three, and so on.) As the course of alcoholism in women is studied more fully, a similar chart may be drawn up to describe the typical progression for them.

Another area of special note is the much publicized fact that mood-altering drugs are prescribed much more frequently for women than for men. This would suggest a very careful drug history as well as an alcohol history and a wary eye to the possibility of cross-addiction. It seems that women often use a "spice rack" approach to their problems; a little of this, and a little of that, and they can come up with a real witches' brew. It brings to mind the theory that adding vinegar will counteract too much sugar accidentally put in the sauce. It seems to be rare to be more careful with the sugar in the first place.

Women are not, in general, free from society's biases toward them. A great problem in the identification and treatment of women with alcohol problems is the general view that it is "worse" for a woman to drink to excess. This view is widely held, and held equally by women. Several possible results follow from this. One is that a woman will delay coming for treatment and deny her problem until no other course is open to her. Her family will also make more effort to deny and/or cover up the possibility of an alcohol problem. If she does appear for treatment, her self-respect is likely to be very low or nonexistent. She holds a very low estimate of herself. She may be so guilt-ridden that she is unable to see any acceptable way out of her dilemma. Since she has delayed seeking treatment, she may be physically and emotionally in worse shape than her male counterpart. Unfortunately, she may be faced by rejection in her first attempts to gain help. One cannot expect that caregivers are untouched by society's views.

Being aware of these factors is important in treatment. Because the disease is telescoped in women, you will need to be alert to the possibility of physical problems beyond those expected in men who have been drinking for similar periods of time. In other words, short duration of drinking is not necessarily a good indicator of a woman's physical condition.

Another consideration will be to help her build her self-esteem to the point where she can see recovery as possible and desirable. Introducing her to recovering, productive, and vital women alcoholics can enhance her chances of seeing this. In talking with them, she'll discover they, too, were once in a position virtually identical to her own. This builds hope, helps allay fears, and provides indisputable proof that recovery is possible. Such an approach is being found helpful in other chronic or serious medical conditions, for example, women with breast cancer who are about to undergo mastectomies are introduced to a woman who has had the surgery. This also opens up an avenue for asking questions the woman may feel are silly or out of place.

In the early stages of treatment some attention to grooming and personal appearance can be important in enhancing self-esteem. (The very same thing is true for men.) As her alcoholism progressed, her outward appearance may have become an accurate mirror of her deteriorated emotional and physical condition. By her own standards, she may have become a real mess. Wearing an outfit that is pressed, has all its buttons, is matched instead of looking like the first thing on the top of the clothes heap, plus having her hair done, may yield quite a transformation. The difference won't be lost on her either as she looks in the mirror. Although externals are not everything, they are something.

One caution to male counselors working with women. If you are the first person in many years to accept her, and if you have been making attempts toward raising her self-esteem, she may mistake her gratitude for this for a personal emotional involvement with you. Your recognition of this "error" is imperative. By providing her contacts with other recovered women alcoholics, she may be better able to recognize this pitfall as well.

Mothering and sexuality

Mothering and female sexuality are two aspects of self-esteem unique to women. If the woman alcoholic has children, some of the questions she may well be asking herself are: "Am I a good mother?" "Can I be a good mother?" "Have I hurt my children?" "Can I ever cope with my children if I don't drink?" These may not be explicit in the alcohol counseling, but they do cross her mind. They begin to be answered, hopefully positively, as she gains sober time. Family meetings may also be one way she gains answers to these questions. However, in some cases where there has been child abuse or a child is having special difficulties, a referral to a children's agency, a family service agency, or a mental health clinic may be important in dealing with these situations. One of the things any alcoholic mother will need to learn to regain her self-esteem as a mother is a sense of what the "normal" difficulties are in raising children.

In terms of her sexuality, there may be a number of potential questions. If there has been a divorce or an affair, she may well be wondering about her worth and attractiveness as a woman. Even if the marriage is intact, there may be sexual problems. On one hand, the sexual relationship may have almost disappeared as the drinking progressed. On the other, it may have been years since she's had sexual intercourse without benefit of a glass of wine or a couple of beers to put her "in the mood." Again, sober time may well be the major therapeutic element. But couple's therapy and/or sexual counseling may be needed if marital problems are not resolved.

What about single women, or women caught in an unsatisfactory marriage. It is not uncommon for them to find themselves "suddenly" involved in an affair or an extramarital relationship. With a little bit of sobriety, they are very ripe to fall in love. This may have several roots. She too may be questioning her femininity, and the attentions of a man may well provide some affirmation of her status as a woman. Also possible is that with sobriety comes a sense of being alive again. There's the reawakening of a host of feelings that have long been dormant, including sexual feelings. In this sense, it may be like the bloom and intensity of adolescence. A romantic involvement may follow very naturally. Unfortunately, it can lead to disaster, if followed with abandon. (To avoid being labeled "sexist," we want to add that this can be equally true for men.)

Another area of great concern when treating women is

children. If she has young children, long-term residential treatment may be very difficult to arrange. Remember, nine out of ten women alcoholics have no husbands in the home. But, for that very reason, it may be all the more important. Models of treatment to overcome this problem are being tried in many areas throughout the country. But in most places the usual facilities are still the only ones available. You will need to stretch your creativeness to the limit to deal with this problem. Potentially, friends, extended family—even if they are called in from a distance—or a live-in sitter can be used. There may be no way to allow her the optimum advantage of a two- to three-week stay in residential treatment. If this is the case, possibly daily outpatient visits, intensive AA contact, or day care can be used. Even if inpatient care can be arranged, you will be faced with her intense guilt over her children and her resistance to leaving them. Part of the task will be to assist her in seeing that she is being responsible to them by devoting her attention to her recovery. There are no easy formulas, and the counselor is left to work out the best solution possible in each individual case.

Another uncomfortable reality is the lack of a supportive family in many cases. Even in the one out of ten situations in which the family is intact, husbands of alcoholic women seem less willing to become involved in family treatment than are wives of alcoholic men. You cannot drag him in by his hair, so you must simply aid her in attending to her problem drinking despite the lack of a supportive spouse. The effects of alcoholism on the family have been discussed. It is clear that the most desirable and effective treatment includes family members. But it is also clear that recovery from alcoholism can and does take place under less than optimum circumstances.

Of late there have been some suggestions that when women are given more opportunities to develop satisfactory life-styles, they will no longer have the need to drink. Since women and men from all walks of life do develop alcoholism, this would seem to be a simplistic view. Also, there are too many women trapped in unsatisfactory life situations who do *not* develop alcoholism to make this a valid theory.

One note on women and AA. Latest figures from the General Services Board of AA indicate that over a third of the new members coming into AA are women. It appears that whatever the differences between male and female alcoholics, AA manages to achieve the same rate of success with both. It is equally as important to make a referral to AA for your female clients as for your male clients. A few trips to local meetings should assure her that it is no longer the male stronghold it once was.

Being aware that alcoholism, alcohol problems, and treatment issues are not identical for men and women is most of the battle. It will keep you alert to the differences and their effects on the treatment course. We can all look forward to the developments to come as more research on alcohol and women is conducted and reported. There is no doubt that many developments will occur before this volume reaches print. But until there are better maps to guide us in the treatment of women with alcohol problems, each counselor will in a sense be an explorer, searching for the best route in each individual case.

THE ELDERLY

On Art Linkletter's show several years ago, he was interviewing children, and they came up with the following answers to a question he posed: "You can't play with toys . . . the government pays for everything . . . you don't go to work . . . you wrinkle and shrink." The question was "What does it mean to grow old?" The responses of the children contain many of the stereotypes our society attributes to the elderly. They also show that this negative picture develops from a very early age. There is a stigma to growing old. The notion is that for the elderly there is no play or fun, no money, no usefulness, and no attractiveness.

Dishonor not the old: we shall all be numbered among them.

APOCRYPHA: BENSIRA 8:6

It is important to recognize that in considering the elderly, we are really talking about ourselves. It's inevitable. We will all age; we will all become the elderly. A participant at a recent geriatric conference reported being asked by a friend, "Give me the inside scoop . . . what can I do to keep from getting older?" The response the person received was simple: "Die now!" There is no other way to avoid aging. So, in thinking about the elderly, imagine yourself years in the future, since many of the circumstances will probably be the same.

Of the approximately 250 million persons in the United States, 20 million are over age 65. This is the group arbitrarily defined as the "elderly," or "aged." Each day, 3,000 die and 4,000 reach their sixty-fifth birthday, so there's a net gain of 1,000. By the year 1990, it is estimated that over 35 million persons will be over age 65; this will represent a larger percentage of the population than ever before. Consequently, the problems of the elderly that will be discussed are going to become a growing concern for our society.

Coping styles

Despite the inevitability of aging and despite the inevitability of physical problems arising as the years pass, there's an important thing to keep in mind. It's been said many times and in many different ways that you are as young as you want to be. But this is only possible if the person has some strengths going for him. The best predictor of the future, specifically how someone will handle growing old, is how the individual has handled the previous years. Individuals who have demonstrated flexibility as they have gone through life will adapt best to the inevitable stresses that come with getting older. These are the people who will be able to feel young, regardless of the number of birthdays they have celebrated.

Interestingly, as people get older, they become less similar and more individual. The only thing that remains alike for this group is the problems they face. There's a reason for this. Everyone going through life relies most heavily on the coping styles that seem to have served them well before. With years and years of living, gradually individuals narrow down their responses. What looks, at first glance, like an egocentricity or eccentricity of old age is most likely a lifelong behavior that has become one of the person's exclusive methods for dealing with stress. An example illustrating this point arose in the case of an elderly surgical patient for whom psychiatric consultation was requested. This man had a constant smile. In response to any question or statement by the nurses or doctors, he smiled, which was often felt to be wholly inappropriate. The treatment staff requested help in comprehending the patient's behavior. In the process of the psychiatric consultation, it became quite understandable. Friends, neighbors, and family of the man consistently described him as "good ole Joe, who always had a friendly word and a smile for everyone, the

You are as young as your faith, as old as your doubt; as young as your self-confidence, as old as your fear; as young as your hope, as old as your despair.

S. ULLMAS, From the Summit of Four Score Years

nicest man you'd ever want to meet." Now under the most fearful of situations, with many cognitive processes depleted, he was instinctively using his faithful, basic coping style. Very similarly, the person who goes through life with a pessimistic streak may become angry and sad in old age. Or the people who have been fearful under stress may be timid and withdrawn in old age. Or the people who have been very organized and always reliant on a definite schedule may try to handle everything by making lists in old age. What is true in each case is that the person has settled into a style that was present and successful in earlier life.

Main stresses

In working with the elderly, to understand what is evolving in an individual case, it is imperative that helping persons consider every possible piece of information. Integration of data from the social, medical, and emotional realm is essential for understanding what makes the elderly person tick in order to make an intelligent treatment plan. Four areas of stress need to be considered in dealing with the elderly: stresses that arise from social factors, biological or physical problems, psychological factors, and, unfortunately, iatrogenic stresses due to the helping professions as they serve (or don't adequately serve) the elderly.

Social stresses. These can be summarized under the phenomenon of the national addiction to youth. TV commercials highlight all types of products that can be used to disguise the process of aging. There's everything from hair colorings to dish detergents, which if used will make a mother's hands indistinguishable from her daughter's. Look around you. Who's being hired and who's being retired? Aging is equated with obsolescence and worthlessness. People who have been vital, contributing members of an organization suddenly find themselves with the title "honorary." It is often not an honor at all! It means these people have become figureheads, they have been replaced. The real work has been taken over by someone else.

Next let's consider social stresses due to the biases of the helping professions. The National Institute of Mental Health in a recent year spent 1.1% of its budget for research on problems of the elderly. Only 1% of its budget for services went to provide for care of the elderly. This is now changing, but it gives a graphic picture of the relative importance placed on this group of people in the recent past. The real issue is one of *attitude*. If one examines the dynamics behind this attitude, then one can see why there has been "disinterest" and "avoidance." Generally, the medical profession and other helping people, including family and friends, are overwhelmed by the multiplicity, chronicity, and confusing nature of the disorders of aging. Caregivers often feel helpless with the elderly and harbor self-doubts about whether they can contribute, both in a satisfactory manner and in a manner that is personally gratifying. To put it another way, most of us like to see results, to see things happen, to believe there is a "before" and "after" picture, in which the difference is clear. Also, it's important to feel that the part we have played, however big or small, has influenced this difference.

Helpers like it when someone puts out his hand and says "thank you," and the elderly often say, "Don't bug me . . . I don't want help." If you check who voluntarily comes into most clinical agencies, it's not the elderly. Those who come are usually coerced into it. Helpers do not like complainers. What do the elderly say? "This hurts, that hurts . . . you're not nice enough . . . you don't come soon enough . . . my old doctor was much better . . . do this, do that." Helpers like patients who receive maximum cures in the minimum of time. This certainly is not the elderly. There are more visits, more problems, more time. Helpers like patients who get well. How many of the elderly get cured? How can you take away their diabetes, their arthritis, the pain from the memory of a lost spouse? Helpers like patients who take their advice. With the elderly, you suggest A, and they'll often do B.

These interactional dynamics are not wrong per se, but on the surface they may rub the helpers' instincts the wrong way. The result is that many potential caregivers decide they don't like working with the elderly, and it shows. Very few clinicians volunteer to take on elderly clients. If an elderly client comes into a helping agency, the chances are good that the person who sees the client may soon decide to transfer the case to someone more "appropriate" or refer the patient to another agency.

Another factor that gets in the way of their receiving adequate care from helping people is that *they may resent the helper's youth, just as the helper fears their elderli-*

ness. Also, the elderly generally dislike the dependent status that goes along with being a client and patient. It is the opposite of what they want, which is to be independent and secure and feel a sense of worth. Being in treatment implies that something is wrong with them. It also means that someone else is partially in charge and telling them how to run their lives.

Psychological stresses. The common denominator is loss. No matter how you slice it, the elderly must constantly deal with loss. The elderly may try to handle loss in a number of ways. One is the widely used defense of *denial.* In response to an observation that a client's hand is more swollen, he may well say, "Oh no, it's no different than it's always been." If a close friend is in the hospital and very seriously ill, she may dismiss the seriousness and claim it is "just another of her spells, she'll be out, perky as ever in a day or two." Another common way of handling loss is by *somatization.* This means bringing the emotional content out in the open, but "saying" it in terms of the body hurts. This is why so many of the elderly are termed hypochondriacal. When he says his knee hurts and he really cannot get up that day, what he also may be saying is that he hurts inside, emotionally. Since he may not get attention for emotional pains, having something wrong physically or "mechanically" is socially more acceptable. Another way of handling loss is *restricting affect.* Instead of saying it does not exist, as with denial, there is a withdrawing. They become less involved, so they don't hear about the bad things happening. By being less a part of the world, they are less vulnerable. Unfortunately, all these defenses boomerang and work against the elderly. How are love, affection and concern expressed? Through words, behavior, and many nonverbal cues—a smile, a nod, a touch. After so many years of living, the elderly certainly know the signs of affection and caring or of distancing and detachment. By withdrawing when they are fearful, they may well see others withdrawing, and they are left without any source of affection, interest, and caring. This they in turn read as dislike, and they may feel their initial withdrawing was justified. Therefore, one of the prime treatment techniques with the elderly is to reach out to them, literally. Smile, touch them, sit close to them. Attempt to reach through the barrier they may have erected with the "protective" psychological defenses mentioned.

The elderly frequently overinterpret what helping persons instinctively say when reaching out to the aged. There are often statements like "you're lucky to be alive . . . quit worrying about things . . . grow old gracefully." What the elderly hear is someone telling them to ignore their losses, or that the person making such statements does not want to get close to them. Their response is that they do not want to grow old gracefully, they do not want to be "easy to manage," they want to go out with a bang, leave a mark—they want to be individuals to the last day.

Loss. In the geriatric population losses are steady, predictable, and often come in bunches. And even if they do not, they are still numerous. What are the specific losses?

There is the loss that comes from the *illnesses* and *deaths* of family and friends. The older you get, statistically the more likely that those about you will begin to falter. So there are the obvious losses of supports and companionship. Not necessarily as obvious is that the deaths of others also leads to questioning about loss of self, anticipation of one's own death. This may sometimes be the source of anxiety attacks among the elderly.

There is the loss that comes from the geographical *separations of family.* This begins earlier in life, as children go to school and later leave home for college, the service, and eventually to marry. For the elderly, this may be especially difficult, since 50% of all grandparents do not have their grandchildren living close by. As new generations are being born, they are not accessible to the older generation whose lives are coming to a close.

There is the loss of *money* through earned income. Whether income is supplemented through pensions, social security, or savings, the elderly do not have as much money as earlier in their lives. Dollars not only represent buying power, they also have symbolic values. Money represents power, stature, value, and independence. Lack of money has obvious implications in these vital areas of self-esteem.

There are the losses that accompany *retirement:* loss of status, gratification, and often most important, identity. With retirement, you lose who you've been. This doesn't refer only to retirement from a job. It includes retirement from anything, from being a mother, or a grandmother, or from being a person who walked around the block. Often accompanying retirement is a loss of privacy. For married couples, retirement may mean more togetherness than they have had for years. Both will have to change routines and habits and be forced to accommodate the presence of the other. The expectations may also be tremendous. Retirement, in most people's fantasies, is thought to usher in the "golden years," provide the opportunity to do the things that have been put off. There may well be a letdown.

There is also the loss of *body functions and skills*, which may include a loss of attractiveness. Older people may develop body odors. They lose their teeth. They are more prone to infection. For women, the skin may become dry, including the skin of the vagina, which can lead to vaginal discharges and dyspareunia (painful intercourse). For men, there is a general loss of muscle tone. Everything begins to stick out where it shouldn't. As physical problems arise, this may lead to loss of skills. The carpenter with arthritis or the tremors of Parkinson's disease will be unable to do the things that were formerly possible and rewarding.

How about sex and the elderly? The most prevalent lay myth is that the elderly have no interest in sex. Physiologically, aging of itself need not greatly affect sexual functioning. With advancing years, it takes a little longer to achieve an erection, a little more time to the point of ejaculation, orgasm is a little less intense, and a little more time is required before orgasms can be reexperienced. But if they are physically healthy, there is no reason why the elderly should not be sexually active. The biggest factors influencing sexual activity in the elderly are the availability of a partner and social pressures. Among the elderly, when a partner dies, the survivor is often not encouraged to date or remarry. What is considered virility at age 25 is seen as lechery after age 65. Even when both partners are alive, if they are living in an institution or in the home of children, sexual activity may well be frowned on, or "not allowed."

Another loss is of *sensation*. With aging, the senses become less acute. What this means is that the elderly are then deprived of accurate cues from their environment. This may be a big factor in the development of suspiciousness in older persons. Any paranoid elderly patient should have hearing and vision evaluated.

The most powerful loss, the loss no elderly person is prepared to understand or accept, is the loss of *thinking ability*. This may happen imperceptibly over a period of time. It comes from the loss of cortical brain function. Suddenly a person who has been an accountant or a schoolteacher, for example, is adding $2 + 2$ and it doesn't equal 4 every time. They become embarrassed and scared and may reveal that they can stand losing other things, but to "lose their mind" is the ultimate indignity.

The result of all or any of these losses is that self-respect, integrity, dignity, and self-esteem are threatened. The implication can be that usefulness is questioned and life is ebbing away. The feeling may well be that "my work is over."

Biological stresses. Of the elderly, only 5% are institutionalized in nursing homes, convalescent centers, or similar facilities. However, 45% of the elderly have some serious physical disability such as heart disease, diabetes, lung disease, or arthritis. About 25% also have a significant functional psychological problem, with depression the most prevalent. Understandably, as life expectancy increases and we live longer, there is more vulnerability to the natural course of disease. For this part of the population, receiving medical care and paying medical bills can mean additional big problems. The elderly have twice as many visits to a physician, their average hospital stay is three and one-half times longer than for persons under age 65, and the hospital stay costs five times more than for the under 65 group. Ironically, for this medically fragile group, insurance coverage (including Medicare) is often less adequate than is coverage for younger persons. Thus, those with the most need for medical care, the greatest medical expenses, and the least ability to pay have the poorest insurance coverage of any group.

Alcoholism is also a big problem for the elderly. Dr. Robert Butler of the National Institutes of Health, the Division on the Elderly, estimates that 20% have a significant alcohol problem. These problems are also ignored for many of the same reasons that sex in the elderly is dismissed without a further thought. "That nice old lady drinks too much (or is interested in sex)!" "Never!" Some of these elderly have had a long history of alcohol use and abuse; they may have been alcoholic for a good long time, but with adequate medical care have somehow lived to old age. However, with the overall deterioration of physical functioning, the alcohol use may begin to take a heavier toll

Portrait of an old man who gets drunk on sacramental wine

Let us eat and drink; for tomorrow we die.

I CORINTHIANS 15:32

and become an increasingly difficult problem. Also among the elderly are persons who do not have a prior history of alcohol abuse; their alcoholism may be described as late onset. The stresses of aging may have been too great or come too fast and at the wrong time. They have turned to alcohol as a coping mechanism. The subgroup of the total population with the highest risk for alcoholism is widowers over age 65. Whatever the variety of alcoholism present, intervention is important. All too often alcohol treatment workers are likely to dismiss the elderly with "what do they have to live for anyway . . . they have been drinking all these years, they'll never stop now . . . I don't want to be the one who asks them to give up the bottle."

Depressive illness is very prevalent among the elderly. There may well be a physiological basis for this. The levels of neurochemicals (serotonin and norepinephrine) thought to be associated with depression change in the brain as people get older. These depressions, then, are not necessarily tied solely to situational events. But because so many things are likely to be going on in the surrounding environment for the elderly, it is too easy to forget the potential benefits of judiciously prescribed antidepressants. Malnourishment is all too common in the elderly. This can cause several syndromes that may look like depressions. Many physical ailments, due to disease processes themselves, manifest as depression. Depression in the elderly may not present like depression in younger persons, with tearfulness, inability to sleep, or loss of appetite. Some of the tips for recognizing depression in the elderly are an increased sensitivity to pain, refusing to get out of bed when physical problems don't require bed rest, poor concentration, a marked narrowing of coping style, and an upsurge of physical complaints. Often, the poor concentration leads to absent-mindedness and inattentiveness, which is misdiagnosed as defective memory and ultimately as "senility" with the depression unrecognized and untreated. Senility is really a useless clinical term. The proper phrase should be dementia, which means irreversible cognitive impairment. However, all cognitive impairment should be considered reversible (delirium) until proven otherwise. The elderly deserve an aggressive search for potentially treatable, reversible causes of organic brain syndromes.

Suicide among the elderly is a very big problem.

Twenty-five percent of all persons who commit suicide are over age 65. The rate of suicide for persons over 65 is five times that of the general population. After age 75, the rate is eight times higher. In working with the elderly, a suicide evaluation is not to be neglected, since so many depressions are masked in their appearance.

Iatrogenic stresses. Unfortunately, the medical problems of the elderly may be aggravated by the medical profession's insensitivities to the psychological and basic physiological changes in the elderly. All too often there is overprescription of medication in attempts to keep behavior controlled rather than diagnosed. Too few clinicians take into account the dramatically altered way the elderly metabolize medications, which means that fewer medicines in combination and lowered doses of any drug are required. Rarely is there any thought of whether the patient can afford the medicine prescribed. Also there is an overestimate of the patient's ability to comply with directions for taking medications. A poignant example of this was the case of an elderly woman who was discharged from the hospital with a number of medications. She had been admitted in severe congestive heart failure but had responded well to chemical treatment of hypertension and fluid retention. Within two weeks of returning to her home, her condition began to deteriorate, which was a source of dismay and consternation to her physicians. The patient was thought surely to be purposefully causing her ailments, and a psychiatrist, who was asked to consult on the case, decided to make a home visit. The woman knew which medications to take, when, and for what conditions. But yes, there was one problem. As she handed the bottle of capsules to the psychiatrist, with her crippled arthritic fingers, the "diagnosis" became obvious: the child-proof cap! She had been unable to open the bottles and therefore unable to take the medicine. This is a vivid reminder of the need to consider *all* the available information in assessing the problems of the elderly.

Practical treatment suggestions

1. If the elderly have some symptoms of psychological problems or physical problems, including a problem with alcohol, provide the same treatment you would for someone younger. Too often, problems of the elderly are dismissed under the assumption the elderly are just complain-

ers, "senile," unlikely to benefit, likely to die soon, or incapable of appreciating help.

2. In making an evaluation of an older person, do a comprehensive assessment rather than just a symptom-oriented search. Pay attention to the social, financial, emotional, medical, cognitive, and self-care status. The latter is often overlooked. Is the person able to do the daily activities required for well-being such as preparing meals, getting groceries, taking medications as prescribed.

3. Since many elderly persons are reluctant to seek or receive professional help, a family member is often the person to make the first contact. This will initially be your best source of information about the person. Be sure to find out the family's views of the situation, their ideas and fears. Whatever the problem, the chances are good that something can be done to improve the picture. Let the family know about this optimism. It often comes as a surprise to them that their elderly relative may get better.

4. Sometimes the family will appear to you as unhelpful, unsympathetic, or uncaring. This may be infuriating and annoy you. Even if this happens, do not alienate the family. Whatever problems there may be with the family, it is possibly the only support system the client has.

5. In dealing with the elderly, remind yourself you are working with persons who are survivors. The fact that they have made it even this far means they have some strengths. These people have stuck their necks out in the past and taken risks. Find out how they have done it, and see if you can help them replicate that. Also, raise their expectations that indeed they can "make it" again, just as they have before.

6. Use all the possible resources at your disposal. In many instances the elderly need to become reinvolved in the world around them. Meaningful contacts can come from a variety of people, not just from professional helpers. The janitor in the client's apartment building, a neighbor, or a crossing guard at the street corner may all be potential allies. If the person was once active in a church group, civic organization, or other community group, but has lost contact, get in touch with the organization. There is often a member who will visit or be able to assist in other ways. Many communities have senior citizen centers. They offer a wide range of resources: everything from a social program,

to Meals-on-Wheels, to counseling on Social Security and Medicare, to transportation. If there is a single agency to cultivate, this is the one.

7. In your interviews with the elderly, the importance of reaching out, showing interest, and having physical contact has already been mentioned. Also be active. Do not merely sit there and grunt from time to time. Your quietness may too easily be interpreted by them as distance and dislike. Another very important thing to do is to provide cues to orient the elderly. Mention dates, day of the week, current events. For anyone who has had any cognitive slippage, good cues from the environment are very helpful. In conversation with the elderly, don't stick with neutral topics like the weather all the time. Try to engage them in some topics of common interest to you both (such as gardening, baseball, etc.) as well as some controversial topic, something with some zip. This stimulates their egos, since it implies you not only want *their* opinions, but you want *them* to listen to yours.

8. If you give specific information to the client, also write it down for him in legible handwriting. This makes it much easier for the client to comply. If family members are present, tell them the directions too. In thinking about compliance and what can be done to assist the elderly in participating in treatment, take some time to think about how your agency functions. What does it mean for an elderly client coming to see you? Are there long waits at several different offices on several different floors? Does it require navigating difficult stairs, elevators, and hallways in the process? Are there times of day that make the use of public transportation easier? Consider such factors, and make adjustments to make it much easier for your elderly clients. In specific terms, make every effort to do things in as uncomplicated, convenient, nonembarrassing, and economical a fashion as possible.

9. Separate sympathy and empathy. Sympathy is feeling sorry for someone. The elderly don't want that; it makes them feel like children. Empathy means you understand, or want to understand. This is what they would like.

10. Be aware that you may be thought of and responded to as any number of important people in your client's long life. Also, you may alternately represent grandchild, child, parent, peer, and authority figure to them at various points

in treatment, even in the same interview, and at the same time.

11. Display integrity with the elderly. Do not try to mislead them or lie to them. They are too experienced with all the con games in life. If they ask you questions, give them straight answers. This, however, does not mean being brutal in the name of "honesty." For example, in speaking with a client you might well say, "Many other people I talk with have concerns about death, do you?" The client responds, "No, I have pretty much come to terms with the idea of dying." You don't blurt out, "Well, you better think about it, you only have six months to live." That is *not* integrity.

12. In working with elderly clients, set specific goals. Make sure that the initial ones are easily attainable. This means they can have some surefire positive experiences. With that under their belts, they are more likely to take some risks and attempt other things.

13. Make home visits. Home visits are the key to working with this group. It may be the only thing that will break down their resistance and help them get treatment. Very few will seek help on their own initiative. So, if someone is not willing to come to your office, give him a call. Ask if you can make an appointment to see him at home. If the response you get is, "I don't want you to come," don't quit. Your next line is, "Well, if I'm ever in the area, I'd like to stop by." And try to do that. Bring some small token gift, such as notepaper or flowers. After your visit, you may well find the resistance has disappeared.

The home visit can be vital in making an adequate assessment. Seeing the person in his own home, where security is at its peak, provides a much better picture of how the person is getting along, as well as the plusses and minuses of the environment. It also allows the patient to be spontaneous in emotions and behavior.

If you regularly make home visits, beware of making the person "stay in trouble" in order to see you. Don't just visit in a crisis. But instead, stop in to hear about successes. Your visits may be a real high point for the person, who may not like to think of losing this contact. Make a visit the day after the client's first day on a new volunteer job, for example.

14. Beware of arranging things for the elderly that will be seen as something trivial to occupy their time. If there

is a crafts class, the point ought to be to teach them a skill, an art, not to keep them busy. Many of the elderly also have something they can teach others. The carpenter who is no longer steady enough to swing a hammer and drive a nail will be able to provide consultation to do-it-yourselfers who want to remodel their homes. The elderly have a richness of life experiences and much to contribute.

15. Thoroughly evaluate symptoms of memory loss, disorientation, and behavioral changes to uncover potentially treatable causes of organic brain syndrome. Have patients show you *all* their medicines, including over-the-counter types. Coordinate medical care to avoid duplication of prescriptions.

In closing, the task in working with the elderly is to assist them in rediscovering strengths, getting involved with people, and discovering life is worth living, at whatever age.

ADOLESCENTS

Adolescence is indeed a special period of life. It lies at the back door of childhood yet at the very doorstep of adulthood. There is no comparable time in life when more physical and emotional changes take place in such a narrow span of time.

Adolescence as a term is less than 150 years old. Prior to that time, one grew straight from childhood into adulthood. The needs of family and culture demanded earlier work and community responsibilities. Survival depended on it. With increasing industrialization, children left the factories and fields to spend more time in school, play, and idle time. Society became increasingly aware of the presence of teenagers as a group who had and still have as yet fairly undefinable roles and rights. Most texts define adolescence from 12 to 21. Physical and legal determinants would suggest otherwise. Physical changes indicative of the beginning of adolescence may begin as early as age 7 and not end until the midtwenties. Legal age has fluctuated within state and federal differences. Varied drinking ages, youthful draft requirements, and reduced voting age have clouded the definition.

Physical changes

The most striking aspect of adolescence is the rapid physical growth. These changes are mediated by the sex

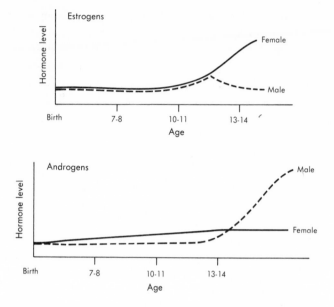

hormones. The rough charts above indicate that the first recognizable change in the male is due to fat increase dictated by a small but gradual increase in estrogen. Every boy gains weight at the expense of height during these years. Some boys due to become tall and muscular men are actually chubby and effeminate looking during these early adolescent years. To add insult to injury, the next body part to grow is his feet, then thighs, which make him appear short waisted and gawky. This slows, allowing the rest of his body to catch up. Androgen influence may not come for a few years, with often unrecognizable pigment changes in the scrotal sac, then enlargement of the penis, testes, the beginning of pubic hair, and early voice changes. His first nocturnal emission or "wet dream" may occur as early as age 10 or as late as age 15. Even so, the majority of boys remain "relatively sterile" till age 15. The major male growth spurt appears at age 14½ and is due to growth in the backbone. This averages 4 to 4½ inches over an eighteen-month period. Some boys will shoot up 8 to 10 more inches during this time. Axillary and facial hair soon follow. Facial hair may develop entirely in one year. Other boys, equally normal but with different genes, may not complete the facial and body hair growth till the mid to late twenties.

We are indeed taller than our ancestors, which can be shown from historical evidence. Clothing, doorways, and furniture were made for shorter men and women. Better nutrition is mainly responsible for the changes seen.

A girl's first hormonal response is around age 7 or 8 with a normal vaginal discharge called *leukorrhea*. Her feet then grow, but this is rarely as noticeable a change as in the male. A breast "button" begins about age 11 under the skin of one breast first, to be followed in weeks or months under the remaining breast. The breasts develop into adult breasts over a span of four to five years. Pubic hair begins approximately six months after breast button stage. Her hips widen, and the backbone gains 3 to 4 inches before she is ready for her menses. Although a critical body weight is not the only initiator, the body is influenced by this. If other criteria are met, such as developing breasts, pubic hair, widened hips, and growth spurt, a sample of American girls will begin their menses weighing from 100 to 105 pounds. Nutrition has a great deal to do with the menarche (first menses); girls in countries with poor nutritional standards begin their menses two to three years later. The mean age for menarche in America is 12. (Pilgrim girls, who suffered from many nutritional deprivations, often had menarche delayed until age 17.) A regular menstrual cycle is not established immediately. Quite commonly a girl will have anovulatory (no egg) periods for six to eighteen months before having ovulatory periods. This change may bring an increased weight gain, breast tenderness, occasional emotional lability, and cramps at the midcycle. These are consequences of progesterone, a hormone now secreted by the ovary at the time of ovulation. An adult pattern in ovulation will not be completed till the early twenties.

Until puberty, boys and girls are equally strong in muscle strength (if corrected for height and weight). Total body fat increases in girls by 50% from ages 12 to 18, whereas a similar decrease of 50% occurs in boys. Muscle cell size and number increase in boys, muscle cell size alone increases in girls. Internal organs such as the heart double in size. Blood pressure increases with demands of growth. Pulse rate decreases, and the ability to break down fatigue metabolites in muscle prepares the male, especially, for the role of hunter and runner that was so important for survival centuries ago.

Marked fatigue coupled with overwhelming strength is

often difficult to fully appreciate. An adolescent may wolf down several quarts of milk, a full meal or two, play many hours of active sports, and yet complain bitterly of severe fatigue at all times! This human metabolic furnace needs the food and rest as well as the drive to have the machine function and test itself out. These bodily inconsistencies often show in mood swings and unpredictable demands for self-satisfaction and physical expression.

The rapidity of these changes tends to produce almost a physiological confusion in many adolescents. Quite commonly, they become preoccupied with themselves. This can lead to an overconcern with their health. In some instances it is almost hypochondriacal. Adolescents may complain of things that to an adult appear very minor. The thing to remember is that their concern is very real and deep. Attention needs to be paid to their concerns. Remembering the rapid rate of physical changes that confronts the adolescent makes their preoccupation with their bodies understandable.

Characteristics

Adolescence characteristically is an extremely healthy time of life. In general, adolescents don't die off from the kinds of things that strike the rest of us such as heart disease. The major causes of adolescent deaths are accidents and suicide. The result of this healthiness is that adults tend to assume that adolescents with problems are not really sick and do not give their complaints the hearing they deserve.

Another characteristic of adolescence is a truly tremendous need to conform to their peers. There's the need to dress alike, wear the same hairstyle, listen to the same music, and even think alike. A perpetual concern of the adolescent is that he or she is different. Although the sequence of physical development is the same, there is still variation in the age of onset and the rate of development. This can be a big concern for adolescents, whether the teenager is ahead, behind, or just on the norm. Worry about being different is a particular concern for the adolescent who may want or need professional help. The adolescent won't go unless it is "peer acceptable." Kids often stay away from caregivers out of fear. A big fear is that if they go, sure enough something really wrong will be found. This, to their minds, would officially certify them as *different*. They can't tolerate that.

Also characteristic of adolescence is wildly fluctuating behavior. It frequently alternates between wild, turmoiled periods and times of quiescence. A flurry of even psychotic type thinking is not uncommon. This doesn't mean adolescents are psychotic for a time and then get over it. There are just some periods when their thinking really only makes sense to themselves and possibly to their friends. For example, if not selected for the play cast, he may be sure that "proves" he will be a failure his entire life. Or, if she is denied the use of the family car on Friday, she may overreact. With a perfectly straight face, she may accuse her parents of *never* letting her have the car, even as she stands there with the car keys ready to drive off.

Let us eat and drink for tomorrow we shall die.

ISAIAH 22:13

Adolescence is very much a time of two steps forward and one back, with an occasional jog to one side or the other. Despite the ups and downs, it is usually a continuing, if uneven, upward trip to maturity.

Another point of importance: in early adolescence, the girls are developmentally ahead of the boys. At the onset of puberty, girls are physically about two years ahead. This makes a difference in social functioning because social development takes place in tandem with physical development. This can cause problems in social interactions for boys and girls of the same age. Their ideas of what makes a good party or what is appropriate behavior may differ considerably. The girls may consider their male peers dumbos. The boys, aware of the girls' assessments, may be shaken up, while the girls feel dislocated too. With the uneven development of boys and girls during early adolescence, girls have an edge in school. In reading skills, for example, the girls may be a year ahead of the boys. There is a catching up period later, but in dealing with younger adolescents, keep this disparity in mind.

Four tasks

When does adolescence end? There are fairly clear-cut signs that mark the beginnings of the process. There is more to adolescence than just physical maturation. Defining the end can lead to philosophical discussions of "maturity." Doesn't everyone know a 45- or 65-year-old "adolescent?" There's more to assigning an endpoint than just considering a numerical age.

One way of thinking about the adolescent period is to assign to it four tasks. From this point of view, once the tasks have been reasonably accomplished, the person is launched into adulthood. These tasks don't get tackled in any neat order or sequence. It is not like the consistent pattern of physical development. They are more like four themes that are interwoven, the dominant issues of adolescence.

One task of adolescence is *acceptance of the biological role*. This means acquiring some degree of comfort with your identity as either male or female. This is an intellectual effort. It has nothing to do with sexuality or experimentation with sexuality.

A second task is *the struggle to become comfortable with heterosexuality*. This doesn't mean struggling with the question of "how to make out at the drive-in!" It's the much larger question of "How do you get along with the opposite sex at all, ever?" Prior to adolescence, boys and girls are far more casual with one another. With adolescence, those days are over. Simply to walk by a member of the opposite sex and say "Hi" without blushing, giggling, or throwing up can be a problem. To become a heterosexual person—able to carry on all manner of social and eventually sexual activities with a member of the opposite sex—does not come easily. It is fraught with insecurity and considerable self-consciousness. If you force yourself to remember your own adolescence, some memories of awkwardness and uncertainty come to the fore. Thus, there is the adolescent who doesn't ask for a date because of the anticipated *no*. Being dateless is much more tolerable than hearing a no.

Another task is *the choice of an occupational identity*. It becomes important to find an answer to "What am I going to do (be)?" There are usually several false starts to this one. Think of the 5-year-old who wants to be a fireman. He probably never will be, but he gets a lot of mileage for awhile just thinking he is. It is not so different for adolescents. It is not helpful to pooh-pooh the first ideas they come up with. Nor is handing over an inheritance and saying "Go ahead" recommended. They need some time to work it out in their heads. A fair amount of indecision, plus some real lulu ideas is to be expected.

The fourth task is *the struggle toward independence*. This is a real conflict. There is the internal push to break away from home and parents, and, at the same time, the desire to remain comfortably cared for. The conflict shows up in rebellion, since there aren't many ways to feel independent when living at home, being fed, checked on, prodded, and examined by parents. Rebellion of some type is so common to this period of life that an adolescent who does not rebel in some fashion should be suspect.

Rebellion. Rebellion can be seen in such things as manner of dress and appearance. It is usually the opposite of what the parents' generation accepts. Little ways of testing out crop up in being late from a date, buying something without permission, arguing with the parents over just anything. The kids are aware of their dependency, and they don't like it. There is even some shame over being in such a position. It is important that the parents recognize the rebellion and respond to it. In this era of Dr. Spock and "Be friends with your kids," a lot of well-meaning parents have accepted *any* behavior from their kids. For example, if the kids, for the sake of rebellion, brought home some grass to smoke, their parents might light up, too. Often the kids will do whatever they can, just to get their parents angry. They are so often reminded by others of how much they look or act like their father or mother. And they don't want that. *Adolescents want to be themselves.* They don't want to be carbon copies of their parents, whom they probably don't much like at the moment. Going out and doing some drinking with the gang, doing something weird to their hair that Mom and Dad will hate, not cleaning their rooms, helping the neighbors but not their parents are all fairly usual ways of testing out and attempting to assert independence.

Destructive rebellion can occur when the parents either don't recognize the rebellion or don't respond to it. It can take many forms, such as running out of the house after an argument and driving off at 80 or 90 miles per hour, getting really drunk, running away, or, for girls, getting pregnant despite frequent warnings from their overrestrictive parents to avoid all sexual activities.

There are many roadblocks to completion of these four basic tasks. One results from a social paradox. Adolescents are physically ready for adult roles long before our society allows it. Studies of other societies and cultures point this out. In some societies adolescence doesn't cover a decade or more. It is about a one-hour trip! Light a fire, beat a gong, send the boy into the woods to pray to the moon; when he returns, hand him a spear and a wife, and he's in

Hi Dear, why don't you invite your friends in, and we can all sit around and smoke some joints.

business. Our society dictates instead that people stay in an adolescent position for a frightfully long time: junior high school, senior high school, college, graduate school. . . . Another social paradox comes from the mixed messages. On the one hand, it's "be heterosexual, get a date" . . . "get a job" . . . "be grown up." On the other, it's "be back by 1 AM" . . . "save the money for college" . . . "don't argue with me." The mixed-upness of "grow up, but stay under my control" can introduce tensions.

The above is a very brief overview of adolescence. There are many excellent books on the subject should you want a more in-depth study. For our purposes here, it will suffice as a context in which to consider alcohol use.

Alcohol

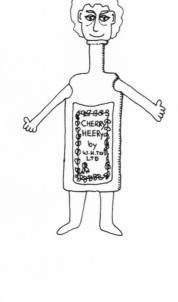

Adolescents do use alcohol, and in many different ways. Some of these ways are a normal part of the whole process. The "try it on" thread runs throughout adolescence. Alcohol is just one of the things to be tried. It is, after all, a massive part of adult society. So it's natural that the adolescent struggling toward adulthood will try it. Drinking is also attractive for either rebellious or risk-taking behavior. It is most usually introduced in a peer group. At present, it is not very acceptable to say, "No, thank you." Here again, the need to conform comes into play. Alcohol use to some degree is a part of the adolescent experience. Statistics now show that by age 18 the number of drinkers is the same as for the adult population. In a recent survey of high school youth, at least one half said they are in social situations where alcohol is served once a month or more. Of this group, one-half said they drink "once a week, twice a week or more." Beer is the beverage most often drunk by both the frequent drinkers and those who had only tried drinking a few times. Most adolescents do not know that beer is as intoxicating as distilled spirits. Forty-two percent thought five to seven cans of beer could be drunk in two hours without risk of intoxication. They are short on facts and tend more than adults to rely on myths. Seventy percent believed cold showers could sober someone up, and 62% thought coffee would do it. Very few realized that only time takes care of it.

They also minimize the consequences of drinking. Only 8% thought their driving ability would be "much worse"

under the influence. They don't feel they are likely to get stopped by the police for drinking, or that the consequences could be severe if they were. They also don't consider their being in an accident a real possibility, much less one that might result in serious injury or death.

The children of alcoholics might use alcohol for other reasons, as well. They're dreadfully ashamed of their parent's alcoholism. They really hate it. They might deliberately, and very openly, come in drunk as a way of saying, "See what you're doing!" They are also quite likely testing out. They are very worried that they might turn out like Mom or Dad. Although they have grown up with alcoholism, their knowledge of it is quite superficial, spotty, and filled with fantasy.

This is why Al-Anon, Al-Ateen, or educational support groups are so important for them at this time. They try alcohol, and their logic goes, "I can go out and drink on Friday or Saturday, but on Monday I don't have to. I can leave it alone. See, I am different; I can handle it." Even explaining that alcoholism doesn't usually show up instantly, that almost everyone can handle it at first, isn't very convincing. They have a hard time accepting this. Adolescents are very oriented to the present. There is just this day. If they think about the future at all, they base it on how they feel *right now*. They sincerely feel they have proved their immunity from alcoholism forever if they don't show all the problems from the time of their first drinking experiences.

Alcohol problems and alcoholism

Since drinking is so prevalent during adolescence, it should not be a surprise to discover that alcohol problems and even alcoholism show up in this age group. Much press coverage has been given lately to "teenage alcoholism." Whether it is indeed more prevalent or simply being detected earlier is not easily answered. Some of both is probably true. That it exists is no longer arguable. A caregiver who does not take a drinking history from an adolescent is being either an ostrich or knowingly negligent. The whole range of alcohol problems besides alcoholism are also happening to adolescents: driving while intoxicated, accidents, fights, arrests, injuries. Driving while intoxicated, in fact, may be quite prevalent, since the young person lacks experience in both driving and drinking. Education about alcohol use or early intervention when a problem is detected is vital, more so than in almost any other age group. It is very important to question the role alcohol plays in their lives.

Considerations in working with adolescents

There are some general things to consider when dealing with adolescents. The issue of confidentiality comes up. It can be a mistake to guarantee that "nothing you say will ever leave this room." The counselor does have the responsibility for others as well as the adolescent client. Given blanket protection, what happens when the kid announces he plans to rob the local deli, or another says she plans to drive the family car off the road at the first opportunity? A different approach is suggested by Dr. Mac-Namee. He tells whomever he sees that while most of what they say will be held in confidence, if they tell him anything that scares him about what they might do, that would be harmful to themselves or others, he is going to blow the whistle. He makes it clear he won't do it without telling them. But nonetheless, he will do it. Adolescents will usually accept this. It may even be a relief. It may help to know that someone else is going to exert some control, especially if they're none too sure about their own inner controls at the moment. In a similar vein, Dr. MacNamee suggests keeping the adolescent posted on any contacts you have with others about him. If a parent calls, start off the next session by informing the adolescent, "Hey, your Dad called me, and he wanted . . . ." Or if a letter needs to be written to a school, probation officer, etc., share what you are writing with the adolescent. The chances are fairly good his fantasy about what you might say is worse than anything you would actually say, no matter what the problem. Since trust is such an issue with adolescents, it is important that you be willing to say *to* them what you would say *about* them behind their backs.

It's also wise to avoid obvious authority symbols, such as white coats, framed diplomas dripping off the walls, and a remote clinical attitude. They are probably having some degree of difficulty with authority figures anyway, and they don't need you added to that list. Being somewhat informal in dress and setting can remove one barrier. On the other hand, wearing beads, playing records, sitting on a floor cushion, and sucking on a "roach" when they arrive won't go down too well either. They want you to know about those things, but not be into them. Unless of course you really are. (Even, then, leave the roach at home.) An attempt to fake out the adolescent will fail. They are a hard group to fool, and they place a high premium on honesty. Respect this and honestly be yourself. This means asking for a translation of their vocabulary if you aren't familiar with the lingo.

Empathy is the goal rather than sympathy. This is true of all therapeutic relationships. Sympathy is feeling like the other person. Empathy is knowing how the person feels, understanding it, but not feeling like he does at the moment. It is simply not helpful to be depressed along with him, for instance.

In general, there are three types of therapy done with adolescents. One involves *manipulation of the environment*. This can include arranging for the father to spend more time with his child, getting the kid who hates Shakespeare into a different school program, or organizing a temporary placement for the child whose parents are nonsupportive at the time. These can be very valuable interventions.

Standard insight therapy—psychological, psychiatrically oriented traditional therapy—is not often used. There are not too many adolescents who are ready for, or even could benefit from, this kind of therapy. The ones who can tend to be "bright," advantaged young people, who seem more capable and older than their peers or their chronological age would suggest.

The most commonly productive therapy is what could be termed a *relational approach*. This requires time for you to become well acquainted and for the adolescent to feel comfortable with you. The counselor is supportive without doing it for him. The counselor is a neutral person, available to him in a very different way than parents or peers.

For the adolescent with an alcohol problem, how might AA be of use? The first thought might be that the adolescent would never identify with a group of predominately 35- to 55-year-olds. In many areas that stereotype of the AA group doesn't necessarily hold true; there are now in some locales what are called "young people's groups." There the average age is the low to mid twenties. Even if there are not any young people's groups in your vicinity, age need not be a barrier to an adolescent's affiliating with AA. On the contrary, there are several features of AA that might attract and intrigue the adolescent. It's a group of adults who will definitely not preach at him. Furthermore, given the collective life experiences within AA, the members are not likely to be shocked, outraged, or, for that matter, impressed by any of the adolescent's behavior. The members will generally treat the adolescent as an adult, presumably capable of making responsible choices, although cognizant that to do so isn't easy for anyone. There is within AA a ready assortment of potential surrogate parents, aunts, uncles, and grandparents. The intergenerational contact, possibly not available elsewhere to the adolescent, can be a plus. Also, AA remains sufficiently "unacceptable" so as not to automatically be written off by the adolescent wary of what he considers traditional, staid, "establishment," and out-of-it adult groups. Since being alcoholic is still a stigmatized condition, the parents may be more uncomfortable than their children about AA attendance for adolescents. The counselor may need to help parents with this. In making a referral, the same guidelines outlined in the section on AA would apply. The adolescent is full of surprises; his receptivity to AA may well be another.

Changing times

In closing, some comment on the changing times and some speculation on its impact on adolescence seems in order. Much of adolescence is concerned with sexual maturation, acceptance of biological roles, adaptation to a heterosexual world, and selection of an occupational identity. What impact does the sexual revolution, the women's movement, gay liberation, or the counterculture have on these tasks? Adolescents appear to be faced with a wider range of choices than previous generations were in the struggle to answer the question "Who/what will I be when I grow up?" How many adolescents' parents had to seriously consider whether they'd marry or just live with someone? Or whether to finish school or hitchhike across the country? Or whether they were straight, gay, or bisexual? Or whether they'd go to graduate school or become a potter?

Having to deal with such questions conceivably leads to healthier adults. But it would also seem to make accomplishing the tasks of adolescence more complicated. And, conceivably, it leads to more casualties along the way. Adolescents do not have culturally agreed on stereotypes to rely upon and provide guidance as they attempt to navigate this period of life. Potentially, part of the role of the helping person in contact with the adolescent is to help him discover which of the many possibilities fits him. The relationship with the counselor can be an important point of reference as the adolescent attempts to chart a course.

The questions the adolescent is grappling with are heavy ones. It will not be helpful if the counselor finds them gut-wrenching. In no other area is it more necessary for the caregiver to be aware of personal biases and hangups. If the counselor is not comfortable in dealing with some of the issues the adolescent raises, the only course open is to make a referral to another worker better equipped to deal with the issues.

THE EMPLOYED

The majority of alcoholics are members of the work force. One estimate, probably a conservative one, is that 8% of the nation's work force is adversely affected by the use of alcohol. Business and industry are beginning to recognize the costs to them of employees with alcohol problems. As a result, there has been a rapid development of special programs by employers to identify problems and initiate alcohol treatment. These programs, generally called either *employee assistance programs* or *occupational alcohol programs*, will be discussed later in this section. What is much less often discussed is how being a worker may influence the development of alcohol problems and the course of treatment.

Although not often mentioned, drinking is interwoven into work. And why not? As noted in Chapter One, drinking is tied to all other parts of life. For some concrete examples of its intrusion into work, consider the office party, the company picnic, and the wine and cheese reception. There are martini lunches, the "drink date" to "review business," and the bar car on the commuter train. What is the good old standby gift for a business associate? A fifth of good liquor. A round of drinks celebrates the close of a

Abstaining is favorable both to the head and the pocket.

HORACE GREELEY

Portrait of a man who stops in a bar for 3 drinks on his way home from work every night.

business deal. The construction crew stops off for beers after work. T.G.I.F. has become a catch phrase and an occasion for a drink. The company bowling team is cheered by beer. The list could be extended.

How might the almost universal presence of alcohol around the work setting be explained? To our knowledge, this has not been systematically, or even haphazardly, investigated. Based on observation, there does seem to be one common denominator to any drinking connected with work. The Kinney-Leaton Law states that alcohol will be conspicuously present at any social gathering composed of people who know one another primarily from work. As a corollary, people who may not associate drinking with social gatherings of friends, family, or neighborhood folk will choose to drink at a social function that's tied to work. It would seem that being initially ill at ease at social gatherings, which is a common feeling, might be more threatening if the function consists of co-workers. And alcohol is often used to lessen anxiety. On the other hand, drinking with co-workers may be considered "time-out"; co-workers may be far more tolerant of one another's getting a little "tanked" than they would be if the drinking were being done with spouse, family, or close friends.

What is common to many work situations is that drinking is not only accepted, it is expected. This is not to imply that nondrinking is frowned upon, but it is considered unusual. The only perceived reason for supplying a nonalcoholic alternative is for the few who never drink. The assumption is that if you drink at all, you'll certainly want to take advantage of the opportunity!

If the use of alcohol is tolerated, the potential for alcohol problems among susceptible individuals rises, and more so if drinking is subtly encouraged. Employers have generally not been considered responsible for their employees' drinking practices. After all, employers are not making employees drink. Or are they? Several recent court rulings have held that an employer, in certain situations, is responsible. The following two cases demonstrate this. From the *New York Times:*

Douglas M. Jolly, A District of Columbia policeman, proved overqualified for an undercover assignment that required him to spend a lot of time in bars, a civil service board ruled Thursday, so he will get a tax-free pension of two-thirds of his $13,000 annual salary. Testimony showed that although Mr. Jolly had been a "health fiend" who seldom touched alcohol, his assignment as a narcotics and liquor-law investigator produced such a case of alcoholism and resulting medical conditions that he had been retired on full disability. He has also stopped drinking.

Laurie Johnston

Also from the *New York Times:*

Office Party Blamed in Death of Employee

San Francisco, Oct. 31 (UPI)—The widow of a man killed in an auto accident after he became intoxicated at an office party is entitled to receive workmen's compensation, the California Supreme Court ruled yesterday.

The court said the "proximate cause" of death of Daniel McCarty originated with his employment at a plumbing concern, which gave a party on company time during the 1971 holiday season.

"An employer who tolerates and encourages employee drinking in connection with the job may not later assert that the injury was caused by the intoxication of the employee," the court ruled.

Although a job can't be said to cause alcoholism, it can contribute to its development. Some of the factors in a job that may be conducive to the development of alcohol problems are noted in the following discussion.

High-risk factors

Certain types of work and work situations appear to aggravate and reinforce alcohol abuse. This statement is substantiated by the high percentage of managerial, white collar, and professional people reported to have alcohol problems. Alcoholism is also a serious problem for, among others, the military, physicians, executives, and airline employees. What do all these diverse occupations have in common? According to Trice and Roman, they have "job-based risk factors." The two major categories of these are absence of supervision and low visibility of performance. It might be useful to review these twelve risk factors:

- Absence of clear goals (and absence of supervision)
- Freedom to set work hours (isolation and low visibility)
- Low structural visibility (e.g., salespeople away from the business place)
- Work addiction
- Occupational obsolescence (especially common in scientific and technical fields)
- New work status

The contract of the National Brewery Workers of America specifies that union members may drink beer in unlimited quantity during breaks. (Do they have an industrial alcoholism program?)

- Required on-the-job drinking (e.g., salespeople drinking with clients)
- Mutual benefits (informal power struggles in upper organizational levels may lead to heavier drinking)
- Reduction of social controls (occurs on college campuses and other less structured settings)
- Severe role stress
- Competitive pressure
- Presence of illegal drug users (less an issue for alcohol abusers)

An interesting conclusion from their research is that deviant drinking is not concentrated in any one social class or occupational group.

The workplace cover-up

If bringing up the drinking practices and potential problems of a family member or close friend makes someone squirm with discomfort, the idea of saying something to a co-worker is virtually unthinkable. There is a separation that almost everyone accepts between work and home or professional and private life. The reticence people feel about butting into someone else's life, especially around drinking, is as true in the work setting as anywhere else. What happens on the job is the legitimate concern of the business and co-workers. Anything outside the job setting is considered someone's own private affair. So until the alcohol problem flows into the work world, the worker's use of alcohol is considered no one else's business. That doesn't mean that no one sees a problem developing. It's our suspicion that someone with just a little savvy can spot potentially dangerous drinking practices. The office scuttlebutt or work crew's bull sessions plus simple observation make it common knowledge who "really put it away this weekend" or the "poor devil who just got picked up DWI" or "you can always count on Sue to join in whenever anyone wants to stop for a drink after work."

Even if an employee does show some problems on the job, whether marginal to or directly related to alcohol use, co-workers may try to "help out." This may mean covering up any work difficulties so that supervisors or management don't find out, by doing extra work, or not blowing the whistle. Co-workers are also not immune to the alcoholic's deceptions. Out of misguided sympathy, they may well feel they are helping the alcoholic "until the pressure's off about

_____ ." Since employee assistance programs, if they are present, are based on identifying work deterioration, any attempt by co-workers to help cover up job problems makes spotting the alcohol problem all the more difficult. If a company does not have a program to help alcoholics, odds for a cover-up by co-workers are greater. It may well be true that if management does spot a problem, the worker will be fired. Co-workers, knowing how important that paycheck is, believing promises by the alcoholic to shape up, and fearful of what dire things may follow the loss of the job, are likely to minimize and conceal the problem.

Another important party in this concealment strategy is the spouse. With the predictable strains in the emotional realm, parental roles, and sexual relationship, the last straw is the potential loss of financial support. The spouse usually doesn't want to do anything to threaten the paycheck. So spouses will do whatever they can to get the alcoholic to work. On the other side of the coin, they'll make excuses whenever possible for those occasions when work is missed. The spouse may buy the alcoholic's rationalization that the drinking is a product of stress at work. Therefore the spouse may support job changes in the hope that they will relieve the drinking and consequent problems.

Eventually the problems become too diffuse for the cover-ups to work anymore. Or the spouse leaves, or the co-workers get sick of the whole thing, or the alcoholic comes in drunk or has an on-the-job accident, etc. At this point, in the past the alcoholic usually got fired. It can be assumed that this still happens in many companies. The employee is out, and the company may have lost a formerly valuable and well-trained worker. Statistically, this is a costly problem for companies all over the country. There are, however, other solutions to this dilemma. Of the 1.5 million companies in the United States, six hundred have employee assistance or occupational alcohol programs. Basically, the thinking behind these programs is that it is cheaper for the companies to identify problems earlier and then use the job as leverage to get the employee into treatment and back to work at an efficient level.

Cost-effectiveness

In a study conducted by Dr. Carl J. Schramm, an economist at the School of Hygiene and Public Health at Johns Hopkins University, employee programs were found to be cost-effective. The three-year study, begun in 1972, involved unions and management in twelve companies employing 134,000 people. In the Baltimore project, where the cost for 206 referred patients was $230,000, the twelve employers saved $454,000 in reduced absenteeism the first year of the program and $600,000 the second year. Savings are expected to be $1 million in the third year and to grow geometrically. Absenteeism was the only factor analyzed in this particular study because it is the most easily measured. But there are a number of other areas that have been identified as potentially beneficial to the employer, including reduction of on-the-job accidents, less equipment damage, and improved morale, leading to increased productivity.

Why so few programs

If all this cost-effectiveness be true, how come only 600 companies have programs? There's no clear-cut single reason, but several possibilities can be mentioned. One is company size. Small companies may be quite informal and have a more personal approach. They may also not have funds or the need to hire a professional to set up and run a program just for them. Consortiums are one emerging answer to this one.

Another frequently mentioned roadblock is the executive or "president alcoholic," who is certainly less likely to institute a program that is personally threatening. It is often said that programs are designed to identify alcoholics at all levels *lower* than that of the person approving the program. It would clearly be difficult for the personnel manager to set up or OK a program when he feels sure that his immediate superior already has a problem. One way out of this bind would be to apply the program to all levels below this.

And, of course, the pervasive American idea that alcoholism is a choice and those who choose it deserve what they get is just as influential in business as elsewhere. There are surely a host of other reasons for the paucity of programs but with slowly changing attitudes, publicity about successful programs, and better available insurance coverage, there is hope that the future will be brighter for the employed alcoholic.

Now on to a bit about identification of troubled employees, types of programs, etc.

Philosophy, the bottom line, or toward a more productive work force

Facts and experience suggest that the occupational environment may be one of the most efficient and economical means of providing an opportunity for early identification and treatment of alcoholism and alcohol-related problems. The problem drinker's daily contact with other employees, supervisors, union stewards, medical department, and personnel staff increases the possibility of others noticing the behavioral changes and impaired job performance that accompany a developing alcohol problem. This early recognition and confrontation is critical; otherwise, the problem drinker tends to use employment as the indicator that he's still OK. After all, he can still go to work!

Chances for recovery are also increased by reaching the alcoholic at an earlier stage, for the following reasons:
1. Physical health has not deteriorated significantly.
2. Financial resources are not as depleted.
3. Emotional supports still exist in the family and community.
4. Threat of job loss is present as a motivator.

Program approaches

The two major approaches to occupational programming are the *broad brush* and the *alcohol-only*. The former (*troubled employee* or *employee assistance*) is directed at all employees, regardless of the type of problem affecting work performance, which may include personal, family, financial, legal, drug, or alcohol problems. The alcohol-only approach is limited to employees with alcohol problems that inhibit their productivity.

An advantage of the broad brush approach is that alcoholism is not the only factor that affects employee behavior or work performance. And the moral stigma that is still attached to alcoholism inhibits many people from seeking help or referring others. Thus, the neutrality of Employee Assistance Program on the door allows certain workers to enter without fearing others will know the particular problem that they might have.

The argument for the straight alcoholism approach is that such directness cuts through the denial and manipulation of the alcoholic and is thus more effective.

There are two things that will be believed of any man whosoever, and one of them is that he has taken to drink.

BOOTH TARKINGTON

Program components

Regardless of approach, staff, or program model, any organization that determines a need exists for developing a program will find there are certain components critical to all:

1. A *written policy* must be issued, one which is supported by management and labor. If there are unions at the facility, these groups should be represented at every level of planning, implementation, and review. As many companies have sorrowfully discovered, without the cooperation and representation of all elements of the work force, a program cannot succeed because there will be competition and distrust.

2. A trained and qualified *Program Coordinator* should be hired. This individual will be responsible for determining the program approach and developing and implementing program, policy, and procedures. This person might function under the umbrella of a medical department, personnel department, a separate department, or at an outside service agency.

3. *Training sessions* should be offered to supervisors, managers, and union stewards to help them recognize problems and also to teach them the referral process.

4. *Information* and *education* should be available to all employees on a continuing basis to ensure proper and full utilization of the program.

5. *Total confidentiality* must be guaranteed to the employee/client. The Federal Privacy Act of 1975 provides strict guidelines regarding client information sharing and record keeping.

6. A *program description*, via a brochure or handbook, is important so that employees will know what services are being offered. Also, information should be given about referral procedures, emplo*yee* responsibility, and emplo*yer* responsibility.

7. *Payment options* need to be determined and then clearly stated, so that the employee/client will be prepared. Some companies include this service with employee health benefits. Others prefer a different arrangement, and the employee might then be asked to assume responsibility for some part of the payment.

8. An *evaluation* or *review* component is critical. It might be administered by the program coordinator, an advisory board, or a joint labor-management committee. The purposes would be to provide for accountability, monitor program implementation, review and advise, disseminate information, and conduct a cost-benefit analysis.

Special features of treatment

It is important for alcohol counselors to be knowledgeable about occupational programs. They can then better coordinate treatment efforts for the employed alcoholic or problem drinker. One method of learning about this client is to obtain a comprehensive job history and job "picture." Among the areas that should be covered are a description of work tasks and responsibilities, relationships to co-workers, attitudes toward the job, length of time employed at this company, how referred to this treatment facility, etc. Based on knowledge of occupational programs, the counselor would also want to know whether or not the client's company has a program, the name of the coordinator, the types of services being offered, and the type of insurance coverage available to pay for the treatment services of the agency. Another critical area to explore with the employed client is current job status. In other words, has a disciplinary procedure already been instituted, or has the employee been informally warned and referred for treatment. And, to avoid future conflict, learn about any union involvement. The information the counselor obtains about clients' jobs can help in the formulation of realistic treatment plans.

An important technique in dealing with the alcoholic employee is sometimes called *intervention, constructive coercion,* or *confrontation.* The technique is used in the work setting to motivate the individual to seek help to improve job performance and retain the job. The use of "job leverage" can also be an excellent tool for the alcohol counselor to use in cooperation with the employer to keep the employee motivated and involved in treatment.

Confrontation is actually a process that occurs within the company's normal evaluation and disciplinary procedures. A supervisor, manager, or union steward who notes certain behaviors and signs of deteriorating job performance documents them. Some of the most common signs and symptoms used to identify the problem drinker are the following:

- chronic absenteeism
- change in behavior
- physical signs
- spasmodic work pace
- lower quantity and quality of work
- partial absences
- lying
- avoiding supervisors and co-workers
- on-the-job drinking
- on-the-job accidents and lost time from off-the-job accidents

One can see the importance of training supervisors and others in recognizing these signs, so that early detection can occur. Training is also critical to helping employers to document and not diagnose. In organizations where there has been no such training or education, the common response to the problem drinker is to "kill him with kindness." His co-workers and supervisors cover up, advise, threaten, and finally give up.

If there is a company program, the procedure would be to identify, document, and then confront the employee with the facts and an informal offer of referral for help. If unsuccessful, the next phase would be a stepped up disciplinary procedure, including a time limit and a formal referral with the "threat" of job loss if performance is not improved.

It is important for the counselor to be sensitive to the policies and politics of the employed alcoholic's work setting. Without this knowledge and awareness, there is the danger of violating the client's confidentiality or, conversely, of not fully taking advantage of the opportunity to cooperate with the employer on the client's behalf. If there is a company policy, learn about it, in order to plan realistically and avoid treatment/work conflicts. The type of medication, if any, will also be affected by the nature of the client's work. A follow-up plan must consider the working person's hours and geographical location. The flexibility and accessibility of the treatment facility can be a key factor in the successful rehabilitation of the employed alcoholic. Evening office hours and early morning and weekend appointments may have to be arranged by the counselor, so that treatment will not interfere with the individual's job. You may also find that some clients will have to receive outpatient care even when inpatient services appear more appropriate. The employee may not be able to take the time off or may not have adequate insurance coverage.

The counselor is faced with a different situation when the person comes from an organization where there is no program. Or the employee may not allow the counselor to contact the workplace. This decision may be realistic, based on the employee's awareness of punitive attitudes and policies in the company. At other times, the alcoholic employee is attempting to continue the usual pattern of denial and manipulation. It's possible that he's trying to hide his problem from his employer and also hide the seriousness of his job situation from the counselor. Regardless of the reason, the counselor must respect the client's decision.

This is a challenging and exciting time. Occupational programs have made significant progress in demonstrating that the "human approach" is good business. But there is still a great deal to be done, and it can only be accomplished if there is better cooperation among those involved in the occupational program field, regardless of approach.

The alcohol worker has an important role to play in the future development of effective programs: by bringing community resources to the workplace, by sharing special knowledge and expertise as consultant and educator, and by participating as part of the occupational treatment team.

IN CLOSING

As alcohol services expand, as alcohol knowledge grows, more attention is being paid to how treatment can best be provided to different groups of people. Recall the impact culture has on the development of alcohol problems. It also influences treatment. Culture influences where people turn for help and their ability to accept it. Culture will dictate the circumstances most likely to trigger a resumption of drinking. The culture will assign the degree of stigma to a member's having an alcohol problem.

The United States is not a homogeneous collection of people. Age, sex, race, ethnic background, where one lives —these factors make a difference. They are forces that mold how we each think, behave, and feel.

Portrait of a man who thinks he's clever when he's drunk

When it comes to alcohol, persons from the same group are likely to share basic attitudes and face similar problems. Any counselor who does not become familiar with the distinct features of major client groups is placed at an unnecessary disadvantage. Anyone who encounters a client clearly from different circumstances than the "normal" agency clientele and who doesn't ask how this might alter treatment is ignoring some important information.

In reading this chapter, we hope you have been confronted with some new ideas. We hope this not only alters the way you approach clients who are women, employed, adolescent, or elderly, but also prods you to find out more about other special populations. Further reading is one way, but not the only way, or even the best. Another is to temporarily put aside what you think you know, and approach it with fresh eyes. Go find someone from a particular group, and ask him what it is like to be a member of that ethnic, racial, religious, or minority group. And *listen*. Sitting in our little rural New England town, we do not presume to even attempt a description of the black, Chicano, Native American, urban, southern, or West Coast experiences. Also, we don't expect you to necessarily be knowledgeable about the Vermont Yankee farmer or the Franco-Americans. Wherever one finds oneself, there is some important homework to be done if treatment efforts are to have maximum impact.

RESOURCES AND FURTHER READING
Women

Gomberg, Edith S. Women with alcohol problems. In Nada J. Estes and M. Edith Heinemann (Eds.), *Alcoholism: development, consequences, and interventions.* St. Louis: The C. V. Mosby Co., 1977.

MacLennan, Anne (Ed.). *Women: their use of alcohol and other legal drugs.* Toronto: Addiction Research Foundation, 1976.

Schuckit, Marc. The alcoholic woman: a literature review. *Psychiatry in Medicine,* 1972, 3(11), 37-43.

Wilsnack, Sharon. Femininity by the bottle. *Psychology Today,* April 1973, p. 36+.

The elderly

Butler, Robert N., and Lewis, Myrna I. *Aging and mental health: positive psychosocial approaches* (2nd ed.). St. Louis: The C. V. Mosby Co., 1977.

Adolescents

Communications strategies on alcohol and highway safety. Vol. II. Washington, D.C.: U.S. Department of Transportation, National Highway Traffic Safety Administration, 1975.

Globetti, Gerald. Teenage drinking. In Nada J. Estes and M. Edith Heinemann (Eds.), *Alcoholism: development, consequences, and interventions.* St. Louis: The C. V. Mosby Co., 1977.

The employed

Follmann, Joseph, Jr. *Alcoholics and business, problems, costs, solutions.* New York: American Management Associations, 1976.

Sadler, Marion, and Horst, James F. Company/union programs for alcoholics. *Harvard Business Review,* September-October 1972.

Schlenger, William, Hallan, Jerome, and Hayward, Becky. *Characteristics of selected occupational programs.* Report from Human Ecology Institute. Raleigh, N.C., 1976.

Schramm, Carl. *The Baltimore Report.* Baltimore: Johns Hopkins University School of Hygiene and Public Health, 1977.

Social services in the work place: starting where the client is and the community isn't. National Conference on Social Welfare. New York: Columbia University Press, 1973.

Spirits at work revisited: needed priorities in occupational alcoholism programming. In Morris Chafetz (Ed.), *Proceedings of the Fourth Annual Conference on Alcoholism of NIAAA.* Washington, D.C.: U.S. Government Printing Office, 1974.

Trice, H. M., and Roman, P. M. *Spirits and demons at work: alcohol and other drugs on the job.* Ithaca, N.Y.: Cornell University Press, 1972.

Weiner, Hyman, Akabas, Shelia, and Sommer, John. *Mental health care in the world of work.* New York: Association Press, 1973.

Jack FiN
e could
drink
NO Wi
Ne — H
iS WiF
E Could
driNk
No liquo
R — But ST
ill they both
goT drunk each nig
ht — though he got'd
runk much quicker...

La pauvre Presse

Brattleboro, Vt.

from the Collecred Do
ggerel of 18TH CenTury
France — by J. ANzolone

THINGS LEFT OUT

There are other topics we consider relevant for alcohol counselors. Space and time limitations prevent us from doing more than just mentioning them here. The whole area of "indirect services" is missing. This awkward phrase is used to cover all the other things a counselor is often required to do, in addition to directly serving clients. Public education, case consultation, and planning for community programs are just a few examples. These indirect services are vital to alcohol treatment efforts. Adequate treatment, early intervention, and prevention all require the efforts of a range of helping people. But in order for others to become involved, they need information and knowledge of alcohol and the problems it can cause. After you develop clinical skill, you might next consider how you can best equip yourself to share what you have learned with other helping people.

Another area that has not been discussed is that of prevention. This is receiving attention at the national, state, and local levels. The goal of any prevention effort is to reduce the numbers of persons who develop alcohol problems. A wide variety of techniques and programs to do this are being explored. In the process, a great many people are trying and saying a great deal. What is clear is that preaching the evils of alcohol and the dangers of alcoholism is ineffective. And we all know how well Prohibition worked. The responsible use of alcoholic beverages is the current thrust of many of these efforts. While much is being done, the results aren't in yet. Attending special workshops and national meetings is one way to familiarize yourself with the philosophy and techniques of prevention efforts.

Another area of current interest centers around the movements to certify and/or license alcohol counselors. Within virtually every state, an attempt is being made to establish minimum standards for counselors in alcohol treatment. In some states, this effort is being led by an Alcohol Counselor's Association. In others, the impetus is coming from the state alcohol programs. Reaching a consensus on what alcohol counselors need to know and what skills they must possess to be credentialed is not easy. Yet, despite the difficulties, there is growing agreement that this is essential for protection of clients, agencies, and workers.

There is also the whole area of alcohol research. Some of the areas in which considerable research is under way have been mentioned earlier. As more and more research is conducted and reported, keeping up to date is a challenge. Sometimes sorting through the emotional debates research findings spark is an even greater challenge. For example, although not a new issue, abstinence vs. controlled drinking is again—or continues to be—a controversy. An open mind and careful examination of the evidence on both sides is essential. This will require you to dig behind newspaper accounts of research findings. Either search out the articles being discussed or find some levelheaded persons who have and can "interpret" them for you.

It has been said that the "half-life" of medical knowledge is eight years. This means eight years from now half of what will be known has not yet been discovered. And, on the other hand, half of what is now taken as fact will be out of date. Consequently, education must be a continuing process.

As with any specialty, the pressure of day-to-day work makes keeping current a real problem. Subscription to a journal or two, plus getting on NIAAA's mailing list, can help, if you can make the time to read them. Area meetings of alcohol workers of all disciplines are also a way to keep posted on such topics as counselor certification, treatment center accreditation, etc. In this relatively new and growing field, the search for new and better ways goes on. It helps to know what's happening.

THE REAL WORLD
Being a professional—what it is . . .

Alcohol counseling is a growing profession. The professional counselor has mastered a body of knowledge, has special skills, and has a code of ethics to guide in the work. Being a professional does not mean you have to know it all. Do yourself a favor, right now. Give yourself permission to give up any pretense that it's otherwise. Feel free to ask questions, seek advice, request a consultation, say you don't know. Alcohol treatment requires diverse skills and talents. Treatment programs are staffed by people with different training, for the very reason that no one person or specialty can do the job alone. Being a professional also means constantly looking at what you're doing, evalu-

ating your efforts. There's always more than one approach. You can't make sober people by grinding drunks through an alcohol treatment machine. Being open to trying new things is easier if you aren't stuck with the notion that you are supposed to be the big expert. And of course you'll make mistakes—so what else is new?

And what it isn't . . .

There are overwhelming numbers of alcoholics needing and asking for help out there. The tendency is to over-burden yourself because of the obvious need. Spreading yourself too thin is a real problem and danger. It creates resentment, anger, frustration, and a distorted view of the world. "No one else seems to care! Somebody's got to do it." It's a trap. Unless you're an Atlas, you'll get mashed. You are important as a person, and must keep that in mind. Save your own space. Collapsing might give you a nice sense of martyrdom, but it won't help anybody. Better to be more realistic in assessing just what you can do pro-ductively, devoting your energy to a realistic and limited number of clients, and giving your best. Keep a clear eye on your own needs for time off, trips, visits to people who have nothing to do with your work.

The people who live with you deserve some of your attention too. It's hard to maintain a relationship with any-one if all you can manage is "What a day!" lapse into si-lence, and soon fall asleep. It isn't going to be easy to han-dle, but some rule of thumb needs to be set in your own head to handle the calls that come after working hours. Some workers ruefully decide on unlisted home phone numbers. Drinking drunks and their upset families are not notoriously considerate. Telephone-itis sets in with a few drinks. You may decide you do want to be available at all hours. But whatever rules you set, try to be consistent. Take a good look at the effects on the important people in your life. Some compromise may be necessary between your "ideal counselor" and your own needs. Give it some thought. State your rules clearly to your clients, prefer-ably when they're sober, and then stick to them. If you said no calls when a client's drinking, then don't get caught listening to a drunk-a-logue at 3 AM for fear he'll do some-thing rash. Being inconsistent may be more dangerous in the long run. When you've had some experience, you'll be

able to tell when you must break your own rules. And you can say that to your clients: "I did say I don't take home phone calls, but you do seem to be in a real bind . . ."

You can't take total responsibility for clients. Rarely does someone make it or not because of one incident. This doesn't mean adopt a laissez-faire policy. But just as you can't take all the credit for a sober, happy alcoholic, neither can you shoulder all the blame when it doesn't work out that way.

CONFIDENTIALITY

For the counselor, as for anyone in the helping professions, confidentiality is a crucial issue. Most of us simply don't consider how much of our conversation includes discussion about other people. When we think about it, it can be quite a shock. It's especially difficult when we are really concerned about someone and are looking for aid and advice. There is only one place for this in a professional relationship with a client. That is with your supervisor or therapist co-workers. It is *never* OK to discuss a client with spouse, friends, even other alcohol workers from different facilities. Even without using names, enough usually slips out to make the client easily identified some time in the future. Unfortunately, this standard isn't kept all the time. There are occasional slips by even the most conscientious of workers. You'll do it accidentally, and you'll hear it from time to time. All you can do is try harder in the first instance, and deliberately forget what you heard in the second. What your client shares with you is privileged information. That includes where he is and how he's doing. Even good news is his alone to share.

If you are heading up an out-reach office, rather than acting as part of a hospital or mental health clinic, it's up to you to inform your secretary about confidentiality. The same is true for any volunteers working in the office. They have some knowledge about the people being seen, at the least, who they are. It must be stressed that any information they acquire there is strictly private. You don't need to get huffy and deliver a lecture, but you should make the point very clearly, and set some standards in the workplace.

ETHICS

Being a professional also means being allied to a set of ethical standards. These might not be written down, but they are nonetheless understood by your professional co-workers. They are there as guidelines. They have a history and have developed from experience. This discussion is not intended to set forth any suggestions for your private life. It is intended to point out what is expected of helping persons that may not be expected of others. Maintaining confidentiality, for example, is one standard of behavior taken for granted. In general, professionals are expected to avoid romantic entanglements with clients. If a romantic inclination on the part of either client or counselor begins to show up, it needs to be worked out—and not in the nearest bed. This is the time to run, not walk, to an experienced co-worker. It may be hard on our egos, but the fact is that people with problems are as confused about their emotions as everything else. They may be feeling so needy that they "love" anyone who seems to be hearing their cry. It really isn't you personally. If they had drawn Joe or Amy, then one of them would be the object of the misplaced emotion right now. So talk it over with a supervisor, guide, or mentor, not just a buddy. And then, follow their advice. It may need to be worked through with the client, or changing counselors may be necessary. The ethical standards are not arbitrary no-nos set up by a bunch of Puritans. They are protections designed to keep both you and the client from any needless hurt. The hurts can be emotional or range all the way to messy court actions. The counselors who have walked the road before you have discovered what keeps up-

sets to a minimum, your sense of self-worth realistic, and your helpfulness at its optimum level.

Clients will occasionally show up with presents. While they are actively working with you, the general guideline is no gifts. This is especially true if something of real monetary value is offered. In such cases it's important to discuss what is being said by the gift. But use your common sense, there are times when clearly the thing to do is accept graciously. (If you have a fantasy of an MG being delivered anonymously to your door, and it comes true . . . unfortunately, our experience doesn't cover that.)

Similarly, social engagements with the client alone or his family are not recommended. It could be a plot to keep you friendly and avoid crunchy problems that need to be worked out. In the office time, deal with the invitation, and gently refuse. Hopefully, in your first years of counseling, you'll have a supervisor to help you through such sticky wickets. Use him or her. The real pros are the ones who used all the help they could get when they needed it. That's how they got to be pros.

Another ethical concern is directed at keeping professional life and private life separate. Don't do your counseling number on your friends. You are likely to end up with fewer of them if you do. When you see a friend exhibiting behavior that you think indicates he's heading for trouble, it's hard not to fall into your professional role. *Don't*. Bite your tongue. He knows what business you're in. If he wants help, he'll ask. Should that day come, refer him to see someone else. And stay out of the picture. Counseling friends and relatives is another no-no. Vital objectivity is impossible. No matter how good you are with your clients, almost anyone else will be better equipped to work with your family or friends.

COUNSELORS WITH TWO HATS

Many of the workers in the alcohol field are themselves recovering alcoholics. Long before national attention was focused on alcoholism, private rehabilitation centers were operated, often staffed by sober alcoholics. In the evolutionary process of recovery, many alcoholics find themselves working in many capacities, in many different types of facilities. We must say here that we don't hold to the belief that simply being a recovering alcoholic qualifies one to be a counselor. There's more to it than that. That view ignores the skill and special knowledge that many alcoholics working in the field have gained, on-the-job, and often without benefit of any formal training. They've had a harder row to hoe and deserve lots of respect for sticking to it.

Being a recovering alcoholic has some advantages for a counselor, but also some clear disadvantages. It may at times be the most confusing for the recovering alcoholic who is also in AA. Doing AA Twelfth Step work and calling it counseling won't do, from the profession's or AA's point of view. Twelfth Step work is voluntary and has no business being used for bread earning. AA's traditions are clearly against this. AA is not opposed to its members working in the field of alcoholism, if they are qualified to do so. If you are an AA member and also an alcohol counselor, it is important to keep the dividing line in plain sight. The trade calls it "wearing two hats." There are some good AA pamphlets on the subject, and the AA monthly magazine, *The Grapevine*, publishes articles for two-hatters from time to time. A book, *The Para-Professional in the Treatment of Alcoholism*, by Staub and Kent, covers a lot of territory on two-hatting very well.

A particular bind for two-hat counselors comes if attending AA becomes tied to their jobs more than their own sobriety. They might easily find themselves sustaining clients at meetings and not being there for themselves. A way to avoid this is to find a meeting you can attend where you're less likely to see clients. It's easy for both you and the clients to mix AA with the other therapy. The client benefits from a clear distinction as much, if not more, than you. There is always the difficulty of keeping your priorities in order. You can't counsel if you are drinking yourself. So, whatever you do to keep sober, whether it includes AA or not, *keep doing it*. Again, when so many people out there seem to need you, it is very difficult to keep from overextending. A recovering alcoholic simply cannot afford this. (If this description fits you, stop reading right now. Choose one thing to scratch off your schedule.) It is always easy to justify skimping on your own sober regimen because "I'm working with alcoholics all the time." Retire that excuse. Experience has shown it to be a counselor killer.

Another real problem is the temptation to discuss your

job at AA meetings or discuss clients with other members. The AAs don't need to be bored by you any more than by a doctor member describing the surgical removal of a gallbladder. Discussing your clients, even with another AA member, is a serious breach of confidentiality. This will be particularly hard, especially when a really concerned AA member asks you point-blank about someone. The other side of the coin is keeping the confidences gained at AA and not reporting to co-workers about what transpired with clients at an AA meeting. Hopefully, your nonalcoholic co-workers will not slip up and put you in a bind by asking. It's probably OK to talk with your AA sponsor about your job, if it is giving you fits. However, it is important to stick with *you*, and leave out work details and/or clients' parts.

Watch out if feelings of superiority creep up toward other "plain" AA members, or nonalcoholic colleagues. Alcoholic status doesn't accord you magical insights. On the other hand, being a nonalcoholic isn't a guaranteed route to knowing what is going on either. Keep your perspective as much as you're able. After all, you are all in the same boat, with different oars. To quote an unknown source: "It's amazing how much can be accomplished if no one cares who gets the credit."

• • •

Be good to yourself. Treat yourself to a movie tonight. And on your way home, remember to look at the stars.

RESOURCES AND FURTHER READING

Staub, George, and Kent, Leona (Eds.). *The para-professional in the treatment of alcoholism.* Springfield, Ill.: Charles C Thomas, Publisher, 1973.

Publications

Alcohol Health and Research World, NIAAA. (Available through National Clearinghouse for Alcohol Information, Box 2345, Rockville, Md. 20852.)

NIAAA Information and Feature Service. (Available through National Clearinghouse for Alcohol Information, Box 2345, Rockville, Md. 20852.)

The Journal (monthly newspaper). Addiction Research Foundation, 33 Russell St., Toronto, Ontario, Canada M5S 2S1.

The U.S. Journal of Drug and Alcohol Dependence (monthly newspaper). 7541 Biscayne Blvd., Miami, Fla. 33138

Index